NATIONAL DREAMS

National Dreams

MYTH, MEMORY, AND CANADIAN HISTORY

Daniel Francis

ARSENAL PULP PRESS
Vancouver

ARSENAL PULP PRESS
Suite 101, 211 East Georgia St.
Vancouver, BC
Canada V6A 1Z6
arsenalpulp.com

The publisher gratefully acknowledges the support of the Canada Council for
the Arts and the British Columbia Arts Council for its publishing program,
and the Government of Canada (through the Canada Book Fund) and the
Government of British Columbia (through the Book Publishing Tax Credit
Program) for its publishing activities.

Typeset by Dennis Priebe, Vancouver Desktop Publishing Centre

Printed and bound in Canada

Library and Archives Canada Cataloguing in Publication

Francis, Daniel.
    National dreams

    Includes bibliographical references and index.
    ISBN 978-1-55152-043-8

    I. Canada—History. 2. Popular culture—Canada. I. Title.
FC95.F72 1997   971   C97-910740-7
F1021.F72 1997

Contents

Acknowledgements

During the lengthy period it has taken me to complete this book I have received assistance from many people—librarians, archivists, academics, friends—without whom the work would have been impossible. Two in particular require mention: Ken Osborne, who supported the project even though he could not possibly have imagined that it would end up in the form it has, and my friend and editor Stephen Osborne (no relation). To them my special thanks, and to the Canada Council and the British Columbia Ministry of Tourism, Small Business and Culture, both of which provided grants along the way.

The Story of Canada

... nations are narrations.—Edward Said.[1]

Like so many books, this one began as something completely different. Several years ago I became interested in writing about the Red Scare, the fear of imminent Bolshevik revolution which gripped Canada following World War I. The more I looked into the Scare, the more it became clear to me that each side in the 1919 debate was a prisoner of its own image of the other. Leftists and labour radicals conjured up images of rapacious capitalist oppressors; employers and government authorities responded with outlandish images of Bolshevik revolutionaries, funded by Moscow, rampaging through the streets of Canadian towns and cities in an orgy of free love and mindless violence. I am not exaggerating. Never has political discourse in Canada been so removed from reality as it was in 1919.

As I studied this period, I became interested in the divergence between image and actuality, particularly in the disjunction between the squeaky-clean image of the RCMP as a stalwart defender of the law and the reality of the force's role during the Scare, when it was used to spy on Canadians and to subvert their rights. The story of the RCMP is one of the great heroic myths of Canadian history. Yet here was the force acting like the secret police in some foreign dictatorship. This led me to begin questioning images and myths in Canadian history generally. What were some of the major myths I had been taught to believe in? Who originated them, and for what purpose? It turns out that many of our cherished myths were invented by government agencies or private corporations for quite specific, usually self-serving, purposes. Canadians as a whole then embraced them because they seemed to express something that we wanted to believe about ourselves. It is this process of myth formation which became my theme.

The Red Scare remains, but as a single chapter in a book about a far wider subject, a book about memory, mythology, and Canadian history.

A few years ago I wrote a book called *The Imaginary Indian* which described some of the ways non-Native Canadians have imagined Native Indians. Lacking any real knowledge of Native people, non-Natives have felt free to imagine all manner of things about them. Indians were (are) savages; Indians were (are) natural mystics; Indians were (are) militant warriors; Indians were (are) disappearing; Indians were (are) the original environmentalists. I concluded that the Indian was a white man's fantasy, a screen on which non-Natives projected their anxieties and assumptions about their place in the New World.

National Dreams is a similar exercise. It attempts to locate and describe some of the most persistent images and stories in Canadian history. These are the images and stories that seem to express the fundamental beliefs that Canadians hold about themselves. They are the "core myths" which settle out from the welter of historical detail, like silt at the bottom of a river. With repetition they come to form the mainstream memory of the culture, our national dreams, the master narrative which explains the culture to itself and seems to express its overriding purpose. This is the story of Canada, we say, the story which contains our ideals, which gives our experience continuity and purpose. This is who we are.

A nation is a group of people who share the same illusions about themselves. All nations are "imagined communities," to borrow Benedict Anderson's evocative phrase: "the members of even the smallest nation will never know most of their fellow-members, meet them, or even hear of them, yet in the minds of each lives the image of their communion."[2] These images of communion are expressed in the stories we tell about ourselves. Because we lack a common religion, language or ethnicity, because we are spread out so sparsely across such a huge piece of real estate, Canadians depend on this habit of "consensual hallucination"[3] more than any other people. We have a civic ideology, a framework of ideas and aspirations which expresses itself in allegiance to certain public policies and institutions. The CBC, the social safety net, universal health care, hockey—these are just some of the components of our civic ideology. But unlike religion, language or skin colour, a civic ideology is not something we come by naturally. It has to be continually recreated and reinforced. This is one function of history, to provide a rationale for the civic ideology. History explains where our institutions and values came from. Out of this shared experience of the past is supposed to emerge a "national identity" which unites all Canadians and makes us unique from, say, the Chinese or the Germans or, particularly, the Americans. How exactly this works remains a bit of a mystery, but most of us are convinced that it does, that there is such a thing as a national identity and that it is a good thing to have one.

I have used the word "myth" in referring to the important images, stories, and legends which emerge from Canadian history. I do not mean to suggest by this that they are necessarily false or misleading. My purpose is not simply to argue with these stories, to prove that they are right or wrong. I do not wish to deconstruct them into oblivion, cast them out like family retainers who have served their purpose, at least not all of them. It is not hard to show that many of our core myths are invalid, that they do not describe history as we now know it to have been. That is one meaning of myth: falsehood, distortion, inaccuracy, lie. It is the meaning implied by Bernard de Voto's famous dictum about American history, that it "began in myth and has developed through three centuries of fairy stories."

But myths are not lies, or at least, not always. Rather, they express important truths. They usually do not provide a precise record of events, but that is because they serve other purposes. Myths idealize. They select particular events and institutions which seem to embody important cultural values and elevate them to the status of legend. In Canadian history that would be the Mounties, to take an example, or the transcontinental railway, or the North. Conversely, myths demonize. They vilify, or at least marginalize, anyone who seems to be frustrating the main cultural project— Indians, for example, or communists, or Quebec separatists. Myths organize the past into a coherent story, the story of Canada, which simplifies the complex ebb and flow of events and weaves together the disparate threads of experience. Myths are echoes of the past, resonating in the present.

Memory implies its opposite—forgetfulness. As a community, we forget as much as we remember, and what we choose to forget tells as much about us as what we choose to remember. For example, it is known, but not often recalled, that the successful, and relatively peaceful, settlement of Canada by European newcomers was possible largely because a vast number of the original inhabitants, the First Nations, were wiped out by terrible plagues against which they had no defence. This holocaust is arguably the most important episode in Canadian history, yet most of us pay it far less attention than Confederation or the Quiet Revolution or the latest referendum in Quebec. Similarly, we recall with pride the legend of the RCMP, and forget the force's long tradition of repression and illegality. Or we describe ourselves as an inclusive cultural mosaic, while forgetting that racism was at the heart of Canadian culture for generations. The creation of myths—or to put it another way, the creation of unity—requires some forgetting. In order to live together, we try to get over our differences, put aside our grievances, show a united front. History is as much about forging a liveable consensus as it is about remembering.

Obviously, many people are excluded or marginalized by the core myths of Canadian history. That is why so many of the myths are under attack at the moment; they do not express a reality of which many Canadians recognize themselves to be a part. This has always been the case. History is contested terrain. Core myths are usually the property of the elites, who use them to reinforce the status quo and to further their claims to privilege. Again, this does not mean that the myths are false, only that they are partial and constantly at risk of losing their power. In fact, this is exactly what is occurring to most of the core myths which have comforted Canadians for the past few generations. The master narrative has been challenged by counter narratives with their own, very different reading of the past, one which is far less flattering to the elites. The tension between the different versions of Canadian history is also the subject of *National Dreams*.

I

> Those who don't remember the past are condemned
> to repeat the eleventh grade.—James W. Loewen[4]

Like most people, I don't remember much of what I learned about Canadian history in school. There was responsible government, of course, though I still may not be exactly sure how it worked. And Jacques Cartier drinking that stuff made out of tree bark that the Indians gave him to cure scurvy. Drinking was associated with John A. Macdonald as well, though the textbooks hinted pretty strongly that his medicine wasn't tree bark.

Because I grew up in British Columbia I also know that Matthew Begbie was "the Hanging Judge," and Amor de Cosmos's real name was Bill Smith, but I get the feeling that this smattering of random facts would not earn me enough marks to pass an exam if I had to write one today.

Nevertheless, the history courses which I don't even remember must have had an impact because, as a result of what they taught me, I grew up with a whole set of misconceptions about the country which I have spent much of my adult life unlearning. For instance, I discovered that the Indians had not disappeared from the real world as they had from the history books; that Quebeckers are not eternally grateful to have been rescued from French rule by the Conquest; that the sun did set on the British Empire; that women have a history too; and that our prime ministers—a collection of drunks, philanderers and hare-brained spiritualists—were a lot less statesmanlike (and a lot more interesting) than the cardboard cutouts whose stern faces gazed out at me from the pages of my schoolbook.

Seeking an example of what I mean, I need look no farther than the pages of *Our Canada*, a history text in wide use during the 1950s and 1960s when I was at school, written by Arthur Dorland, a professor at the University of Western Ontario. Any student paying attention to Professor Dorland's book would have learned the following "facts": that North American Indians were Chinese in origin and most were cannibals (p. 18); that New France was a "despotism" (p. 59); that the Conquest is something "on which both English- and French-speaking Canadians can look back with pride" (p. 105); that Quebec is a backward province whose people "cling tenaciously to the old French-Canadian ways of living" (p. 353); that "the British Commonwealth of Nations is one of the greatest achievements in human organization in all history" (p. 413); that we should never lose our "rugged spirit of independence" by relying on social assistance, which "should never be a substitute for self help, and should offer no encouragement to the shiftless or lazy" (p. 504). Of course, these are not facts at all. Some are theories, others are opinions, some are outright falsehoods, yet not so long ago they were part of our history, part of what all Canadians were expected to know about their country.

Textbooks are a good place to look for the story of Canada. They are the only history books that most people will ever read, and they are among the few places where the story of Canada is written down in black and white.

That is why I began my search for the core myths of Canadian history by going back to my own high school history textbook, and to the textbooks used by other generations of students before and since. These books remain fascinating not because they explain what actually happened to us, but because they explain what we think happened to us.

Textbooks are only one source for this book. The core myths of Canadian history are revealed as well in the heroes we create, the art we make, the novels and poems we write, the holidays we celebrate, the symbols we acknowledge, even in the advertising images with which we flood the world. I have been interested in them all. One limit I did set was to confine myself almost completely to the history of English-speaking Canada. It is difficult enough to try to understand my own culture; I am not foolhardy enough to attempt to understand another. Quebec is mentioned often in the pages which follow, but always as it is imagined by English Canadians, not as it is imagined by Quebeckers themselves.

No book of this kind can hope to exhaust its subject. My intention is to suggest a way of thinking about Canada so that readers might begin their own process of unlearning history, of re-examining some of the national dreams which preoccupy our waking hours as a nation.

CHAPTER ONE

Making Tracks

THE MYTH OF THE CPR

On the morning of November 18, 1993, as I sat over my morning cereal reading the *Globe and Mail*, I was startled to encounter columnist Michael Valpy's outrage at the desecration of a Canadian symbol. Canadian Pacific had just announced that it was introducing a new corporate logo which would include the American Stars and Stripes along with the familiar maple leaf. "I have a message for those soul-shrivelled, dreary, thick, witless people at Canadian Pacific Railway," Valpy wrote. "You are pathetic."

According to Valpy, CPR was "flushing away" a great Canadian tradition for the sake of making a few more dollars. The railway was, said Valpy, a "wonderful romantic notion," a magnificent technical achievement and one of the enduring symbols of Canadian identity. It had been built in order to preserve the country from the Americans. It was one of the truly great things Canadians had done together as a nation. Yet the "grey faceless bean-counters" in the corporate head offices now planned to betray that legacy by painting the dreaded Stars and Bars on the sides of their rail cars.

In his outrage, Michael Valpy was expressing a common view of the CPR and its relationship to the country. This view holds that without the railway there would be no Canada, certainly not as it exists today. The railway was built chiefly on the backs of Chinese coolie labour, using land obtained for almost nothing from the Indians and capital raised for the most part in Britain. Nevertheless, for many people, it has become over the years a great "Canadian" achievement and a symbol of the bonds which unite us as a people. In 1990, when the Mulroney government introduced drastic cut-backs to national rail service, including an end to the historic route north of Superior known as *The Canadian*, the disappointment and anger were

1. Pierre Berton became something of a national icon himself following publication of his popular two-volume history of the CPR in 1970-71. Already well known as a controversial newspaper columnist and television quiz-show host, Berton's railway books made him the pre-eminent popular historian in the country, our number one National Dreamer. It is impossible to dig too deeply into any aspect of Canada's past without encountering the Berton Version. Here he is instructing Canadians on the history of their national railway in the television miniseries based on the railway books.

widespread. "It's one of the most famous trains in the world," wrote one mourner about *The Canadian*, "right in there with the Orient Express, the Trans-Siberian, the Indian-Pacific. They can't be serious. The history of *The Canadian* is our history."[1] It seemed as if the government was giving up on a noble dream, the National Dream, that once gave meaning to the country. In Canada, a train is, or at least was, much more than a train. It is seen as a visible expression of the determination to exist as a country, against the logic of the geographers and the accountants, Michael Valpy's "grey faceless bean-counters."

"Study the railways and you learn about our people," Silver Donald Cameron once wrote.[2] Where does this idea come from? Most recently it comes from Pierre Berton, who mythologized the history of the railway during the 1970s in three books and a popular television series. Berton's narrative presents the CPR as an heroic endeavour which united the disparate regions of the country in a single, bold dream of nationhood, making Canada "a rare example of a nation created through the construction of a railway."[3] In this narrative, Prime Minister John A. Macdonald is presented as a visionary politician who recognized that Canada was a nation in name only until its two ends were united by the iron road. W. Kaye Lamb, another historian of the railway, agrees. "If he [Macdonald] had not found ways and means of constructing it when he did, Canada would almost certainly not extend today from sea to sea."[4] In the pantheon of nation builders, Macdonald holds front rank, and the railway was his chosen instrument.

The myth of the CPR was in the air long before Berton and Lamb began writing it. Almost every book written about the railway has made the argument that, as R.G. MacBeth put it in 1924, "the country and the railway must stand or fall together."[5] When the Newfoundland poet Ned Pratt was casting about for a suitable epic theme to cap his distinguished career, he saw that the story of the CPR had the necessary ingredients.

> The east-west cousinship, a nation's rise,
> Hail of identity, a world expanding,
> If not the universe: the feel of it
> Was in the air
> —"Union required the line."

His Governor-General's Award-winning epic, *Towards the Last Spike*, presents the railway as a symbol for the completion of the nation.

The myth of the CPR as creator of the country is, in fact, as old as the railway itself, which is not surprising given that it was the railway itself which created the myth. Once the CPR had built the line, it set about promoting its achievement in countless books, pamphlets, stories, and movies. "The construction of the Canadian Pacific consummated Confederation," the company crowed in one of its early publications. The mundane act of constructing a railway was transformed into an heroic narrative of nation building. After a while it was almost impossible to imagine one without applauding the other.

I

Canada is a country without an independence day. Our history reveals no single moment at which the country gained its autonomy.[6] "We cannot find our beginning," Robert Kroetsch writes. "There is no Declaration of Independence, no Magna Carta, no Bastille Day."[7] Canada began as a collection of separate colonies belonging to Great Britain, then evolved by

stages into an independent nation. During the 1840s, responsible government brought a modicum of independence to the local legislatures. In 1867,
Confederation united these legislatures into a single colony, but one which
remained under the protective wing of the Mother Country. The Balfour
Report (1926) declared that Canada was an "autonomous community
within the British Empire," and we began establishing our own embassies
in foreign countries, but the British Privy Council was still our court of last
resort, and the constitution was still amendable only in London. Perhaps
we were not truly independent until 1982, when Canadians attained the
power to amend their own constitution.

Canada accepted its autonomy as a country gradually, almost tentatively,
as opposed to many other countries which seized it enthusiastically and
proclaimed it defiantly. As a result, we have no myth of creation, no narrative
which celebrates the birth of the nation, not even a central image like Uncle
Sam or John Bull to personify the community and sum up what it stands
for. We have no Founders, at least none whom we celebrate. In the absence
of a defining moment, various symbolic ones have been proposed. For the
sake of convenience we celebrate our national birthday on July 1, implying
that Confederation Day, 1867, is Canada's true independence day, even
though it is not. (To make matters more complicated, Quebec celebrates
its "national" day on June 24, St. Jean Baptiste Day.) One familiar narrative
suggests that Canada "came of age" during World War I, that the country
attained a new maturity and the right to speak for itself in the world because
of the carnage suffered by our young soldiers. On the other hand, I
remember getting the impression when I was at school that Canada became
independent with the Statute of Westminster in 1931, even though that
legislation continued to leave important powers in British hands.

One of the most popular candidates for Canadian Independence Day has
been November 7, 1885, the day on which a party of CPR navvies and
notables watched company president Donald Smith drive the last spike at
Craigellachie deep in the mountains of British Columbia. Histories of this
event declare that the two photographs taken at Craigellachie are the most
famous in Canadian history. In his 1924 book about the railway, R.G.
MacBeth suggests that a Last Spike photograph belongs on the wall of every
schoolroom in the country because it captures "the birth of a nation."[8] A
much more recent book about the company calls the Last Spike "the most

2. There are two Last Spike photographs taken by Alexander J. Ross to record
the completion of the Canadian Pacific Railway in 1885. In this one, Donald
Smith stands ready to hammer the spike home. Van Horne is on his right with
chief engineer Sandford Fleming visible between them. The second photograph
shows Smith striking the historic blow. These photographs have been called the
most famous in Canadian history.

important single event in Canadian history."[9] Other countries have produced romantic images of citizens storming the barricades clutching the
flag of freedom. Canada's version is apparently these photographs, showing
a man in a top hat and a wool suit banging at a nail.

If the photographs of the Last Spike are going to be taken as symbolic
representations of the moment of our independence as a nation, it is worth
inquiring how they came to be taken. Textbooks tell us that CPR general
manager William Van Horne wanted a modest ceremony, mainly because

it was all the railway could afford. Chief engineer Sandford Fleming was there, as was Van Horne, Major A.B. Rogers, discoverer of Rogers Pass, and a few other company officials. So were the men who had been busy completing the last stretch of track through Eagle Pass. Otherwise, Van Horne supposedly said, "anyone who wants to see it driven will have to pay full fare."[10] Donald Smith's first blow with the hammer glanced away and merely bent the spike. Another was quickly substituted and, this time more carefully, Smith drove it home. The original, bent spike was taken by Smith and cut up into brooches for the wives of company officials. The second last spike was pulled out following the ceremony to prevent its removal by over-zealous souvenir hunters; it eventually ended up in the possession of Edward Beatty, a later president of the CPR.

The man who took the famous photographs was Alexander J. Ross, a photographer from Calgary. Berton describes him as a hunchback. Beyond that nothing is known about why he was chosen to capture this historic moment on film. Ross remained in the photography business for a few years, then turned to ranching before he died in 1894.[11]

No public officials were present at the Last Spike ceremony, no repre-sentative of the country which, myth has it, the railway made possible. (The Governor-General, Lord Lansdowne, had planned to be there, but was called back to Ottawa on more pressing business.) The Last Spike was an event staged by a group of capitalists to celebrate the completion of a privately-owned railway, albeit one which was generously supported with public land and cash. For them the "trail of iron" was a money-making proposition, not a national dream. "The Canadian Pacific was built for the purpose of making money for the share-holders and for no other purpose under the sun," stated Van Horne.[12] Yet within a few years myth had transformed the railway from a triumph of private capitalism into a triumph of patriotic nation-building. The backers of the CPR were "Empire-builders," not "money-makers," wrote MacBeth.[13] The implication to be drawn is that the real Fathers of Confederation were William Van Horne, Donald Smith, and George Stephen, the men who built the railway.

The narrative of nation-building was reinforced by the fascination which railways exerted over the public imagination during the last half of the nineteenth century. Railways were the emblem of an age which believed fervently in progress and technological achievement. Their promoters

3. Labourers had their own story to tell about the construction of the transcontinental railway. They staged their Last Spike ceremony after the bigwigs
had gone. This photograph reminds us that there are different ways of narrating
history, depending on who is telling the story.

presented them as miracle workers. This "apparently impossible project,"
MacBeth called the CPR; "this modern wonderwork."[14] Railways seemed
capable of transforming the world like magic, spreading wealth, settlement,
and industry in their wake. George Ham, an early CPR publicist, marvelled
at how the road "magically transformed a widely scattered Dominion into
a prosperous and progressive nation."[15] The railway, proclaimed another
enthusiast, is "the magical wand which is destined to people the Great
North West."[16]

Despite all this rhetoric, in the spring of 1885 the yet-to-be-completed
CPR was teetering on the verge of bankruptcy, in desperate need of another
injection of capital. But the patience of the government was wearing thin,
and most observers expected the half-finished project to collapse. Then a
group of disaffected Métis led by Louis Riel and Gabriel Dumont in the
Saskatchewan River country decided to take up arms in support of their

land grievances. They declared a provisional government and routed a party of Mounted Police, raising the spectre of an all-out frontier war. The CPR offered its partially-completed line to move a force of almost 3,000 soldiers quickly westward from Ontario to quell the insurrection. After the Métis and their Indian allies were defeated, the CPR could claim a share in saving the country, and in return a grateful government saved the CPR by approving the money necessary to finish the road.

This co-dependency between the railway and the politicians whose survival depended on its completion goes some way toward explaining the origins of the CPR myth. The railway needed Prime Minister Macdonald and his party to ensure the provision of public funds. Macdonald needed the railway to prolong his political survival and to complete his vision of a transcontinental nation. CPR contributions to the Conservative Party during the 1880s totalled somewhere between $15 and $25 million in today's money.[17] This was taxpayers' money, of course, paid over to the CPR by the government, and then given back to the Conservatives to use to fight their political battles. Locked in such a mutually rewarding embrace, it was not hard for the railway and the Party to convince themselves that the country depended on their success. No wonder the destiny of one became so thoroughly confused with the destiny of the other.

II

The railway preceded settlement, it did not follow it, which meant that once it was completed, there was no one to ride on it. In 1885, the great boom in prairie settlement was still a decade in the future, and almost nobody had any reason to take a train ride across the country. Faced with the challenge of paying for itself, the CPR did two things. First of all, it developed an immigration program for the Prairie West, and secondly it began a campaign to convince travellers that western Canada, and particularly the Rocky Mountains, were attractive tourist destinations. Both objectives could only be achieved by creating a favourable image of western Canada and marketing it around the world. So the CPR embarked on a mammoth selling job, which succeeded beyond its wildest dreams.

In return for building the railway, the CPR had obtained from the government about ten million hectares of land between Ontario and the

THE GRAPHIC

LADY STANLEY RECEIVES A DEPUTATION OF CREE INDIANS FROM THE RESERVE
TO THE NEW WEST WITH THE GOVERNOR-GENERAL OF CANADA OVER THE CANADIAN PACIFIC RAILWAY

4. The CPR promoted western Canada as Indian Country where travellers could expect to see exotic Natives in their natural setting, much like a safari in Africa.

Rocky Mountains (along with $25 million and a variety of other concessions). The company was expected to finance the railroad by selling the land to new settlers. To do so, it created an immigration department which produced a flood of posters, pamphlets, maps, and books in a variety of languages for distribution across Europe and in the United States. This material extolled the Canadian West as a paradise where newcomers would find every opportunity to achieve the good life. Lecturers toured Europe with slide shows designed to impress viewers with the wealth and fertility of the region. In England the railway created a Travelling Exhibition Van which toured the back-country roads like an itinerant circus, carrying the message of the Canadian Eden to all the tiny hamlets where future immigrants might be found. The agent who accompanied the van set up shop in the village market: distributing pamphlets, showing photographs, display-

Canadian National Park

Banff Springs

Glaciers and Mountain Ranges of BRITISH COLUMBIA

CANADIAN PACIFIC LINE

5. Judging by the tourists pictured in this CPR brochure, rail travel to the Canadian West was an opportunity reserved for the well-to-do traveller.

ing samples of grain and other produce. Similar exhibition cars were dispatched to eastern Canada and through the United States, and foreign journalists were conducted across the Prairie at no expense to see for themselves the prairie wonderland. The company even employed the new technology of moving pictures as early as 1902, by commissioning Charles Urban, a British producer, to make a series of thirty-five short films, collectively called *Living Canada*, intended to encourage travel and immigration. A few years later the company ordered a series of thirteen dramatic films, made on location by the Edison Company using a special train placed at its disposal. The films featured melodramatic plots set against the impressive scenic backdrops which were their real subject matter.[18]

This massive sales campaign, reinforced by the government immigration program, paid enormous dividends. By the end of 1883 the company had already made $6.6 million on land sales.[19] Crop failures and government land policies combined to create a slump in the market for a few years, but when the great immigration boom began in 1896, the CPR was nicely situated to profit from its real estate holdings. Much of this valuable land was located in the downtown core of burgeoning western cities like Winnipeg, Calgary, and Vancouver, where even today the CPR continues to profit from the original deal it made well over a century ago.

The efforts which the CPR put into selling western Canada contributed to a new image of the prairie region, which prior to the 1880s had been considered a desert unfit for agricultural settlement. In 1880, a botanist named John Macoun toured the southern prairies on behalf of the federal government and returned to declare that the desert was in fact fertile and just waiting for the farmer's plow to transform it. Immigration promoters, the CPR among them, seized on this revised estimate of the West's potential and spun it into an aggressive campaign to attract settlers. In the process, they manufactured a new identity for the region. No longer was the central interior a barren wasteland better left to the Indians who inhabited it. Now the West was a sunny paradise of grassy meadows, broad rivers, and fertile soil, breadbasket to the world, "the last, best West."

Immigrants were not the only target of CPR propaganda. Tourists were another source of revenue for the railway and a lot of effort went into presenting an image of the West, and particularly of the Rocky Mountains, that would attract visitors. As William Van Horne put it: "Since we can't export the scenery we shall have to import the tourists."[20] In 1884, he engaged the well-known Montreal photographic firm, William Notman and Son, to travel west at the railway's expense to make photographs of the prairie and mountain sections of the railroad. William McFarlane Notman, eldest son of the founder, made a total of eight forays out west, and the photographs he made were used extensively in CPR promotional material and sold separately as postcards, prints, and viewbooks. CPR patronage was extended to other photographers, including Oliver Buell, who used his photographs as lantern slides in his travelling lectures, as well as to several painters who received free rail passes which allowed them to discover the mountains as a new subject matter for their art. The resulting "Railway School" of painters—John Fraser, Lucius O'Brien, Thomas Mower Martin, F.M. Bell-Smith, to name a few—produced a steady stream of mountain portraits. Some of these paintings found their way into the CPR's publicity, as well as into the homes of company executives.

The CPR publicity machine succeeded in turning the country into story. With the help of the company's promotional material, the rail journey unfolded like a book, leaving thoughtful travellers to contemplate the rise of civilization and the majesty of wild nature. The transcontinental trip became a narrative by which visitors interpreted the country as they passed through it, beginning in the settled East where cultivated farms and growing industrial cities gave evidence of a long history of occupation, and progressing onto the plains, which were being transformed into a world granary. Everywhere the signs of industry and growth indicated a prosperous future, while here and there a picturesque Indian village exposed vestiges of the "primitive" peoples who first occupied the region. Finally, visitors arrived at the wilderness of mountains, the ultimate scenic experience.

A further consequence of the CPR's corporate agenda was the system of national parks. The railway created the idea of western Canada as a scenic theme park, promising visitors the chance to see "mighty rivers, vast forests, boundless plains, stupendous mountains and wonders innumerable."[21] Canada was "a paradise for sportsmen," a rare challenge for hikers and trailriders, an unparalleled experience even for someone who just wanted to sit at the window of the observation car and watch the scenery go by. The CPR was involved from the very beginning in the creation of national parks. It pressed the federal government to take control of the hot springs at Banff in order to develop a fashionable spa resort there. Once the government established the Rocky Mountain parks, the CPR took full advantage by touting these wilderness preserves as offering the most spectacular mountain scenery in the world, "1001 Switzerlands Rolled into One" in Van Horne's memorable phrase. It was the CPR which came up with the novel idea of turning the natural wilderness into a profit centre, with great success. By the outbreak of World War I the railway estimated that the Rockies were attracting about $50 million worth of tourism into the country each year.[22] The commercialization of the western mountains persists today in the way we imagine and utilize that part of the country.

The railway also created another narrative: western Canada as Indian Country. Photographs of Native people and their villages sold briskly to travellers wishing mementoes of their visit. Tourists with their own cameras had lots of opportunity to "Kodak the Indians" at stops along the way. "The Indians and the bears were splendid stage properties to have at a station," remarked the English traveller Douglas Sladen.[23] In 1894, the CPR inaugurated Banff Indian Days, an annual summer festival featuring displays of traditional Native cultural practices. The railway realized that wild Indians were a surefire tourist attraction, every bit as exciting as the tribes of darkest Africa, yet available from the safety and convenience of a railway car.

III

The myth of the CPR—the myth that was created by the company and reiterated by most historians ever since—is that the railway made Canada. And perhaps it did. We cannot really know for sure what would have

6. This is one of the Notman photographs that the CPR made available for sale to travellers.

happened had the railway not been built, or not been built as speedily as it was. Without the iron road, the "spine of Canada," the West may well have been absorbed by the United States. Regardless, what remains unarguable is that the CPR did play a leading role in imagining the country into being, which is an entirely different thing. The photographs, paintings, and other images produced by the railway's publicity machine provided the first look most people had of the "New Canada" west of Manitoba. It was impossible even to see the country except by rail; until World War I, the CPR was the only way to do it. Travellers rode in CPR trains, stayed at CPR hotels, ate in CPR restaurants and understood what they were seeing through a veil of CPR promotional material. The CPR "created" Canada not by binding it together with steel rails, but by inventing images of it that people then began to recognize as uniquely Canadian. Canada was the last, best West. Canada was an exotic wilderness. Canada was the breadbasket of the world. Canada was Indian Country. Canada was an imperial highway linking Britain and its distant colonies in a new northwest passage. All these Canadas were conjured into being by the CPR as part of its strategy for becoming the leading transportation and real estate conglomerate in the land.

By 1990, when the federal government closed down most passenger rail service, Canadians had long since given up taking the train. Rail was too slow, too inconvenient, for the modern traveller. But strong public reaction to the cuts demonstrated that the railway nevertheless continues to play an important role in the national fantasy life. We know that the railway no longer holds the country together in fact, but we suspect that it is one of the things which hold it together in our imaginations. Still revered as a fabulous technical achievement, completed against enormous odds, the railway is for many people—Michael Valpy among them—a symbol of our unity, sea to sea. Canadians take pride in the railway as a way of taking pride in the country. You don't just shut down symbols. The protests were expressing a real anxiety, not about the loss of a money-losing rail network, but about the loss of a sense of nation.

CHAPTER TWO

The Mild West
THE MYTH OF THE RCMP

Canadians are the only people in the world who recognize a police force as their proudest national symbol. For a hundred years the Royal Canadian Mounted Police has occupied a special place in our history and our imaginations. The story of how they drove out the American whiskey peddlers and pacified the West is familiar to every school child. Their frontier exploits have been romanticized in decades' worth of movies, books, and television shows. They stand on guard at our national buildings; in gaudy scarlet coats and stiff-brimmed hats, they are present at all our important national ceremonies. They project just the right mixture of stern rectitude and pleasant helpfulness which Canadians like to think we all possess. And, of course, they always get their man.

The Mountie is the face we turn to the world. They are Canada's poster boys, and now girls. They are, as Stephen Osborne has written, "the only souvenir police force in the world."[1] How many thousand postcards of poker-faced police are purchased by visiting tourists each year? Police on horseback, police in front of the Parliament Buildings, police shaking hands with Indian Chiefs. In the past the government has used the image on immigration pamphlets and tourist promotions. For many residents of other countries, the Musical Ride is their first, often their only, exposure to Canada. Not so long ago there was a new beer launched in England which featured a Mountie on its label. So widely known and well regarded is our national police force that in 1995 the Disney Corporation recognized its profit potential by purchasing a license to control the marketing of the force's image.

Our identification with the Mountie reveals something basic about our

understanding of our own history. The narrative of the Mountie subduing
the fiery spirit of the Indian and making the West safe for settlement is one
of our basic cultural myths. It affirms the importance of law and the
subservience of the individual to the community. It expresses our sense of
ourselves as a civilized, orderly society, a "peaceable kingdom." Pierre
Berton has made this a theme of several of his popular history books—the
Canadian desire to maintain order and stability at all cost, sometimes at
great cost. In his book about the Klondike gold rush, Berton returns again
and again to the role of the Mountie in maintaining the peace and showing
the rough-hewn Americans how law-abiding a frontier could be. "Safety
and security, order and harmony—these are qualities that Canadians prize
more highly than their neighbours . . ."[2] In his essay "Why We Act Like
Canadians," Berton returns to "our national preoccupation with peace,
order and good government, by which . . . we mean 'strong government.'"[3]
Berton is not the first, he is just the latest in a long series of popular writers
who have transformed the Mountie into a symbol of a national predisposi-
tion to deference and conformity. Like many of our myths, it has been said
so often that it has become "true."

I

The North-West Mounted Police, the forerunner of the RCMP, was a
frontier police force created by the federal government in 1873 to keep the
peace between Native Indians and white intruders in the area now com-
prising Alberta and Saskatchewan. The familiar narrative relates how a
small army of about three hundred Mounties marched west from Manitoba
in the spring of 1874 across the Plains to southern Alberta where they found
the whiskey peddlers already dispersed. They built a network of log posts
and began dispensing justice British-style. They discouraged horse stealing,
helped to negotiate land treaties, patrolled the railway construction camps,
controlled the liquor trade, and generally imposed order on a restive
frontier. It was a time of transition in the West. The buffalo which had
sustained the Aboriginal lifestyle for centuries were disappearing. Both
Indian and Métis were unsettled by the threat to their traditional economy
posed by the arrival of non-Native settlers. The job of the police was to
make sure that a new society replaced the old with as little upset as possible.

CANADIAN PACIFIC

7. This CPR publicity poster from the 1920s fuses two Canadian icons, the mountains and the Mounties.

It was because they carried out this job so well (and, it must be said, so cheaply) that the story of the Mounties was embraced by a grateful Canadian public.

The transformation of the Mounted Police from historical police force to mythic heroes began with a small group of autobiographers, popular historians, novelists, and Hollywood filmmakers. With the explosion of the dime novel phenomenon near the end of the nineteenth century, the Mountie became a stock figure in fiction. Writers of stories for children picked up the scent—"The scarlet tunic! What a story!" gushed an author in *Chums*, a British adventure magazine for boys—as did bestselling authors like Ralph Connor and James Curwood. They all relied for their material on a handful of published accounts by actual police officers, chiefly Sam Steele's memoir, *Forty Years in Canada* (1915), John Donkin's reminiscences, *Trooper and Redskin in the Far North-West* (1889), and Cecil Denny's history, *The Law Marches West* (1939). To this extent, the Mounties created their own version of history, which then attained the status of popular myth when it was taken over by the professional storytellers. The dime novelist was followed by the Hollywood filmmaker. The first Mountie movie appeared in 1909, and by 1922 one was appearing every couple of weeks. In *Hollywood's Canada*, Pierre Berton estimates that about half the movies made in Hollywood about Canada featured the Mounted Police.[4] These included the 1936 classic, *Rose Marie*, with Nelson Eddy and Jeanette Macdonald, and Cecil B. DeMille's 1940 version of the Northwest Rebellion, *North-West Mounted Police*, starring Gary Cooper. These movies helped to make the Canadian Mountie as familiar to moviegoers as the cowboy and the hard-boiled private eye.

By the time the fictioneers were finished, the reality of the North-West Mounted Police was obscured behind a dense fog of romance and tall tales. The "Great March" of 1874, which in reality was a fiasco of bad planning, in legend became an heroic test of bravery and endurance. The western Plains, where Aboriginal nations had gotten along for centuries without outside interference, were transformed into a savage frontier which was, according to R.G. MacBeth, full of "orgies, brutalities and crimes beyond description."[5] The Mountie myth, as strong today as it was seventy-five years ago, says that the Canadian West was on the brink of a full-scale Indian war which was only averted by the timely arrival of the Mounties who, despite their small numbers, managed to befriend and pacify the Native tribes. "There is no finer chapter in Canadian history," wrote one historian of the force, "than the one in which a mere handful of officers and men of the Mounted Police, with endless patience, unflinching courage and consummate skill in open diplomacy, kept the peace in an area larger than several European kingdoms . . ."[6]

The narrative of the Mounties always emphasizes its own improbability. "How they can accomplish it with such efficiency as they do," wrote the novelist W.A. Fraser in an article in *The Canadian Magazine*, "guarding half a continent, peopled by warlike Indians, so well that a white man may walk from one end of it to the other, unarmed and alone, with greater security than he could pass from Castle Garden to Harlem in New York City, is just a matter of wonder."[7] Historian A.L. Burt actually called the pacification of the West "one of the miracles of Canadian history." How was it possible, Burt wondered, for so few men to "tame" the western tribes? "It is explained by the fact that these were no ordinary men."[8] In Burt's view, they were more like gods: strong, bold, quick-witted, and wise. This hero-worship extended to the descriptions of their physical appearance. "The men looked like models for the statue of Apollo," wrote R.G. MacBeth, "and with clear eye, bronzed faces and alert movement born of their clean and healthful life on the plains, they were godly to behold."[9] Their character, likewise, was unimpeachable. The early chroniclers described the Mountie as unassuming, patient, impartial, self-disciplined, sober, and completely incorruptible. Is it any wonder that Canadians decided to identify so closely with such a paragon?

At the heart of the Mountie legend is the story of the Confrontation, retold again and again in the literature. The details vary, but in essence it is the same event recurring each time. On one side stands the solitary, unarmed Mounted Policeman; on the other side, a much larger number of desperadoes, armed to the teeth and ready to make trouble. The most famous of the Confrontation stories involves the Cree Chief Piapot, who blocks the Canadian Pacific Railway tracks with a large number of warriors in an attempt to extort food for his people. Two Mounties arrive on horseback and give the Cree fifteen minutes to move off. Time passes. The Cree attempt to intimidate the police by shooting their guns and bumping horses. When the time expires, Corporal William Brock Wilde calmly dismounts and knocks over Piapot's tent. He then knocks down another tent, and another, until the Indians realize they are up against an implacable force and meekly withdraw. This story is usually told as if it actually happened. In fact, it was a tall tale invented by William Fraser in an article in *McClure's Magazine* in 1899.

The novelist Ralph Connor tells another version of the Confrontation in *Corporal Cameron of the North-West Mounted Police* (1912), one of his bestselling potboilers. The setting is a Western "gambling joint" popular with "bad men from across the line." Trouble is brewing, when in walks "a tall slim youngster in the red jacket and pill-box cap of that world-famous body of military guardians of law and order, the North-West Mounted Police." Without drawing his own weapon, the Mountie orders the bad guy to put down his gun. Despite the fact that he is surrounded by friends and facing an unarmed man, the American gambler does as he is told and slinks shamefacedly from the room.[10]

These incidents—one told as non-fiction, the other as story—illustrate how the Mountie legend shades from "fact" to "fiction" and back again. They also illustrate the moral force which according to the legend is the real secret of the Mounties' success: the police represent British justice and western civilization. There may only have been a few of them, but they carry the weight of Empire behind them. Indians and other troublemakers are understood to have recognized this immediately. They were easily cowed by the obvious superiority not of the police themselves but of the ideas they represented. Pierre Berton points out that the Mountie is a typical Canadian hero in that he is nameless, faceless, a member of a group rather than an individual.[11] Aside from the self-promoting Sam Steele, history hardly remembers the name of a single Mounted policeman, who, we are told again and again, achieves his goals because of the ideals he embodies.

According to popular legend begun by the Mounties themselves, the Indians were quick to acknowledge that the police were their friends, come to protect them from whiskey traders and other unscrupulous whites. How do so few policemen manage to "keep the Indians down," wonders an American in Connor's novel. "We don't keep them down," responds the Mountie. "We try to take care of them."[12] This is what marks Canadians as different from Americans. South of the border they waged genocidal war against their Native population. In Canada, we sent the Mounted Police to befriend and protect the Indians. Canadians have always believed that we treat our First Nations much more justly than the Americans. It is part of our national self-image. We "know" that the absence of a Wild West in Canada was no accident of history; it was the result of our moral superiority and the superiority of British justice as exemplified in the Mounted Police.

During the early years of their history, the North-West Mounted Police were basically a law unto themselves, acting as arresting officers, judge and jury, imposing order from the top down. The fact that this seemed to earn them respect rather than defiance is often taken to be a sign that Canadians admire deference and pride themselves on respect for law and order. Like any legend, the story of the Mounted Police provides a narrative for understanding our history and expressing our values. According to this narrative, the Mounties in the West were nation builders, laying the groundwork for civilization. "There is absolutely no doubt," affirmed R.G. MacBeth, "that the tide of humanity flowed freely into the vast frontier land by reason of the fact that the scarlet-coated riders had made the wilderness a safe abode and a place of opportunity for the law-abiding and the industrious."[13] The conventional story of the Mounties provides a way of understanding how Canada reached out across the barrier of the Shield country to embrace the western Plains and create a unique society there.

More than that, the Mountie has come to represent a Boy Scoutish quality which according to the master narrative is as basic to our national personality as flag-waving is to the Americans or the stiff upper lip is to the British.

II

The legend of the Mountie was set very early and remained impervious to criticism for a very long time. Given the degree to which Canadians embraced the Mountie image, it is interesting how close the force came to not being created at all, and then, when it was created, how close it came to being disbanded, not once but twice. When the bill to create the North-West Mounted Police was introduced in Parliament during the spring of 1873 there was not a great deal of interest in it.[14] The Pacific Scandal, which would eventually bring down the Conservative government, erupted at about the same time and Prime Minister Macdonald and his followers were naturally preoccupied with their political survival, not events on an unsettled frontier thousands of kilometres away. The legislation passed without debate, but the government wanted to put off the actual creation of the force for another year. It was at this point that a skirmish took place between American wolf hunters and a band of Assiniboine in the Cypress Hills in southern Saskatchewan. About twenty Assiniboine were killed, and promoters of the new police force were able to use this "Indian massacre" to convince the Prime Minister that something had to be done immediately about the American whiskey peddlers and wolfers who were disrupting the territory. As a result, the first contingent of Mounties hurried west to Manitoba in the fall of 1873, not long before Macdonald's government fell, to prepare for the legendary Great March, which took place the following year. R.C. Macleod argues that the new Liberal government, led by Alexander Mackenzie, was more frugal about public spending and would not necessarily have fulfilled the commitment to create a police force had the necessary legislation not already been passed. In other words, Canada's national icon came within a few weeks of never existing at all, leaving Hollywood without *Rose Marie* and Canadians without the musical ride.

The North-West Mounted Police grew in size from about three hundred officers and men to a maximum of a thousand during the 1885 rebellion. During the 1890s, the size of the force began to decline. It had always been conceived as a temporary measure, as a means to pacify the western frontier prior to settlement. By 1900, eastern politicians generally agreed that the Mounties had completed the job they had been sent to do and that the force should soon be dissolved and replaced by the ordinary militia. "The force was not established to remain permanent and perennial," explained Prime Minister Laurier. "It was understood that one day it should cease."[15]

Once again, events intervened to save the NWMP. The outbreak of the Boer War in 1899 diverted all available military personnel to South Africa, and by the time the war ended three years later the Mounties had proven so effective at keeping the peace in the Klondike gold fields and the railway construction camps that western Canadian business leaders were able to convince the federal government yet again to retain the force. This created a constitutional problem, since policing was a provincial, not a federal, responsibility. Nevertheless, when Alberta and Saskatchewan were created as provinces in 1905 it was agreed that the NWMP would remain in place and the new provinces would pay for its services.

But the Mounties' place in history was still not secure. During World War I, the force, now the Royal North-West Mounted Police, once again verged on dissolution. Its contracts with Alberta and Saskatchewan expired, many of its members resigned to join the overseas armed forces, and in eastern Canada another federal force, the Dominion Police, was operating, however ineptly. There appeared to be little reason to keep the RNWMP around.[16] What saved the force, and led directly to its reorganization early in 1920 as the Royal Canadian Mounted Police, was an acute attack of national paranoia known as the Red Scare. In the wake of the war, and the Bolshevik Revolution in Russia, a fear that a "Red revolt" was going to break out in Canada swept the country's ruling elites. Political radicals and labour organizers were labelled revolutionaries; it was believed that they threatened to overthrow the Canadian government. Unwilling to tolerate what it considered to be seditious activity, the federal government took steps to thwart the possibility of revolution by imposing a strict press censorship, banning various political organizations, intercepting mail, deporting so-called "troublemakers," and putting in place an extensive network of undercover agents to spy on anyone who supported radical social change. In effect, what took place in 1919 was a secret conspiracy by the government of Canada against its own people. And one of the main weapons in this conspiracy was a revitalized RNWMP. This is the dark side of the red coat, the counter narrative of the Mounties.

The government campaign against the Reds originated as part of the war effort. With the war dragging on, steps had to be taken on the homefront to produce a narrative that would reinforce the public's resolve to stay the course. As far as the government was concerned, any activity which hampered the war effort smacked of sedition and could not be tolerated. That included workers who opposed conscription and "parlour socialists" who wanted a more equitable social order. Mobilization for war had to be total. As the conflict entered its fifth year the government became particularly attentive to political radicals and labour organizers. There was nothing illegal about their activities, but authorities increasingly portrayed them as harbouring seditious, "bolshevik" ideas. Rumours swirled that foreign money was flooding into the country to fund revolutionary political activity. In May 1918, Prime Minister Robert Borden appointed a special inquiry into the extent of radicalism in Canada, headed by Charles Cahan, a Montreal lawyer. Cahan turned out to be a zealous anti-Bolshevik crusader. His secret report, submitted to the Prime Minister in September, warned that a variety of "revolutionary groups" were actively carrying on "a most pernicious propaganda," especially among recent immigrants from eastern Europe. Much of the labour unrest in the country resulted from this propaganda, which, Cahan claimed, advocated "the destruction of all state authority, the subversion of religion and the obliteration of all property rights."[17] Cahan's report provided a text for the Red Scare, a narrative which demonized virtually all critics of the status quo.

Following Cahan's recommendations, the Borden government passed a series of Draconian Orders-in-Council aimed at smashing radical organizations. One of these measures prohibited the public use of "alien enemy" languages, so that overnight thousands of residents of Canada faced stiff fines and jail sentences for speaking or writing their own language. Another banned a total of fourteen political and labour organizations, mostly belonging to the immigrant communities. Along with the Orders-in-Council, Borden created a Public Safety Branch, with Cahan in charge, "to control, if not to extirpate, the enemy and revolutionary propaganda now being carried on throughout Canada."[18] Increasingly those in authority were blurring the line between legitimate political dissent and treason. In effect, they were applying the force of law to impose a particular reading of reality, a particular narrative of events, and prohibiting any attempt to suggest a counter narrative, even to the extent of banning the languages in which such a counter narrative might be expressed.

Armed with their new powers, police forces across the country went into action. In Winnipeg police arrested Michael Charitinoff, a newspaper editor, for possession of illegal literature. Security forces claimed that Charitinoff was Lenin's "ambassador to western Canada," and that he had been provided by the Bolshevik leader with a seven-thousand-dollar bank-roll to foment revolution. Judge Hugh John Macdonald, son of the former prime minister, sentenced him to three years in prison and a thousand-dollar fine. Meanwhile, in Ontario, police carried out raids on the offices of several banned organizations, seizing literature and arresting forty-four people. In England, where he was preparing for the upcoming peace conference in Paris, Prime Minister Borden received intelligence that the Russian government was smuggling large sums of money abroad to support a massive propaganda effort. He relayed the information to Ottawa, with the warning that his ministers should be prepared to see an organized effort to subvert the government in the new year. Charles Cahan warned of "incipient revolution raising its head, with accompanying civil disorder and bloodshed."[19] His apocalyptic language was echoed by A.P. Sherwood, the retiring commissioner of the Dominion Police, who urged the government to continue its repressive measures until every Bolshevik idea "shall be either stamped out or driven back to the home that gave birth to this dangerous form of madness."[20]

In retrospect, it seems astonishing that Canadians agreed with the government's contention that the country was on the verge of a Bolshevik insurrection at the end of World War I. Nothing of the sort occurred, of course, and it seems perfectly clear now that there was no organized conspiracy to overthrow the government, funded by Moscow or anybody else. The whole thing was a paranoid fantasy, a version of events which managed to gain hegemony over any other version. At the time, however, the example of the Russian Revolution was fresh in everyone's mind, including many labour leaders who delighted in adopting some of its rhetorical flourishes, such as signing their letters "Yours in revolution" and punctuating meetings with shouts of "Long live the Russian Soviet Republic." It was an atmosphere of optimism and anxiety. After years of war and sacrifice, everyone expected a change, but in what direction? "But what a seething time it is in the world!" Senator George Foster wrote in his diary. "What is brewing, what will result? Certainly the foundation of things are being uprooted in a thousand ways—what will be laid down to take their place?"[21] Anything seemed possible, but nothing seemed certain. The political and business elites grew alarmed when workers took seriously the possibility of social and economic change. "Bolshevism" became a convenient way of interpreting, and discrediting, most efforts at real reform.

The RNWMP played a key role in silencing anyone who proposed a counter narrative to the Red Scare. Its agents infiltrated most of the leading labour organizations and sent back alarmist reports that unions were seething with revolutionary intent. In March 1919, union representatives from across western Canada attended the Western Labour Conference in Calgary where they voted to organize a referendum on the formation of One Big Union. The OBU, which passed the referendum and was launched in June, was an attempt to unite all workers in a single industrial union committed to political action and social change.[22] To mainstream unionists, governments, and the public, it was nothing short of Red revolution. "Soviet Plotters Busy in Canada," the *Montreal Daily Star* told its readers. "The Bolshevistic spirit in its worst form lies back of the 'Red' activities of last week's convention," editorialized the *Calgary Daily Herald*. "There is no place, no room for it in Canada."[23]

Robert Gosden, one of the RNWMP's undercover agents, attended the Calgary convention where almost immediately he was identified as "a police spy and stool-pigeon." After a noisy debate, the meeting decided he could stay anyway, but what delegates did not know was that the force had another agent in attendance. He was Frank Zaneth, known in Calgary labour circles as Harry Blask. Posing as an activist, Zaneth/Blask had infiltrated the union movement by getting a job as secretary to one of its leaders. He attended secret meetings of the Socialist Party, conferred with its members, sold its literature on the streets—and reported everything to his police superiors. The first inkling labour leaders had that their friend Harry Blask was not

8. Roger Bray, one of the Winnipeg strike leaders, addresses a meeting at Victoria Park. During the Red Scare, meetings like this one would be guaranteed to attract several police spies. The Royal North-West Mounted Police proved so efficient at undercover work that the federal government reorganized it as a brand new national police force, the Royal Canadian Mounted Police, in 1920.

who he said he was did not come until December when he appeared in a courtroom in Winnipeg in full Mountie uniform to testify against the men arrested during the General Strike earlier in the year.[24]

Meanwhile, Gosden filed reports with the RNWMP under his code name, "Agent 10." In his opinion, the OBU was nothing more than a ruse to solidify the position of radical socialists at the head of the labour movement. Their aim, he reported, was to foment "a social revolution of the Bolsheviki type." By now this way of constructing events was familiar enough, but Gosden proposed a uniquely extreme response. He suggested that the Mounties secretly apprehend several members of the "Red element" and imprison them without trial or publicity in an attempt to terrorize their followers into submission. In other words, he was proposing the use of "disappearances" long before they became favoured by Latin American dictators. "After one or two of these leaders had been picked up at various points in a mysterious manner, and disappeared just as mysteriously, the unseen hand would so intimidate the weaker and lesser lights that the agitation would automatically die down," he wrote. He admitted that "this may not be in strict accordance with technical law," but desperate times called for desperate measures.[25]

Gosden's superiors in the RNWMP characterized his report as "over drawn" and did not carry through on his recommendations. Commissioner A. Bowen Perry was more sanguine. He did not think the "Reds" were plotting a violent overthrow of the government. Nonetheless, Perry did believe that there was cause for alarm. "I do say that they are influencing a section of labour in the West," he warned, "and unchaining forces which, even if they so desire, some day they will be unable to control. Here is grave danger, to the peace and security of the country."[26]

Another important police document influencing government thinking about the labour situation was a "Memo on Revolutionary Tendencies in Western Canada," prepared by C.F. Hamilton, a former journalist and wartime press censor who had become assistant comptroller of the Mounted Police following the war. In his memo, Hamilton argued that there was a small but active band of revolutionaries at work in western Canada attempting to subvert the Canadian government. "Their openly avowed aim is to procure the establishment of a Soviet government, with its concomitants of the disappearance of parliamentary government, the subversion of the rule of the majority, the abolition of private ownership of property, and the destruction of the other institutions upon which society is founded." Hamilton admitted that armed insurrection seemed unlikely, but he argued that there were circumstances in which it could occur and the key was the troubled labour situation. He sketched out a plausible scenario for the "would-be revolutionists." "What they aim at is an intense conflict between labour and capital, embittered by riots and bloodshed; they calculate on a general dislocation of the industrial system, passing into an uprising of the working classes, probably reinforced by masses of discontented returned soldiers. The whole project turns upon the propagation of bad temper and mutual hate between classes . . ." Unlike "Agent 10," Hamilton did not believe that direct repression was the answer. Instead, he called for a campaign of counter-propaganda highlighting the failure of Bolshevism to bring social peace and prosperity to Russia.[27]

As the police flooded his office with alarmist reports, acting Prime Minister Sir Thomas White panicked. In mid-April he cabled Borden, who was still away in Europe at the peace talks, to inform him that Bolshevism was rampant in Canada, especially in British Columbia. There was a revolution brewing, White reported, and he took the surprising step of requesting that Borden ask the British government to dispatch one of its warships to Vancouver as a pre-emptive show of force. Borden, busy making the world safe for democracy, was impatient at White's bothering him with what no doubt seemed like petty domestic problems. "I would very much like to reply, For Heaven's Sake, let me alone," he confided to his diary.[28] Instead he advised White to do the best he could with the forces at his disposal; there would be no request for a British gunboat.

There would, however, be the propaganda campaign that Charles Hamilton of the RNWMP envisioned. Whenever police reports arrived with information about the Reds, it was relayed to members of the print media and via the newspapers to the public. Chief press censor E.J. Chambers did his best to orchestrate a campaign involving the press, university professors, Canadian Clubs, churches, even movies, all fuelled with information of the right type provided by his department. In February he wrote to the presidents of several major universities asking that they make speeches or write articles exposing the fallacies of "extreme red Socialism."[29] Charles Cahan was another busy scaremonger. In January he resigned from his job as director of public safety, but he continued to speak out about the Bolshevik threat. One of his speeches, "Socialistic Propaganda in Canada," was printed as a pamphlet and widely distributed. In it he conjured up the likelihood of actual civil war between capital and labour which would require the army to intervene.

Among the most influential proponents of the Scare narrative were *Maclean's* magazine and its owner, Col. John Bayne Maclean. The January 1919 issue of the magazine contained an article titled "Is Bolshevism

Brewing in Canada?" to which the author, Thomas Fraser, answered an emphatic Yes. "There is a bold, systematic and dangerous effort being made to lay the fuse of Bolshevism from one end of the Dominion to the other," Fraser warned.[30] Labour radicals were allegedly plotting to seize control of all industry and to abolish the wage system. This article earned warm praise from Ernest Chambers, the press censor, who wrote to Maclean urging him to continue to raise the alarm. The Colonel hardly needed encouragement. In the June issue of his magazine, he wrote an article claiming that groups of revolutionaries in Toronto and Ottawa were poised to take over the country. Then, in August, he introduced *Maclean's* readers to the kingpin of the Bolshevik conspiracy in North America, one Santeri Nuorteva, a Soviet information officer in New York who, Maclean said, had bankrolled the recent general strike in Winnipeg and was busily preparing eastern Canada for revolution. Accompanying the article was a photograph of a stocky, bald, bespectacled man whom Maclean characterized as the very face of the Red conspiracy.[31] (Nuorteva was an employee of the Russian Soviet Government Information Bureau in New York and claimed to be promoting perfectly legitimate commercial relations with Russia. He soon returned to the Soviet Union where the regime for which he was supposedly a master spy threw him in jail for a year, then exiled him to Siberia.[32])

The definition of Bolshevism which emerged from all the propaganda generated by the Red Scare was suprisingly flexible. It could be applied to almost anyone whose politics strayed from the mainstream. Some people believed that Bolshevism was essentially an economic doctrine proposing the abolition of the wage system and the transfer of the means of production from employers to workers. Others thought that it primarily promoted free love and the abolition of the family. To others it was nothing more than organized terrorism on a grand scale. For instance, the federal minister of public works, F.B. Carvell, defined a Bolshevik as "a wild-eyed anarchist looting a bank, shooting down all the Bourgeois or property owners in the country and carrying off their wives and children."[33] Pleading for a return to common sense, Liberal Member of Parliament "Chubby" Power pointed out: "It is becoming the habit in this country to designate everyone a Bolshevist with whom we cannot agree."[34]

The Red Scare, a brewing storm of fear, suspicion, class prejudice, and anti-immigrant hysteria, broke over Winnipeg in the spring of 1919. The general strike which began in that city on May 1 was greeted as a prophecy fulfilled. Police agents and the popular press had been warning for months that the Reds were planning a revolt. When the strike began, then quickly snowballed to involve 30,000 workers, bringing the city to a standstill, a government which had been conditioned to expect an insurrection naturally believed that one had broken out. The Winnipeg strike was a stark example of conflicting narratives battling for acceptance. For the strikers, it was about their right to collective bargaining. For many police and government officials and members of the employing classes, it was the beginning of Canada's Bolshevik revolution, what the *Winnipeg Free Press* dubbed "The Great Dream of the Winnipeg Soviet."[35]

The Mounties played a central role in the strike, just as they had played a central role in the undercover campaign leading up to it. The usual Winnipeg detachment of twenty-seven men increased to a force of 245 men, sixty horses, and four armoured vehicles with mounted machine guns. At two crucial moments authorities employed the Mounties as a special strike force against the strikers. Firstly, before dawn on the morning of June 17, police descended on the homes of nine strike leaders and "foreign agitators" and swept them away to Stony Mountain Penitentiary north of the city. The arrests led to the bloody showdown of the strike which took place four days later, on June 21, when a troop of Mounties on horseback was deployed to break up a march of returned soldiers demonstrating in support of the jailed leaders. Assailed by a heavy barrage of stones, bottles, and bricks, the police retaliated, first with clubs, then guns. One man was killed instantly, another died later, and several others were wounded by police gunfire. After "Bloody Saturday" there were no more demonstrations. Workers began drifting back to their jobs. Five days later the general strike officially ended.

"The boil broke in Winnipeg on Saturday," announced George Foster, back from Europe and still keeping his diary. "Some blood was shed but law and order was maintained and probably the issue as to that point was settled for all Canada."[36] Historians still debate the implications of the Winnipeg strike, but most Canadians at the time shared Senator Foster's analysis. The brutal suppression of the strike, followed by a series of police raids on the offices of suspect labour and political organizations right across the country, stopped the "revolution" in its tracks. Later in the year, the show trials of the arrested strike leaders, featuring crucial testimony by Mountie informers, led to convictions and jail terms. The official version of events embodied in the Red Scare narrative had carried the day. As a result, the Scare was no longer necessary and it petered out.

As an organization, the Mounties profited greatly from the Scare. Federal policing was reorganized to combine the RNWMP with the Dominion Police in a single new force, the Royal Canadian Mounted Police. In a little over a year the Mounties had gone from a limited, regional force of 303 men with no clear mandate and apparently no future, to a 2,500-man force with jurisdiction over the entire country.[37] The romantic image of the frontier Mountie pursuing his man to the ends of the earth on dogsled and horseback may have satisfied the requirements of dime novelists and Hollywood filmmakers, but that image had nothing to do with the reality of police work in Canada post-World War I. The RCMP actually owed its success, its very existence, to its clandestine efforts to stamp out not crime, but radical political activity.

III

Though the obsession with Red revolution which gripped the country in 1919 dissipated during the following decade, it never disappeared completely, and the RCMP continued to make itself useful spying on Canadians. In 1921, a group of activists formed the Communist Party of Canada at a secret meeting in an isolated barn near Guelph, Ontario. But the meeting wasn't really so secret; the Mounties had an agent in attendance. For its first three years the CPC was illegal under the terms of the War Measures Act, which was still in effect. In 1924, it surfaced as a legitimate political party, though its activities were severely restricted by the infamous Section 98 of the Criminal Code which banned any organization advocating violent political or economic change. Even the slightest link with such an organization—for example, attending a meeting—could result in a jail sentence.

The Communist Party of Canada was a dedicated but weak and divided group of workers and intellectuals which never succeeded in attracting many members. The party did attract a disproportionate amount of attention from the police, however, especially during the 1930s. When Prime Minister R.B. Bennett promised to grind communism under "the heel of ruthlessness," it was the heel of the RCMP riding boot he had in mind. At the same time as the upright image of the Mountie flourished in books and movies, the force was actually acting as stormtroopers on behalf of a federal government once again obsessed with the fear that the restless unemployed were on the verge of rising up in Soviet-style revolution. It was the Red Scare all over again.

The RCMP's Depression-era war on the Reds began in August 1931 in Toronto, when several members of the force took part in a co-ordinated police raid on the headquarters of the Communist Party and the homes of several of its leaders. Later in the year eight of the men, including Tim Buck, the longtime leader of the party, were convicted under the provisions of Section 98, largely due to the evidence provided by the RCMP. Seven of the eight received five-year terms in Kingston Penitentiary; Tomo Cacic, a Croatian immigrant who was swept up in the raids because he happened to be paying a visit to party headquarters, got two years.[38]

Meanwhile, at the end of September in the coal fields of southern Saskatchewan, striking miners clashed with police in one of the worst incidents of strike violence in Canadian history. The miners, who lived and worked in conditions resembling serfdom, were on strike because mine owners refused to negotiate with their Communist-led union. In defiance of a ban on demonstrations, a cavalcade of miners' cars approached down-town Estevan to attend a meeting, and a cordon of RCMP officers attempted to halt the procession. Fighting broke out, and police began firing into the crowd. Three unarmed strikers died, and many more were wounded. No member of the RCMP was ever held accountable for the deaths. Instead, eleven miners received jail terms for their part in the incident. The attempt to unionize the mines failed and the strike collapsed. The owners had succeeded in passing themselves off as freedom fighters in the war against the Reds. As a result they earned the complete co-operation of the government, including the RCMP.

Authorities were terrified of the Reds beyond all reason. By any objective standard, the Communist Party had almost no support among the Canadian people. In early 1930 in Vancouver the party called for a demonstration among the unemployed, and only thirty-seven people showed up. In the federal election that year, Communist candidates won exactly 7,601 votes. As the Depression deepened, sympathy for the unemployed and destitute increased, but sympathy hardly constituted mass revolutionary ferment. If anything, it was the attempts at suppression of the party which ended up winning it the attention it craved.

In 1932, the government launched a campaign to rid the country of foreign-born "agitators," and the RCMP began rounding up radicals who were newcomers to Canada and had not yet become naturalized citizens. They seized them at home or at their place of work, sequestered them without telling anyone where they were, and spirited them by train to Halifax where they received secret hearings and were summarily deported to Europe.[39] The whole operation was reminiscent of Agent 10's plan to disappear union leaders during the first Red Scare in 1919. At that time the idea was considered too extreme, but by the 1930s the government was prepared to stop at nothing to get unnaturalized radicals out of the country. The occasional voice was raised in protest—the *Toronto Star* called the RCMP the "Canadian Cheka," a reference to the Soviet secret police—but by and large the police had the support of a traumatized public.

The worst instance of RCMP violence occurred in 1935 when thousands of unemployed men from government relief camps arrived in Regina by rail on their way to present their demands in Ottawa. This so-called On-to-Ottawa Trek began in Vancouver and had been gaining momentum as it moved eastward. When the men reached Regina in the middle of June, Prime Minister Bennett decided it was time to call a halt to the protest. The RCMP was deployed to make sure that the trekkers did not get any farther, while federal negotiators met with trek leaders and invited them to send a delegation to Ottawa to talk with Bennett. When this group returned from the capital empty-handed a week later a lot of the steam went out of the trek, but for the time being the protesters had nowhere to go. On July 1, some of them gathered at a rally in Regina's Market Square with over a thousand residents of the city. Mounties and city police surrounded the square, ostensibly to arrest the trek leaders, but at a prearranged signal they stormed into the crowd, swinging their clubs and knocking people to the ground indiscriminately. Confused and terrified, the crowd fought back, and soon a full-scale riot was in progress. The Mounties used tear-gas to clear the square and were battered in return by bricks, bottles, rocks, and sticks, whatever lay to hand. City police fired on the crowd and seventeen people ended up in hospital with gunshot wounds, none fatal. There was

9. According to the Red Scare narrative, these single, unemployed men riding
the rails in search of work were "the enemy within," dangerous radicals who
posed a threat to the social order. The RCMP had the job of spying on their activities. Matters came to a head during the On-to-Ottawa Trek in the summer of
1935 when protesters were set upon by police at a demonstration in Regina.

one death: a plainclothes city policeman beaten over the head. By the time
the riot petered out after about four hours of street fighting, downtown
Regina was a mess of broken plate glass windows, smashed automobiles,
and debris of all descriptions. Four days later the trekkers were allowed to
leave the city, this time heading back West to their homes or to the relief
camps where the whole thing started.[40]

The image of the upright Mountie suffered as a result of these incidents,
at least with the working people and immigrants who were the main victims
of repression. By and large, however, the public shared the government
obsession with "the enemy within" and viewed the RCMP as a bulwark

against domestic revolution. The popular press laid down a tremendous barrage of anti-Red propaganda, fulminating against "foreign agitators" and "Red troublemakers." Most of the victims of police repression were immigrants anyway; their fate was not of much interest to the majority of Canadians. The Red Scare contained a broad streak of xenophobia; Communism was considered a foreign philosophy spread by outsiders. Unlike Americans, Canadians have never officially identified anything called "un-Canadian activities," but if the phrase had been invented it certainly would have been applied to the efforts of the Communists to organize the dispossessed during the Depression.

Just as World War I produced the first Red Scare, so World War II merged into the Cold War and yet another outbreak of Red paranoia in Canada. Once again Mounties were pressed into service as the foot soldiers in a war against "the enemy within."[41] In 1945, Igor Gouzenko defected from his job as a cipher clerk at the Soviet embassy in Ottawa, taking with him a stack of documents revealing the existence of a spy ring active in Canada. This sensational case eventually led to the conviction of eleven conspirators and touched off a wave of public concern about Communist subversives. The RCMP Security Service targeted the Communist Party of Canada and its various front groups for infiltration, along with labour unions, the peace movement, the National Film Board, and any other group leftist enough to draw attention to itself. Communists were considered "masters of deception"—the phrase is Lester Pearson's—working secretly to undermine and overthrow the Canadian government. In reality Communists in Canada were hopelessly marginalized, enjoyed almost no public support, and never posed a serious threat to the stability of the state. But they were useful bogeymen which the government could use to mobilize public opinion in support of its Cold War foreign policy. For the RCMP the Communist had replaced the Indian as the all-purpose threat to peace and stability. According to the original legend, the North-West Mounted Police had averted a savage Indian war and pacified the West. In the modern version of the myth, the Mounties kept democracy safe from radicals and subversives hell-bent on destroying it.

So long as the targets of its activities were criminals, subversives, and "foreigners," the benign image of the RCMP as the stalwart defender of law and order was preserved. No one seemed to care that much of the force's work involved the suppression of legitimate political dissent and freedom of speech. The reputation of the Mountie was associated so closely with the essence of Canadian identity that criticizing the force would have felt like criticizing ourselves.

IV

In the 1970s, the Mounties' image began to tarnish as a series of public inquiries revealed the extent to which the force was breaking the law in its relentless pursuit of "the enemy within." Gradually it came out that the RCMP was tampering with the mail, burglarizing the offices of perfectly legitimate political parties like the Parti Québecois, spying on Aboriginal and black Canadians, and generally behaving like dirty tricksters instead of the incorruptible lawmen of legend.[42] As a result of these revelations, the federal government in 1984 removed responsibility for internal security matters from the RCMP and created a new, civilian agency, the Canadian Security Intelligence Service.

The scandals of the 1970s did irreparable harm to the image of the Mounties. It began to seem much more likely that the vaunted Redcoats were spying on Canadians than standing on guard for them. As a result the Mountie has become more a figure of fun than an authority figure. Take, for example, the television show *Due South*, which lampoons the lantern-jawed image for an American audience, or Corporal Renfrew, comedian Dave Broadfoot's dimwitted version of the Mountie. Canadians seem to have lost faith in most of our traditional institutions; there is no reason why the Mounties should be spared.

Still, the traditional, upright image continues to resonate, or the Disney Corporation would not be interested in marketing it. It seems to stand for something deep in the Canadian character. It has become dissociated from the actual history of the force and stands alone as a symbol of how Canadians like to see themselves: honest, brave, modest, law-abiding, polite. The image of the Mountie is a fabrication, which does not mean that it is untrue, just that its "truth" is psychological, not historical. In this sense, the "Mountie" has become wholly imaginary, a source of pride and identity which provides a pattern to our history and affirms values which all Canadians are presumed to share.

Over the years the imaginary Mountie has been very useful to authorities. With the support of the press and much of the public, governments have consistently invoked the image to protect the Canadian "way of life." As a frontier police force, the Riders of the Plains prepared the western interior for "civilized" occupation. As an urban police force, the RCMP rooted out subversion and spied on political nonconformists. The benign image of the Boy Scout Mountie was the velvet glove in which the iron hand of the state wielded its power.

CHAPTER THREE

Your Majesty's Realm
THE MYTH OF THE MASTER RACE

By the time I began school in the 1950s, the ties which bound Canada to Great Britain, the monarchy, and the old Empire were beginning to fray. A large number of countries on the tattered map of the world hanging on the wall of my classroom were still coloured red, but no one seriously expected us to become little imperialists. I recall being quick-marched up to Tenth Avenue one morning with the rest of my school—it must have been 1959—and told to wave my tiny Union Jack at a passing cavalcade of shiny black limousines. A flash of white glove at the window indicated which vehicle contained Queen Elizabeth and Prince Philip. We redoubled our cheers, but our celebrations had more to do with the novelty of skipping class than with any enthusiasm for the monarchy. I do not recall feeling that this was my Queen. My small heart did not swell with pride at the thought that Canada was a member of the Commonwealth of Nations. The fact that four decades later I still cannot explain why the Common-wealth exists is surely testament to the inadequacy of my education for imperialism.

Not so for earlier generations of Canadian schoolchildren, who were taught to venerate Great Britain and its empire. The Union Jack flew at all the schools (Canada didn't have its own flag yet); students pledged alle-giance to the monarch and sang "Rule Britannia" and "Soldiers of the Queen." (How many of us attended schools named before we were born for members of the Royal Family? Mine was Queen Mary. Our baseball league included teams from Queen Elizabeth, Lord Kitchener, Lord Ten-nyson, and General Gordon. Later I attended a high school named for a British-born Governor-General.) Sir John A. Macdonald's stout defence

10. This classroom in a one-room school near Bruderheim, Alberta, in 1910 was decorated with the same imperial images as my own big-city school fifty years later, including the wall map, the flags, and the pictures of British royalty.

of the colonial connection—"I am a British subject, and British born, and a British subject I hope to die"—seemed the highest form of patriotism. Teachers taught that Canadian institutions derived all their value from British precedent. Until at least World War II the worship of the monarchy and the British Empire enjoyed almost cult status in Canadian society.

I

One way to understand the degree to which Anglo-Saxon ethnocultural pride once pervaded Canadian society is to re-examine what children belonging to generations previous to my own were taught in the classroom. Every subject in the curriculum was expected to reinforce the British connection, but none more so than history. It was in the history classroom, and the history textbook, that young Canadians received explicit instruction in the ideology of imperialism. Until at least the 1950s, students were educated to become citizens of an empire as much as to become citizens of Canada.

Two important elements of the master narrative of Canadian history as it used to be taught in the schools were the superiority of the British form of government and way of life, and the gradual evolution of Canadian society to equal partnership in the imperial enterprise. This imperialist version of history was preoccupied with describing the progress of Canada from dependent colony to self-governing Dominion; "the earnest and unceasing struggle for political liberty," as one book called it.[1] The process much resembled the maturation of a child to responsible adulthood. Given this way of framing the subject, it is not surprising that the details of Canadian history as they were taught in school were almost entirely political, military, and constitutional. The conventional story line begins with the conquest of the French by British arms on the Plains of Abraham, proceeds through the extension of representative political institutions, and concludes with Confederation and the subsequent expansion and consolidation of the Dominion. Events which do not conform to this narrative agenda are to be considered, as Charles G.D. Roberts wrote in 1897, "mere incidents, to be referred to in passing, but not to be confused with matters of deeper import."[2]

Self-government in the Canadian context was not to be confused with independence. Early textbooks made clear that Canada's destiny was to be a member of the imperial flock, not a solitary bird flying alone. According to the imperialist view, it was within the sheltering embrace of the Mother Country that Canada would flourish. This rejection of independence was expressed most forcibly by Roberts—a teacher before he was a poet—who warned his young readers that it would be selfish and ungrateful to think of turning their backs on Britain.[3] More moderate, but no less enthusiastic imperialists, such as Arthur Dorland, writing fifty years later, invoked the analogy of the family. Great Britain was "the mother of a family of free states," each of whom was an autonomous individual but still dependent on its parent for security and favoured treatment.[4] Canada must be one of the few countries in the world to have taught its young citizens that national independence was an irrelevant, even a shameful, aspiration.

This textbook road to nationhood is marked by several familiar

11. "The Death of Wolfe" by the American artist Benjamin West (1738-1820) depicts General James Wolfe expiring on the Plains of Abraham during the Battle for Quebec in 1759. This is one of the most famous paintings in the history of British imperial art. It is entirely rhetorical, a monument to historical fabrication. Almost none of the people depicted in the painting were present at Wolfe's death, which happened away from the field of battle. But West did not care to be constrained by fact. He wanted to move the mind and engage the emotions and for that he needed spectacle; mere accuracy would not do. And, of course, he was right. Exhibited for the first time in London in April 1771, "The Death of Wolfe" was an instant sensation. It was replicated by West himself several times; engraved copies sold like hotcakes and reproductions turned up on drinking mugs and tea trays. Most importantly here in Canada, the painting has appeared in countless schoolbooks where it has been used to convey a view of the Conquest as an heroic victory for British civilization.

signposts, beginning with Wolfe's victory at the Battle of Quebec in 1759, a victory which brings Canada into the imperial fold. According to the imperialist narrative, the Conquest was a victory not just for British but for French colonists as well because it rescued them from the despotic control of the French monarchy. (More on this subject in the next chapter.) The next signpost on the road to self-government is the arrival of the Loyalists in Canada at the end of the eighteenth century. These refugees from the American War of Independence are considered in the imperialist view to be "the real makers of Canada"[5]: they were the best and the brightest that the American colonies had to offer, "people of culture and social distinction," "the best blood in the United States."[6] Unjustly hounded from their homes by rebellious Americans, the Loyalists are construed to have lost everything but their faith in the British constitution. Canadian textbooks were unanimous in their presentation of the American Revolution as unnecessary and self-interested: the American colonists did not want to pay their fair share of taxes, it was as simple as that. The Loyalists' defence of imperial unity is to be seen, in this view, as noble and unselfish, and their struggle to make new lives for themselves in Canada an inspiration for succeeding generations. Modern historians draw a more complicated picture of the Loyalists who, they say, came from all social classes and wanted to sit out the Revolution for all sorts of reasons, some of which had nothing to do with political principle. The imperialist view less subtly presents the Loyalists as unqualified martyrs and heroes who injected a strain of moral seriousness into the Canadian character which remains with us to the present.

Loyalism was tested once again, according to the textbooks, by the War of 1812, which, they tell us, was a war of aggression started by land-hungry Americans. The war was "our baptism in blood," wrote W.L. Grant in 1914, and it gave to Canada "an heroic tradition" of selfless sacrifice.[7] Many lives were lost, but the cause was just and the pride which resulted from the successful resistance to the Americans represented the first glimmering of a Canadian nationality. In the same way that later generations of Canadians have come to believe that a sense of a distinctive Canadian identity was born in the blood and sacrifice of World War I, so earlier generations traced this self-awareness to the battlefields of the War of 1812.

The imperialist view of history casts into the shade the 1837 rebellions in Upper and Lower Canada, which are presented without exception as dreadful mistakes. Some writers treat them as *opera bouffe*, with rebel leaders like Louis Papineau and William Lyon Mackenzie cast in the role of clowns. A majority of the textbooks treat the risings more seriously, but still present them as the work of irresponsible zealots who, by trying to force the pace of constitutional change, actually did more harm than good. This was the "official line" on the rebellions until at least the 1950s.

Most English-language textbooks before the 1960s are more dismissive of the Lower Canada rebels than their Upper Canada counterparts. The Quebec populace had very little to complain about, they argue, and were misled by the impetuous, demagogic Papineau. The grievances of the *habitants* were trivial, claimed the Methodist clergyman turned historian William Withrow in 1876; their leaders were "restless and designing demagogues" who duped an ignorant populace into taking up arms in support of completely unreasonable demands.[8] Other writers took a more sympathetic view of Papineau, describing him as eloquent, cultured, charming, and dynamic, but in the end, however, they came to similar conclusions about the armed rising: a basically loyal populace misled by a small group of scheming radicals into acting against its own best interests. As *The Story of Canada*, a popular text in wide use during the 1930s and 1940s, put it: "This Papineau seemed to have summoned his dupes to arms and then to have run away . . ."[9]—a reference to the fact that Papineau fled to the United States when fighting broke out. It was basic to the imperialist view that the vast majority of French Canadians did not join the rising; that they were content with British rule and had no serious grievances against it.

In Ontario, on the other hand, the same textbooks agree that injustices prevailed, principally in the concentration of power in the hands of a small, ruling clique, the so-called Family Compact. Still, this in no way is seen to justify the violent response of Mackenzie and his followers. In almost every book Mackenzie is dismissed as a vain, posturing, impulsive agitator: his heart may have been in the right place, but he had no "workable solutions" for the problems of the day.[10] Only one textbook, *Canada: A Nation and How It Came to Be* (1948), positions the events of 1837-38 as a popular, democratic uprising. "The Rebellions were American Revolutions in miniature," write its authors, Lower and Chafe, "and though at the time they seemed to have failed, they cleared the way for self-government; and just beyond

12. No friend of the French, Lord Durham has been hailed in English Canada as a far-sighted visionary who gave Canada responsible government and the world a revitalized British Empire.

self-government stood national life."[11] Every other book characterized the rebellion as a complete failure, and a lucky one at that, because if the rebels had succeeded they would have set back the evolution of "democratic reform." The imperialist view admitted that the Family Compact had too much power but argued that its members were nonetheless able, dedicated men whose vision for society was outdated but not necessarily dishonourable. The true textbook heroes of the rebellions were "constructive reformers" like Robert Baldwin and Joseph Howe, men who rejected violence and worked peacefully to bring about constitutional change.

According to the textbook version of history, far and away the best thing about the rebellions was that they brought Lord Durham to Canada. It is hardly possible to overstate the adulation which generations of Canadians have heaped on Durham, who arrived in the colonies in 1838 in the wake of the risings to report on their causes. He only remained in Canada for five months, but the result of his investigations, published in 1839 as *Report on the Affairs of British North America*, has been hailed ever since as the inspiration for the granting of responsible government to the North American colonies a few years later. Plus, his recommendation that Upper and Lower Canada be united, a recommendation which the British acted on in 1841, has commonly been seen as a forerunner to Confederation.

Whatever his accomplishments, Lord Durham belongs to a long line of textbook saviours who at a time of national peril arrive in Canada from somewhere else to make everything right again. Examples of earlier white knights leap to mind. Governor Frontenac twice came from France to pacify the Iroquois and save the tiny colony of New France. When the marauding sea captain William Phips lay seige to Quebec City, Frontenac famously answered that he had no reply "other than from the mouths of my cannon and muskets." Governor Guy Carleton also gets credit for saving Canada not once but twice: the first time by winning over the suspicious *habitants* immediately after the Conquest, then for preserving Quebec City from invading Americans in 1775-76. Isaac Brock, a British general, died heroically on the slopes of Queenston Heights defending against another American invasion during the War of 1812 and has been widely depicted as the saviour of Canada. It is a pattern which repeats itself in all the early renditions of our history, and it conveys the unspoken but unmistakable inference that Canadians were not capable of getting out of their own predicaments. In the same way as the imperial theme encouraged youngsters to direct their patriotism overseas, so the white knight syndrome encouraged them to look elsewhere for solutions to the country's problems.

Of all the stars in the imperialist firmament, Lord Durham shone the brightest. "It was the supreme good fortune of Canada and of Great Britain that the hour and the man coincided," wrote W.L. Grant in 1914.[12] In 1937, A.L. Burt called Durham's report "perhaps the most famous government report in the English language."[13] He was "fearless, honest and generous."[14] The reason for all this praise was that Durham's report, as presented in the imperialist narrative, transformed the British Empire and thus, in a sense, the world. His special contribution was that he found a way to accommodate colonial desires for increased self-government without sundering the bonds of imperial unity. Canada, the textbooks declared, could evolve toward real democracy without having to indulge the republican fantasies of radicals like Mackenzie and Papineau. The extension of responsible government to the colonies meant that officials appointed by Britain were responsible to the will of locally-elected legislatures. Once responsible government was introduced, which it was in 1848, home rule was said effectively to have been achieved.

This was not just a local solution to a local problem. Generations of schoolchildren learned that Canada's example was a beacon to the rest of the world, illustrating how the British Empire could transform itself into a federation of self-governing societies without disintegrating in the process. "He [Durham] was the first British statesman to see it," enthused A.L. Burt, "and, seeing it, he gave the idea to the British world. In this lies the supreme greatness of his report."[15] In rejecting rebellion, Canada turned out to be a pioneer of orderly, non-violent political change, and as such was a model to the world.

There was one major problem with Durham's report: his views on the French "question." In a famous passage, he wrote: "I entertain no doubts as to the national character which must be given to Lower Canada [Quebec]; it must be that of the British Empire; that of the majority of the population of British America; that of the great race which must, in the lapse of no long period of time, be predominant over the whole North American Continent." In Durham's opinion, French Canadians were a backward race, a people without literature or history. His solution to unrest in the lower province was to recommend the unification of Upper and Lower Canada. Once the colonies were unified, Durham predicted, the French would abandon "their vain hopes of nationality" and assimilate to the English-speaking majority. In 1841, union was carried out, although it would never accomplish its main purpose.

Reviewing these events, most English-language textbooks, at least until the 1960s, skim lightly over Durham's anti-French bias, either ignoring it or forgiving it as a singular lapse in an otherwise magnificent achievement (a "blind spot," as Chafe and Lower called it[16]). When union is dealt with at any length, it is generally presented not as a scheme to assimilate the French but as a far-sighted prelude to Confederation, and French objections are dismissed as misguided. Certainly Durham's very limited understanding of French Canada is never allowed to detract from his status as one of the most important "makers of Canada."

In the early textbook version of Canadian history, Confederation more or less completes the slow march from colony to nation. The marriage of the four British North American colonies into a new Dominion in 1867 is seen as a triumph of compromise. "In the hour of trial," explained Emily Weaver in 1900, Canada's politicians "set aside party differences and worked shoulder to shoulder for the common good."[17] Confederation, in other words, was an administrative accomplishment, representing a practical solution to a political problem, not an expression of some great

13. "The Fathers of Confederation" was a group portrait by Charlottetown painter Robert Harris (1849-1919). Art critic Dennis Reid calls it "the most important official commission ever to be offered in Canada." The painting was a tribute to the statesmen who created Canada. It took Harris two years to complete and hung in the Parliament Buildings from 1883 until it was destroyed by fire in 1916. All that remains is this large oil sketch prepared by Harris before the final work.

principle. None of the textbooks cared much that the people of Canada had no say in it. George Brown called Confederation "a triumph of statesman-ship," readily admitting that "only a minority in any province was really ready for it." Luckily, continued Brown, the compromising spirit of the politicians was infectious "and people were swept off their feet by the example of unselfish leadership and the hope that a great accomplishment would come of it."[18] (Brown did not explain how he knew that the people were so enthusiastic about Confederation, since in the only place they were actually asked to vote on the question—New Brunswick—they rejected it.) Confederation is presented as an indisputable blessing; the textbooks do not acknowledge that there might have been any opposition at all.

According to the imperialist view, Confederation did not imply any loosening of the tie with the Mother Country. The new arrangement was another signpost on the road to self-government, but Britain continued to retain ultimate responsibility for foreign relations and constitutional matters. And even if the formal lines of authority between Mother Country and colony were fraying, the imperial connection did not rely on formal authority anyway. It was held to be a bond of sympathy, history, and culture. No matter how far down the road Canadians travelled in the direction of self-rule, they would remain British and a part of the British family of nations. This was the great privilege of being Canadian, wrote Arthur Dorland in 1949, to be part of "one of the greatest achievements in human organization in all history."[19]

For some of the textbooks, the constitutional evolution of Canada did not end with Confederation, or even in 1931 with the Statute of Westminster, which confirmed the equality of Britain and its dominions. The last chapter was yet to be written: it would involve the ultimate creation of a formal Imperial union in which Canada would take its place as an equal partner in a worldwide federation of British nations. "Our recent history, our growth from weak and divided provinces to one great and united Dominion, should encourage us to look forward to the still wider federation of all the lands which fly the Union Jack."[20] Once again the imperial bias encouraged Canadian youngsters to submerge any nationalist aspirations in loyalty to a "greater" cause.

II

The importance of imperial themes in schoolbooks mirrored their importance in Canadian society at large. The period before World War I was the high-water mark of imperial feeling, an era when "imperialist" was not a dirty word. As Carl Berger showed in his book, *A Sense of Power* (1970), a great many English-speaking Canadians believed that the destiny of the country lay in a closer connection, even a federation, with Great Britain and its Empire. Organizations like the Imperial Federation League and the British Empire League attracted a great deal of support. "Belief in England was in the blood," wrote Sara Jeanette Duncan in *The Imperialist*, her novel about turn-of-the-century, small-town Ontario. On its own, these people felt, Canada was a nullity, possibly even facing absorption into the United

States. But as part of a union of Anglo-Saxon nations, and an Empire which embraced a quarter of the world's population, Canada could participate in the great mission of spreading justice, freedom, and prosperity around the world, and incidentally find support for its independence from the U.S. These ideas achieved caricature in the puffed-up militarism of Colonel George Taylor Denison, the Toronto magistrate, avid cavalryman, and enthusiastic member of the Imperial Federation League. (Among Denison's many schemes was a school essay contest on the subject of "The Patriotic Influence of Raising the Flag over School Houses." He was the contest's only judge, and he awarded the winning essay from each Ontario county a huge Red Ensign.) But a great many other prominent writers, academics, and politicians espoused the imperialist cause.

R.B. Bennett, future prime minister of Canada, was just a rank-and-file member of parliament in 1914 when he gave a speech outlining his version of the imperial ideal. "We are the only colonizing race that has been able to colonize the great outlying portions of the world and give the people the priceless boon of self-government," he told his audience, "and we have educated men year after year until at last those who were once subjects became free, and those who were free became freer, and you and I must carry our portion of that responsibility if we are to be the true Imperialists we should be...." This opportunity to tote the white man's burden, Bennett explained, comes with membership in the Empire: Why would Canada wish to shirk its responsibility by becoming an independent nation with insufficient clout to have any impact on the world? "Eight or nine million people could not discharge the responsibilities that have come down to us; we cannot be true to the race from which we are sprung," except as part of a Greater England. "An independent Canada means this, that we Canadians are afraid of responsibility and the obligation of power, afraid to accept the responsibilities of our race and breed; afraid to think we are Britons, afraid to face the future in the eye."[21]

With opinions such as these, it is no wonder that after he was retired by the voters Bennett decamped for England where he lived on a country estate as a titled gentleman for the rest of his life. Nor was his anglophilia unusual among the political elite. Bennett's predecessor as leader of the Conservative Party, Arthur Meighen, shared this enthusiasm for the Mother Country. His biographer writes: "For him England, whose history and literature he had read and loved, was always a shining Citadel of all that was worthwhile in life."[22] For these men, and many others like them, a Canadian was simply another word for a Briton who happened to be living abroad. "I do not care to speak any longer of Canada and the other countries constituting the Empire, as Colonies," declared Donald Smith, Lord Strathcona, high commissioner to the United Kingdom from 1896 to 1914, and one of the country's leading capitalists. "They are English quite as much as is Great Britain, and to remain so to all time is the desire of Canada and all other possessions of the Empire."[23] The imperial allegiance penetrated to the most distant corners of the country. Martha Black, wife of the Commissioner of the Yukon, recalled how the audience at a theatre in Dawson City stood as one to sing "God Save the King" when told of the outbreak of World War I. "Although eight thousand miles of mountain, land and sea separated us from London, the heart of the Empire, yet England's King was our King, and England's Empire was our Empire."[24]

R.B. Bennett's remarks quoted above were made at an Empire Day banquet in Toronto. Empire Day was an orchestrated outpouring of public spiritedness dreamed up as a way of promoting patriotism among schoolchildren.[25] The idea was broached originally by Mrs. Clementine Fessenden, a Hamilton clubwoman, who wrote to Ontario's minister of education, George Ross, in 1897, suggesting that he set aside a special day in the school year for students to indulge in organized expressions of loyalty to Queen and country. Armed with an encouraging response from the minister, Mrs. Fessenden set to work organizing Flag Days in schools across southern Ontario. Children were asked to write essays about the Empire, sing patriotic songs, and listen to uplifting speeches. The timing could not have been better. Queen Victoria was celebrating her Diamond Jubilee that summer with lavish parties and processions in London. For Canadians there was special significance: their prime minister, Wilfrid Laurier, was knighted on the morning of the Jubilee. Citizens of Greater England were seized in a paroxysm of racial self-congratulation. Amid the boom of cannon, the endless unveiling of statues, and the pomp of ceremony, everyone agreed that there was nothing finer than to belong to the mightiest empire in history. Canada commemorated the imperial connection the next year by issuing a postage stamp showing a map of the world, the Empire in red, with the slogan, "We hold a vaster Empire than has been."

Quick to adopt the spirit of the times, George Ross climbed on board the bandwagon set rolling by Mrs. Fessenden and on May 23, 1899, Ontario schoolchildren celebrated their first Empire Day. (The date was the last school day before the May 24 holiday in honour of Queen Victoria's birthday. Victoria Day was another Canadian invention; it has never been celebrated anywhere else. It began as an annual public holiday in Toronto in 1849 and gradually spread to other cities and other provinces until by the end of the century it was considered the official beginning of summer, more important than July 1.) The name Empire Day betrayed the conviction that Canadian schools should be promoting a wider patriotism that honoured not just Canada but Britain and all of the Empire as well. "There is no antagonism . . . between Canadianism and imperialism," explained Ross, who became premier of Ontario in 1900. "The one is but the expansion of the other."[26]

Support for Empire Day spread across the country and it soon became a national celebration, the Canadian equivalent of the Fourth of July. It was by no means a holiday. A rigorous schedule of events took place and students were expected to attend. Schoolrooms were festooned with bunting, maple leaves, flags, and portraits of the Queen. Choirs gave fervent renditions of "God Save the Queen," "Rule Britannia," and our very own "The Maple Leaf Forever," written by a Toronto schoolteacher.

> In days of yore, from Britain's shore,
> Wolfe the dauntless hero came,
> And planted firm Old England's flag,
> On Canada's fair domain!
> Here may it wave our boast, our pride,
> And joined in love together,
> The Thistle, Shamrock, Rose entwine,
> The Maple Leaf forever!

Students paraded through the streets of towns and cities and gathered in parks to watch historic tableaus, listen to recitations (Kipling was a favourite), and participate in flag exercises.

Empire Day acquired a martial spirit with the addition of rifle drills and cadet parades. As of the 1890s, Ontario high schools began to receive funding for military instruction. Then, after the Boer War, Donald Smith donated a quarter of a million dollars to fund physical and military training in the schools and the federal militia department kicked in with weapons and training for instructors.[27] The department saw the cadet program as a way to develop a standing army-in-waiting, especially after Sam Hughes took over as minister in 1911. The trooping of the cadets became a highlight of Empire Day activities: by the mid-1920s in Toronto as many as 10,000 uniformed boys marched to Queen's Park, accompanied by girls in white blouses carrying baskets of flowers; in 1931, there were more than 44,000 cadets in Ontario's schools available to add pomp to Empire Day. Most civic and educational leaders believed that military training promoted good health, moulded character, encouraged discipline and loyalty, eradicated vice, and, not least, trained a force of young soldiers for the defence of the Empire.

Empire Day was an unabashed celebration of Anglo-Saxon superiority, a day on which Anglo-Canadians (and many Francophones who accepted the myth of the beneficent Conquest) gloried in their membership in the Master Race. "Empire Day," Governor-General Earl Grey told an audience of schoolchildren in 1909, "is the festival on which every British subject should reverently remember that the British Empire stands out before the whole world as the fearless champion of freedom, fair play and equal rights; that its watchwords are responsibility, duty, sympathy and self-sacrifice; and that a special responsibility rests with you individually to be true to the traditions and to the mission of your race."[28]

III

Empire Day was an annual excuse for Canadians to celebrate their British heritage. Much less frequent, and for that reason much more exciting, was a visit from a member of the Royal Family. The first official Royal visit to Canada occurred in 1860 when the Prince of Wales (son of Queen Victoria, and later Edward VII) toured the Atlantic colonies, Quebec, and Ontario. Among his many official functions, the Prince laid the cornerstone for the new Parliament Buildings in Ottawa. By the time the next Royals arrived—

the Duke and Duchess of Cornwall and York (he was later George v)—the Canadian Pacific Railway was ready to carry them coast to coast. It was 1901 and the visit generated enormous enthusiasm. The CPR built a nine-car train especially for the tour featuring mahogany and walnut panelling in the compartments, electric lights, and velvet curtains. As the Royals made their way across the country—it was, wrote a senior government official, "a stately pageant, a unique spectacle, a royal progress the like of which Caesar had never dreamed"—they were greeted at every stop by ecstatic crowds, brass bands, displays of fireworks, and salutes by gun and cannon. It was the first Royal visit to western Canada and seemed to confirm the great work of settlement and civilization that was going on there.[29]

In 1919, it was the turn of Edward, the Prince of Wales, later Edward VIII. Once again the CPR provided a special train, described by a Calgary newspaper as "the most palatial train that has ever been assembled in North America."[30] And once again the crowds were large and enthusiastic. "It was a moving thing," wrote newspaper reporter Frederick Griffin, who covered the tour for the *Toronto Star*, "to see, to feel, the joy, the exaltation, which a glimpse of him provoked in long vistas of Canadians strung on the sidewalks or massed in the streets."[31] Another veteran of the tour left this poignant description of Canadians' devotion to the monarchy: "Sometimes in the depth of night, as we sped along, we could hear through the windows of our sleeping section a faint and ghostly cheer of people who had gathered for their Prince—infinitely lonely yet infinitely loyal creatures, who in some way had heard a whisper of the Prince's coming and had come themselves to do him honour."[32] In Alberta, Edward spent a day at the Bar U Ranch near High River (now a national historic site) where he was so impressed with the cowboy life that on his return trip across the country he arranged to purchase his own cattle ranch near the Bar U. The E.P. (Edward Prince) Ranch remained in royal hands until 1962, though he only visited the property five times in forty-three years.[33]

The most impressive Royal tour of Canada was the visit in 1939 of King George VI and Queen Elizabeth, parents of the present Queen.[34] Just as members of later generations would be able to remember exactly where they were and what they were doing the day President Kennedy was shot, so our parents' generation can recall with equal precision their encounter

14. Young children await the arrival of King George VI and Queen Elizabeth during the 1939 Royal tour. These children represent the deep loyalty many Canadians had to the monarchy and the Empire and the myth of Britishness they embodied.

with the Royals in 1939, which was after all the first time that a reigning monarch had come to Canada. Knowing how popular the King and Queen were, the prime minister, Mackenzie King, took advantage of their reflected glory by accompanying them for their entire stay in the country. He even manoeuvred around the governor-general, Lord Tweedsmuir, so that when King George stepped ashore at Quebec City it was the portly figure of the prime minister who greeted him with the words: "Welcome, sire, to Your Majesty's realm of Canada." People turned out in vast numbers to cheer the Royals. On the first day of the visit 40,000 schoolchildren, most of them French-speaking, massed on the Plains of Abraham waving tiny Union Jacks. The next day in Montreal more than a million people lined the route of the motorcade. And so it went for the entire visit. "Their devotion to the British throne is entirely genuine," reported one of the King's secretaries, "and almost an article of faith." An encounter with royalty was close to a mystical experience. Enveloped in an aura of pomp and ancient tradition, the Royals personified the majesty and power of Britain and the Empire it possessed. The superiority of the British "way of life" was still unquestioned. "It is a very strange . . . but none the less indisputable fact," wrote novelist Frederick Philip Grove, "that the average Anglo-Saxon considers himself superior to all the other races of the world. . . ."[35] A Royal visit provided an opportunity for Canadians to feel a part of something far greater than themselves. It allowed them to celebrate their participation in a superior form of government, a superior morality.

IV

One fine morning in turn-of-the-century Alberta, a young newcomer from England, Abee Carter Goodloe, went out to sample some local culture at Fort Macleod, only to find herself overwhelmed by the sense that she was back in the Old Country. "In the morning there is polo," she wrote, "and one sees young English fellows in patent-leather boots and baggy khaki riding trousers, for which they have sent all the way to England, dashing up and down and 'running the whole show.' The Indians standing around look like aliens, like visiting strangers. The Englishman doesn't insult or bully the Indian. He simply ignores him, and by pursuing a life as nearly as possible like the one he would lead in England, and by appropriating whatever suits his interest or fancy, he makes the Indian understand that it is his country."[36]

Goodloe captures the arrogance of a colonial elite at its leisure, what Sid Marty calls the "Raj on the Range."[37] This vision of cowboys in polo helmets was replicated everywhere across the country, with regional variations, whether it was the tea-sipping, croquet-playing gentlefolk on Vancouver Island, or the colony of remittance men at Saskatchewan's Cannington Manor, or the ersatz Ontario gentry familiar from the best-selling Jalna novels of Mazo de la Roche. These were the self-confident purveyors of the British ideal who anticipated molding the new dominion of Canada in the image of the Mother Country. Blacks, Jews, Asians of any type, Slavs,

15. Many British immigrants to Canada attempted to replicate familiar aspects of the Old Country in their new setting; as, for example, these polo players in frontier Alberta.

need not apply for membership in this elite. In the words of Professor W.G. Smith, an "expert" on immigration, "British-born Canadians" were "the elect of the earth."[38] This was the dark side of Canada's British inheritance, a virulent sense of racial superiority which placed beyond the pale anyone who was not English speaking, fair skinned, and devoutly Christian.

As Goodloe's description makes clear, one group which in particular suffered the fallout from this ethnocentric view of the country was the Aboriginal people, whom the newcomers pushed aside as if they hardly existed. The past three decades have seen an explosive growth in interest in the history and traditional culture of Canada's Native population. Treaty rights and land claims have shot to the top of the public agenda, and the century-long policy of assimilation has been discarded in favour of a formal commitment to some form of Native self-government. There has been nothing short of a revolution in the thinking of non-Native Canadians about the Aboriginal "question." Given such a changed climate of opinion, it is easy to forget how different the mainstream Euro-Canadian view was just a generation ago when Aboriginals, if they were considered at all, were dismissed as backward savages. No matter how familiar one is with the sad history of Aboriginal-white relations in Canada, one is not prepared for the sorry stew of smug, racist propaganda which, until quite recently, passed for informed opinion about Indians.

Just as school textbooks are an excellent place to examine the ideology of imperialism, they are also an excellent source for the kinds of stereotypes non-Native Canadians used when they thought about Aboriginal people. What emerges from the pages of these books is a cluster of images which might collectively be labelled the Textbook Indian. The Textbook Indian was the Indian in whom Abee Goodloe's polo-playing cowboys believed, the Indian which the anglocentric view of Canada invented in order to justify its own hegemony.

The earliest schoolbooks virtually ignored the Indian. A few pages at best, a few lines at worst, this was about all the attention Aboriginal societies received. W.H.P. Clement, for example, in his award-winning 1898 text, took eleven sentences to sum up the "character and habits" of the Indian. Another book concluded a brief discussion of the subject by dismissing its importance: "Much more might be said, but it would be tedious to do so in this place."[39] John George Hodgins's text, *A History of Canada*, in wide use in Ontario at the time of Confederation, included a nine-page chapter on "The Principal Indian Tribes," but prefaced it with the following note: "The Teacher can omit this chapter at his discretion."[40] Perhaps it was just as well that many teachers did, for the chapter is an appalling collection of stereotypes and misinformation. By the 1920s, the status of the Textbook Indian had improved to the point that most books presented at least some sort of an overview of Native societies. Still, as late as mid-century, the Canadian and Newfoundland Education Association, the national organization of educators, proposed a standardized outline of Canadian history that did not even include Native people as a topic worth studying.

Textbooks which did mention Native people adopted a fairly standard approach, beginning with a brief overview of the Indian Tribes, then moving on to more important matters. Students could not help but notice that French and English colonists received far more attention than the indigenous people. At the same time as Clement devoted eleven sentences to the Indians, for instance, he took eight and a half pages to describe the career of Samuel de Champlain.

The material which was devoted to Aboriginal cultures focussed almost entirely on what they lacked. Texts made much of the fact that Indians did not have a written language and therefore had no books, no laws, no schools; that they did not have sophisticated technology; that they did not live in houses; that they had no discernible religions ("As they were heathens, of course, they knew not the true God of the Christians."[41]). Native people were portrayed as overawed by the superiority of European technical achievements. Here is George Wrong, head of the history department at the University of Toronto, describing the meeting between Jacques Cartier and a party of Micmac: ". . . he scattered among them glass beads, combs and other trinkets for which they scrambled like eager children. They were a wretched company, and Cartier thought they must be the poorest people in all the world."[42] Cartier may well have thought so, but the textbooks did nothing to suggest their readers might think otherwise. A relentless ethnocentrism pervaded all descriptions of the Textbook Indian.

The dominant theme of all these books was the expansion of European civilization in America. Given that way of framing the story, there was no real place for Native people, except insofar as they obstructed this process. History was something that happened to white people. "They had no history or written language," John Calkin assured his young readers.[43] Once the Iroquois wars end, the Indians go missing from the textbooks, reappearing briefly during the War of 1812 and again during the disturbances in western Canada in 1869 and 1885. Otherwise they have no role to play. By their very nature they were inimical to the main story line.

Until the 1960s, Textbook Indians were sinister, vicious figures, without history or culture. They inhabited the New World as wild animals inhabited the forest. They were introduced to young readers not as another civilization with which Europeans came into contact, but as part of the landscape which had to be explored and subdued. Contact, a term familiar to modern readers, implies that two civilizations meet and interact. This was not the way youngsters thirty years ago, myself included, were taught to understand what took place. We were taught that the Indians were savages; that is, beings without civilization—and that the arrival of Europeans in America was a process of discovery and conquest, not contact.

Early texts portrayed Indians as bright-eyed animals peering out from their hiding places in the dark woods; "wolf-eyed, wolf-sinewed, stiller than the trees," as the poet Marjorie Pickthall put it. Descriptions focussed on their physical characteristics. The Indians were "a strange race," wrote Duncan McArthur. "They belonged to the country almost as the trees or the wild roaming animals."[44] They were "human wolves," wrote W.L. Grant.[45] Like animals, their senses were particularly keen. "They had bright, black eyes that could see ever so far, and ears that could hear clearly sounds that you would never notice."[46] And their strength was notable. "The Indians . . . were tall athletic people with sinewy forms. . . . They were capable of much endurance of cold, hunger and fatigue; were haughty and taciturn in their manners; active, cunning, and stealthy in the chase and in war."[47] Their lodges were crowded and filthy like animal dens, and their ferocity was like the wild beasts tearing at the heart of the European settlements.

War was the favourite, almost the exclusive, pastime of Textbook Indians. "But to go to war was the most important part of an Indian's life," wrote J.N. McIlwraith in *The Children's Study of Canada*; "he cared for nothing else."[48] "The customs and character of the American aborigine turned, mainly, upon war," declared Castell Hopkins.[49] Before the arrival of whites, Textbook Indian life was taken up by fighting amongst themselves; afterwards they made a sport of preying on the colonists. And sport it seemed to be, since the textbooks never seriously paid attention to any rational motives Native people might have had for their behaviour. Colonists had political and economic objectives; Textbook Indians ("these forest tigers, these insatiable scalp-hunters"[50]) had only appetites and superstitions. Like beasts, they seemed to lack the ability to reason out their own best interests.

The double standard employed by Charles G.D. Roberts was typical. After condemning Iroquois bloodthirstiness for a hundred pages, he turns to a description of the expulsion of the Acadians from Nova Scotia by the British in 1755. Not surprisingly, Roberts finds reason to forgive this admittedly ruthless act. There was a war going on, he explains, and bad things happen in wartime. "If the step now decided upon seems to us a cruel one, we must remember to judge it by the standards of that day rather than this."[51] An excellent piece of advice but one which Roberts had not thought to give when he was portraying the Indians as "painted butchers," "shrewd, red schemers." It was simply not admitted that Native people had a point of view worth trying to understand.

Textbook authors did admire certain martial qualities attributed to Textbook Indians, who were held to be fiercely brave in combat and, when captured, "gloried in showing that they could not be made to heed pain."[52] As far as the texts were concerned, however, these qualities were corrupted by the Natives' whole approach to warfare: whereas Europeans fought honourably, out on the open battlefield, Textbook warriors skulked through the forest and attacked from ambush. They did not abide by the code of the gentleman; the textbooks use words like *ruthless, cunning, cruel, sinister, ferocious,* and *bloodthirsty* to describe their behaviour. Indians were not soldiers, they were predators. "War is not a pretty thing at any time," wrote Agnes Laut, a popular writer for children, "but war that lets loose the bloodhounds of Indian ferocity leaves the blackest scar of all."[53] Textbooks liked to linger over the hideous tortures inflicted on the colonists, entertaining their readers with the smell of burning flesh and the sound of tearing limbs.

The entire approach to the early history of Canada in these textbooks, both French and English, serves to demonize the Indians. The history of New France is depicted as the struggle of a small band of brave colonists to gain a toehold in the St. Lawrence Valley while fighting off first the Indians, then the English. The bold *habitant* farmers with a plow in one hand, a gun in the other. The founding colonists endure unspeakable suffering; Indians are the implacable foe which give meaning to this suffering. Every text highlights the same familiar series of events as they review the history of New France for their readers. First, Adam Dollard des Ormeaux singlehandedly holds off an Iroquois war party at the Long Sault. This was "Canada's Thermopylae," declare the textbooks. Then Madeleine de Verchères, the teenaged farm girl, defends the family fort against marauding Iroquois; and the Iroquois attack on Lachine in 1689 is always presented as the worst instance of Indian depravity. It hardly matters that modern historians have shown that many of these events did not happen the way the textbooks say they happened. These stories long ago transcended mere fact to become the myths which explain the origins and survival of the country. Together they established what has been called our "trial-by-fire tradition," a tradition of suffering and sacrifice which animated, and to a great extent still animates, the textbook version of the early history of Canada.[54]

An important premise of the trial-by-fire tradition is that colonists were the innocent victims of Indian aggression. This premise is usually taken for granted. When made explicit, however, it shows how even the most glaring contradictions appear to make sense in the absence of an alternative point of view. In his *History of Canada*, J. George Hodgins spends about a hundred pages on the wars between the French colonists and the Iroquois, including the several attacks by French soldiers on Iroquois villages, after which he concludes, rather astonishingly, "that Canada was one of the few countries which was not originally settled by (or for purposes of) conquest. The pursuits of her inhabitants were always peaceful, not warlike. She has always acted on the defensive, and never as the aggressor."[55] Hodgins never offers his readers the opposite point of view, that Native people were fighting to protect their homelands against what amounted to an armed invasion by European soldiers and settlers. Instead, students were encouraged to believe that no colonist ever killed an Indian who wasn't asking for it.

At the centre of the trial-by-fire tradition is the figure of the Jesuit missionary. Textbooks pull out all the stops when they come to describe the efforts of these itinerant priests to convert the Native people not just to Christianity, but to civilization itself. "Their record among the savages is one of imperishable glory," wrote Charles Roberts, whose praise of the missionaries is bathed in eroticism. "Their faith was a white and living flame, that purged out all thought of self. Alone, fearless, not to be turned aside, they pierced to the inmost recesses of the wilderness."[56] The Jesuits were "pioneers of civilization," "a glorious army" sent to subdue the savage heart of America. The Indian represented the untamed, uncivilized essence of the New World. The Jesuits were special heroes because they went up against that essence armed only with a bible and a cross. Their suffering gave the colonial enterprise a moral purpose. And so it was described in gory detail, often purely imaginary: the necklace of red-hot hatchets, the dripping heart torn from the chest and devoured, the severed tongues and roasting flesh, the screams of agony. "The boys and girls who read these pages will never be called upon to witness such scenes in our country again," writes G.U. Hay in his *Public School History of Canada*; "but it is well that they should know of the toil, suffering and hardship of its founders, and be themselves willing to undergo, in a less degree, trials that may come to them. This is the duty of the patriot."[57]

The deification of the Jesuits meant the demonization of the Indians: Native people were the villains of New France. As one historian has written, "martyrs must have murderers."[58] That was the role assigned to the Textbook Indians: they stood in the way of civilization; it was natural that they should be brushed aside. Textbooks constructed the story of New France in such a way as to justify policies of forced assimilation which the government had been practicing in Canada since Confederation. The derogatory image of the Textbook Indian was not created in a vacuum. It reflected the inferior status of Native people in Canadian society and Canadian historiography. In Quebec, prior to the Quiet Revolution of the 1960s, the Catholic Church exercised pervasive power and influence. The Church operated the school system and priests wrote the textbooks. Not surprisingly, the Catholic version of Canadian history disparaged Native people as superstitious savages and praised French colonists and missionaries for planting the One True Faith in the New World. To Catholics, which meant to the majority of Quebeckers, New France represented the triumph of Christianity over the dark forces of paganism. This was the meaning of Quebec's early history.

Until only recently, Native people everywhere in Canada were considered second-class citizens, and the declared aim of government policy was their assimilation. Most Canadians firmly believed that Indians had no future as Indians, that their culture was unsuited to modern, industrial civilization, that their only hope for survival was to join mainstream, white society. Natives were segregated socially, silenced politically, and marginalized economically. No wonder, then, that textbooks read back into history the inferior status of the Native which was everywhere evident in contemporary Canada.

When early textbooks turned their attention to the Métis of western Canada, it was usually with the same superficiality that characterized their treatment of the First Nations of New France. The Métis only appear in early textbooks when they clash with European settler society, so readers meet them for the first time at Seven Oaks on the Red River in 1816 when a party of Métis led by Cuthbert Grant skirmished with a party of Lord Selkirk's settlers. Responsibility for this event, which resulted in the deaths of twenty-two people, has been argued by historians ever since, but the textbooks show no hesitation in handing out blame. Seven Oaks was a "crime," declared A.L. Burt, committed by "half-civilized Métis" under the thumb of unscrupulous fur traders.[59] Chester Martin agreed that the Métis had no will of their own, that their "Indian blood" was "aroused to frenzy," that the "hideous massacre" was all their fault. It was "the worst orgy of bloodshed among men of British race that ever stained the western prairie," he told his readers.[60] The Selkirk settlement on the Red River represented an extension of European civilization into the wilderness; by opposing it, the Métis were seen to have put themselves beyond the pale. None of the textbooks admit that the Métis possessed a unique culture or played a pivotal role in the economy of the West. Charles G.D. Roberts was typical when he contemptuously dismissed their claim to be a "New Nation" as simply "vainglorious."[61]

The next textbook appearance of the Métis is the Red River insurrection of 1869-70. Most authors admit that the federal government was to blame for not dealing sooner with the legitimate fears of the Métis for the security of their land tenure. But this did not mean that they condoned armed rebellion. To the contrary, they invariably portray the Métis and their leader, Louis Riel, as impatient, excitable, and unstable. Whatever cause the Métis may have had to complain about their treatment at the hands of an indifferent federal government, they are said to have had no cause to take the law into their own hands. What especially outraged the textbook authors, as it did most English-speaking Canadians at the time, was the death of Thomas Scott at the hands of a Métis firing squad. The execution was "cold-blooded murder"; Scott was shot "like a dog." "It was not an execution," wrote Charles Roberts, "it was a murder, and a peculiarly brutal one."[62]

The North-West Rebellion in 1885 was similarly treated as an act of lunacy. While again admitting that the Métis may have had legitimate grievances, most authors concentrated on Louis Riel and the question of his stability. He was mad, they wrote, a wild fanatic. Chester Martin thought Riel was insane and raises the spectre of an Indian bloodbath.

"None but a madman could think of bringing the savage Indians from their reserves on such a mission against settlers with their innocent women and children."[63] Others portray Riel as clever but "unstable" and "deluded." Once again the distinctive culture of the Métis is ignored, as are their claims to being a "new nation." In the early textbooks, the rebellion is important chiefly for the strain it placed on French-English relations; its implications for the West are largely ignored.

By the 1930s and 1940s the textbook view of the western rebellions was becoming a bit less black and white. The language used to describe the events was less hyperbolic and more credence was given to the Métis point of view. Some books—not all, but some—began to lay a heavier weight of blame on the government of John A. Macdonald for not responding sooner to Métis grievances. Riel still emerges from the books as a highly erratic character, but his cause is considered just. "With all his faults," admits Arthur Dorland somewhat reluctantly in 1949, "Riel's aims in standing up for the rights of the Métis and Indians were not entirely unworthy."[64] Evident in these books are the first glimmerings of the transformation of Riel into the folk hero he would become to later generations.

With the execution of Riel, Native people virtually disappear from the early textbooks, having served their purpose of providing a standard against which the superiority of Euro-Canadian civilization was measured. They had given Canadian youngsters like myself a reason to consider our country superior to the United States. And they had provided a rationale for the policy of forced assimilation which the government of our parents was implementing against Native people. No one cared that Textbook Indians were never really taken seriously as distinct cultures. Their contributions to Canadian history are not mentioned in the books. Issues which affect them are not discussed. There are almost no references to the contemporary land question, to the treaties, to life on the reserves. It is quite probable that as a student in high school during the 1960s I would not even have known that reserves existed. As in contemporary Canada, so in the textbooks, Indians are marginalized and silenced. Their spirituality is dismissed as nothing more than superstition. Their claims to their traditional territories are never even discussed.

Imagine for a moment the impact these ideas would have had on Native students when they encountered them in the residential schools which were established to accomplish their acculturation. Richard Nerysoo, a northern Native man, told Justice Thomas Berger at the hearings of the Mackenzie Valley Pipeline Inquiry in the mid-1970s: "When I went to school in Fort McPherson I can remember being taught that the Indians were savages. We were violent, cruel and uncivilized. I remember reading history books that glorified the white man who slaughtered whole nations of Indian people. No one called the white man savages, they were heroes who explored new horizons or conquered new frontiers. . . ."[65] An analysis of social studies texts in use in Ontario schools during the 1960s concludes: "It is bad enough that any group should be subjected to prejudicial treatment, but the fact that Indians are the native people of this country and that their children are required to read these texts compounds the immorality of such treatment."[66]

Of course, the curriculum was not devised for Native students like Richard Nerysoo. Their discomfort, their shame, was incidental. The curriculum was devised for white youngsters like myself. It was supposed to teach us a view of history which rationalized the assimilationist policies being carried out by our government. In effect, we were being educated for racism. Textbook Indians were vicious children who did not have the good sense to recognize the superiority of the British heritage which could have been their rightful inheritance as citizens of Canada. Assimilation was presented as the only alternative to their extinction. We were taught that we were doing them a favour.

v

The same racism which infected Canadian attitudes to Aboriginal people infected the treatment of almost anybody who did not belong to the white, Christian mainstream. The evidence is familiar and overwhelming. As the tide of immigration to this country swelled in the early decades of the century, all manner of government policies were introduced to keep Canada "British." Chinese were allowed into the country to build the railways, then systematically excluded, first by the use of the infamous head tax, then for twenty-four years from 1923 to 1947 by an outright ban on Chinese immigration. Japanese immigration was limited to a small number of individuals annually, then banned altogether for twenty-seven years from

1940 to 1967. Canadians of Asian origin were subject to a myriad of restrictive laws and regulations that affected their access to public services and their ability to make a living. In 1908, all immigration from India was effectively stopped until after World War II, when it resumed in a very limited way. Anti-Semitism was open and acceptable until at least the 1950s; Jews were denied jobs and professional appointments, excluded from clubs and public facilities, subjected to hiring quotas, and refused admittance to the country, even when their lives were imperilled by the Nazi regime in Europe. All of these restrictions, and many others, were implemented on behalf of the Anglo-French majority in an effort to ensure that it retained economic, social, and cultural pre-eminence.

Curiously, at the same time as Canada was so obviously shot through with racial prejudice, the myth of the mosaic gained widespread acceptance. According to the mosaic principle, Canadian society is characterized by a tolerance for ethnic and cultural diversity quite unlike other countries, and especially unlike the United States. The mosaic conjures up an image of a society in which different groups live amicably side by side, each appreciating the characteristics and contributions of all the others. In the past thirty years, we have turned this metaphor into a widely accepted description of Canadian reality. We have become so used to it that we seldom wonder where it originated.

The mosaic was first used in this context by Victoria Hayward, an American writer, in a book describing a trip she took across Canada in 1922. When she reached the Prairies, Hayward paid tribute to the "sturdy character" of all the "New Canadians" she found there, but her use of the mosaic seems to refer to the patchwork nature of the exotic church buildings erected by the many different religions. ("It is indeed a mosaic of vast dimensions and great breadth, essayed of the Prairie."[67]) In 1926, a writer named Kate Foster prepared a survey of immigration for the Dominion Council of the YWCA and published it as *Our Canadian Mosaic*.[68] Foster used the term as an objective description of the way Canadian society was made up of a number of disparate pieces. It was left to a publicist for the Canadian Pacific Railway named John Murray Gibbon to transform the mosaic from a description into an ideal, a positive metaphor for the way Canadians should live together, and something which set us apart from our American neighbours.

16. John Murray Gibbon, CPR publicist, amateur folklorist, and cultural entrepreneur, deserves credit for originating the mosaic as a metaphor for multicultural Canada.

Gibbon was a respected British journalist, an Oxford graduate well connected in literary circles, when he joined the London publicity office of the CPR in 1907. His first assignment was to conduct a group of British newspaper editors to Canada where the railway gave them the royal treatment aboard the transcontinental all the way to Vancouver. Gibbon continued to promote the CPR across Europe from his base in London until 1913 when he moved to Canada as the company's general publicity agent. For more than three decades he served as a tireless ambassador for the railway and a promoter of Canadian culture. He was the founding president of the Canadian Authors Association, an organizer of countless artistic events, the author of more than thirty books. He has been called "one of the principal figures in imagining the Canadian community in the 1920s and 1930s." Ian McKay goes on to suggest: "Without Gibbon, the now all-pervasive metaphor of Canada as a mosaic might have died an obscure death as an American writer's conceit. It was Gibbon who rescued it as the governing metaphor of the new post-colonial liberal nationalism that gradually overshadowed many Canadians' earlier identification with Britain."[69]

Gibbon was a firm believer in bilingualism and an admirer of French-Canadian folk culture. In 1926, he organized an evening of traditional Quebec folk songs to celebrate the opening of an addition to the Château Frontenac, the CPR hotel in Quebec City. The event was a great success and evolved into an annual Folksong and Handicraft Festival at the hotel,

17. This poster advertises one of the CPR's many folk festivals during the 1920s, staged to attract visitors to the company's hotels.

featuring the songs, dances, arts, and crafts of the province. Banff Indian Days had already been going for several years, and the company sponsored a similar pageant at Desbarats, Ontario, where each summer actors dressed as Indians performed scenes from Longfellow's poem "Hiawatha." Gibbon extended this roster of festivals by launching a Highland Gathering on Scottish themes at the Banff Springs Hotel in 1927, a New Canadian Festival featuring a variety of ethnic performers at Winnipeg's Royal Alexandra Hotel in 1928, a Sea Music Festival in Vancouver, and so on. During the Depression these staged events were the basis for a regular radio program called "Canadian Mosaic," which was also the title of a book Gibbon published in 1938 on the subject of Canada's cultural diversity, which won the Governor-General's Award.[70]

Gibbon's book is a chapter-by-chapter survey of the history and contributions of the country's "racial groups." "The Canadian people today presents itself as a decorated surface, bright with inlays of separate coloured pieces . . . ," he wrote, "and so the ensemble may truly be called a mosaic."[71] It is ironic that he used the word "coloured" since he omitted any mention of blacks or Asians in his book. Gibbon seems to have shared the racialist assumptions of his day that these groups were basically unassimilable by mainstream, white society. The subtitle of his book is "The Making of a Northern Nation"; presumably a northern nation had no place for coloured faces. As well, his fiction reveals a strain of anti-Semitism, so apparently Jews were also excluded from the mosaic.[72]

There are several things to note about the mosaic. First of all, it was an idea originated by the white, Euro-Canadian mainstream and expresses a remarkably benign view of ethnic relations in the country. It celebrated diversity and encouraged mutual understanding, up to a point at least, while ignoring the realities of inequality and racial injustice in Canadian society. Secondly, it was a term employed initially by the CPR to promote Canadian culture as a tourist attraction. Gibbon and the railway encouraged the folk arts of different ethnic groups as something exotic and picturesque to pique the interest of visitors. Thirdly, this folk-arts approach to cultural diversity in which groups are encouraged to retain their distinctive customs in order to make Canada a livelier, more colourful place to live was a precursor of the official policy of multiculturalism announced by Pierre Trudeau's Liberal government in 1971. "The government will support and encourage the various cultures and ethnic groups that give structure and vitality to our society," Trudeau told Parliament at that time. "They will be encouraged to share their cultural expression and values with other Canadians and so contribute to a richer life for us all." In a sense, along with all its other claims to fame, the CPR is the father of multiculturalism in Canada. Lastly, the mosaic gradually came to replace the myth of the master race as a core myth used by Canadians to describe their society. As Canadian society became less and less "British," the mosaic increasingly seemed to be not just an accurate description of reality but an actual prescription for the way Canada ought to be, until today it is as unthinkable to deny the worth of the mosaic as it was to deny the racial superiority of British civilization seventy-five years ago.

VI

If the myth of the master race no longer makes much sense to most Canadians, it nevertheless left a lasting legacy still evident in our institutions, even in ourselves. We Canadians have become used to thinking of ourselves as modest, self-effacing types, quick to beg pardon for imagined rudeness, reticent about putting ourselves forward in any way. We are so polite and unassertive, we believe, that not much happens here. Before tensions can get too high, we smooth things over by apologizing or appointing a royal commission. This is the Canadian way of dealing with divisive issues and we are proud of it, but we feel that it has somehow made us boring. Just as we are personally unassertive, so we are unassertive as a nation. We do not thrust ourselves forward on the international stage. We are known as peacekeepers, not war mongers. Our history is lacking in the dramatic conflicts which mark other countries. And who could possibly wish otherwise? Nonetheless, all this peace, order, and good government has left us with a nagging regret that our fate as a nation is to be on the sidelines of the twentieth century.

We tend to regard self-effacement as part of our immutable national identity, but actually it is relatively new. Only recently has the self-effacing Canadian become a prominent cultural stereotype. Canadians used to be self-confident, perhaps even self-important, sure that we were playing a leading role in world affairs. When Wilfrid Laurier said the twentieth century would belong to Canada, he was not thought to be talking nonsense; he was expressing an assuredness widely shared by Canadians. Not so long ago we knew who we were and knew we were at the centre of the universe. The source of this confidence was our "racial" inheritance, the narrative of imperialism. As members of the Anglo-Saxon race and the great British Empire, we were secure in our superiority. Canadians of British stock experienced this directly. Others—French Canadians, Aboriginals, immigrants from other countries—were expected to be grateful for the opportunity to assimilate themselves to the British mainstream.

So, what happened to sap our self-confidence? First of all, imperialism fell into disrepute. Bearing the white man's burden was no longer seen to be a noble project but rather an exercise in oppression. There was no great pride to be taken from our participation in an empire in full retreat. Our ties to Great Britain withered, and during the inter-war period the influence of the United States grew. But ever since the American Revolution our purpose as a separate nation had been to provide an alternative society to the United States. Canadians have always seen themselves as distinct, morally superior. We could not become a confident part of the American empire. We were allies, but could not consider ourselves equals and did not want to merge our identity in a larger, North American nation. We were the mouse in bed with the elephant. As a result, we have been unable to take the same pride in our role as a minor partner in the American world order as we took from our participation as a major partner in the British Empire.

As well, Canadian society has been profoundly changed by the immigration which has taken place since World War II. During the post-war economic boom, restrictions on immigration loosened as the demand for labour increased and it became obvious that native-born Canadians were not reproducing themselves in sufficient numbers. The population swelled with newcomers from eastern Europe, Asia, and the Caribbean who were chosen more for the economic contributions they might make, or their plight as refugees, than the colour of their skin. As a result, Canadian society became much less homogenous than it had been. By 1991 only about forty percent of the population claimed British or French background, and the number was falling. Fewer and fewer people identified with British traditions so the cultural mythology which had united us lost its hegemony. The old definitions of Canada no longer seemed accurate. As the ground shifted, Canadians began to feel less confident about their place in the world. Instead, a sense of marginality developed, a belief that nothing important ever happens here. There is a story told by the late novelist, Robertson Davies. He was at a party in 1957 when it was announced that Lester Pearson had just won the Nobel Peace Prize. There was a silence, and then Davies heard a woman sniff, "Just who does he think he is?" Today, this joke is instantly recognizable as revealing a distinctive Canadian attitude. In the "old Canada," where the master narrative still had strength, would anyone have understood it?

The fires of imperial enthusiasm died out in Canada between the two world wars. The first war soured most people on foreign entanglements and overseas responsibilities. A residue of loyalty to the British connection remained, of course, as it does even today, but all expectation of a formal Imperial federation was over. Empire Day transmuted into something called Citizenship Day; Dominion Day, our national holiday, became Canada Day; indeed, the word dominion disappeared from our vocabulary altogether. Since World War II the symbols of British hegemony have been patriated one by one. In 1946, we got our own Citizenship Act and were no longer officially considered British subjects. Our first native-born governor-general was appointed in 1952; our own flag replaced the Union Jack in 1965; "O Canada" became the official national anthem in 1967; the constitution came home in 1982. In the classroom, and in the culture at large, the master narrative shed its most fervent appeals to imperial unity. Canada became an autonomous, North American nation, not the overseas extension of Great Britain it was often portrayed as being earlier in the century.

Today, Britishness is a quaint artifact, largely confined to the tourist industry, one "tile" among many in the cultural mosaic. Whether in Nova Scotia, where "Scottishness" has been promoted as a provincial identity, or Victoria, B.C., which sometimes presents itself as the last bastion of the Imperial way of life in Canada, these vestiges are maintained principally to give visitors something interesting to look at. They have more to do with strategies for local economic development than with any cultural reality.

But this does not mean that Canada is no longer a British country. In important ways it still is, in the sense that many of its institutions derive from British precedent. The monarchy, which historian W.L. Morton in 1960 described as "the moral core of Canadian nationhood," is increasingly irrelevant to most peoples' sense of the country, but it is the pillar on which our system of parliamentary democracy rests.[73] English remains the dominant language outside of Quebec; the Canadian constitution and most of our laws originate in England; our school system was founded on an Irish model. The present multicultural reality cannot deny the fundamental significance of British traditions to our history and institutions. As historian Donald Akenson has pointed out, it is in the context of these institutions and traditions that multiculturalism now operates.[74]

The British connection is also responsible for encouraging a set of attitudes which seem characteristically Canadian, or at least English Canadian. First of all, there is the matter of our diffidence. "Canadians," wrote Arthur Dorland in his 1949 textbook, "share to some degree the temperamental reserve and caution of the Britisher, his aversion to sensationalism and to the loose social habits which have sometimes characterized American life."[75] As Dorland's comments suggest, Canadians have been educated to be anti-American. Our schoolbooks have taught us that Americans are headstrong and unstable (to say nothing of expansionist), a result of their excessive indulgence in democracy. The British system, and especially the monarchy, emphasized obedience and deference and as a result produced stability and prosperity. The American system, which placed excessive faith in the people, bred only instability and contempt for authority. The whole purpose of Canada's survival as a separate nation was to create an alternative, superior (i.e., less democratic) society to the United States.

As its criticism of the United States implies, this view of Canadian history was marked by a conservative temper. Compromise and gradualism were believed to be the hallmarks of Canadian development. The evolution from colony to nation occurred slowly and steadily. Not for us the sudden, violent convulsion of revolution. Canadians shared an optimistic faith in progress, certainly, but it was progress measured in increments, not giant leaps. Events such as the armed uprisings in the Canadas in 1837-38 have always been viewed suspiciously for just this reason: they deviated from the pattern of peaceful, orderly change which Canadians told themselves was characteristic of their history. Confederation, on the other hand, has always seemed typically Canadian; it was a solution arrived at by the political elite after long negotiation and compromise. This was, and remains, the dominant image of political change for Canadians. Not heroic figures storming the bastions of privilege, or raising the flag of liberty, but instead, a group of men in suits haggling around a conference table.

Obviously an interpretation of Canadian history and character which made so much of the British connection was unlikely to find favour with the French-speaking majority in Quebec. For the Québecois, their history had an entirely different story to tell, one which highlighted the struggle to preserve French language and culture in North America. Canadians have never resolved this dichotomy in their approach to their own history, though not for want of trying.

CHAPTER FOUR

The Infantilization of Quebec
THE MYTH OF UNITY

When I was in Grade Ten in 1963, I went on a summer exchange from my home in Vancouver to Montreal. This was my first visit to Quebec, my first real exposure to the myth of national unity. The trip was sponsored by the Council of Christians and Jews, and its purpose was to promote national togetherness by exposing French-speaking and English-speaking students to each other's culture. The assumption, of course, was that each would recognize that the other was "just like us" and we would live together happily ever after.

I did not believe for one minute that the Québecois were "just like us." As a product of the Canadian school system, my head was filled with "information" I had picked up in the classroom. Drawing on this knowledge, I expected to encounter a quaint, rustic society, less sophisticated than my own but much more fun-loving and emotional. I "knew" that Quebeckers spoke a form of degraded French quite unlike the "correct, Parisian French" I learned at school, so I anticipated having difficulty understanding and being understood, but generally I was excited to be visiting the land of Radisson and the Plouffes.

As it turned out, none of these stereotypes was fulfilled. The family I stayed with was remarkably like my own, not the Plouffe family at all. I heard no fiddlers, saw no woodcarvers; no one spoke English that sounded at all like a William Henry Drummond poem. But instead of being relieved or enlightened by this, I remember being disappointed that Quebeckers did not fit the image I had of them. I had expected to encounter something that was not there and in its absence I remember being mainly impressed by the climate. My initial impression of Montreal was that it was very hot.

As I disembarked from the train I walked into a wall of air so warm and dank that it took my breath away. It was like stepping into a shower with my clothes on. Can people really live like this? I wondered, wishing I could go home. A few days later I travelled north into the Laurentians with the family with whom I was staying. As we drove up the autoroute a heavy rainstorm swept down on us and the road became a river of water. The rain fell in such quantity and with such ferocity that the wipers could not clear it from the windshield and we had to stop the car until the storm passed. I was from the West Coast, but I had never seen rain like this. Huddled in the back seat of the car, I was terrified listening to the huge drops pound against the roof.

Nothing else about Quebec made such an impression on me as the weather. I got on well with the student with whom I was billeted (though I heard later that he became a separatist at university and have always wondered whether perhaps I was at fault for not making a convincing enough case for the country) and I loved the ancient stone buildings and narrow streets of Old Montreal. But the weather was definitely unfriendly, and I decided that there was little point in venturing east ever again. It turned out that for me the two solitudes were climatic, not linguistic or cultural. So much for national unity.

Many groups aside from the Council of Christians and Jews sent, and still send, English-speaking youngsters to live with French-speaking families. And many young Québecois pay visits in the opposite direction. It is a Canadian tradition. The motive behind all this accumulation of air miles is to promote good feelings between the country's two main linguistic groups. It is often said that we do not understand each other because we do not know each other. It is expected that by demystifying each other these exchanges will relieve some of the antagonism which seems to be at the root of our national disunity.

The irony is that while I and all those other students were spending our summers travelling back and forth in aid of national unity, we were spending our winters in school learning a version of each other that was patronizing, divisive, and completely one-sided. My generation of English Canadians who went to school in the 1950s and 1960s was typical. Armed with "facts" we had picked up in our history classes, and dispatched eastward as young soldiers in the battle for national unity, we must have personified everything our Quebec hosts resented about the country. According to a study of textbooks published by the Royal Commission on Bilingualism and Biculturalism in 1970, we learned a version of Canadian history which presented English-speaking Canadians as superior in almost every way to the French. The overriding concern of the Québecois to preserve their language and culture was hardly even mentioned in our texts, which ignored or belittled French achievement. More recent studies have concluded that things haven't changed much in the twenty-five years since the royal commission.

In Quebec the situation was perfectly mirrored. Here is Premier Lucien Bouchard telling journalist Jeffrey Simpson about his history education at the hands of the Oblates at a *college classique* during the 1950s.

The way they taught history seems so strange now. We spent so much time—years and years—on the French regime before the Plains of Abraham defeat. It was like a golden age for us. Some kind of Arcadia. The French were here. They were building things. They were converting the natives. There were good natives and bad natives: the good ones who supported the French, the bad ones who supported the English. It was a very simplistic view, but that was the way it was.

Then, very late in our teaching, there was the battle of Wolfe against Montcalm. That was the big thing. We spent weeks on that. The battle, before the battle, during the battle, after the battle. The sense of loss and sadness and mourning. It was so sad when Montcalm died—we didn't care much about Wolfe.

The rest of Canada was portrayed as only a blur. It was another country, a country we didn't know. We studied a lot of history of France, Great Britain, Germany, Europe, the United States, Quebec. But what happened in the rest of Canada after Confederation, we didn't know. We were terribly ignorant about English Canada. . . .[1]

Shortly after his election as leader of the Parti Québecois and premier of Quebec, Bouchard offended many English-speaking Canadians by suggesting that Canada was not a "real country." This remark, for which he later apologized, made clear that Bouchard, and by extension the Quebec political "class" to which he belongs, know almost nothing about the part of the

country from which they wish to separate. The Bilingualism and Biculturalism Commission saw a direct link between the kind of history which has
been taught in Canadian schools and the appeal of separatism to Lucien
Bouchard and so many other Québecois. "When we consider that today's
French-speaking youth has received its historical education from these
books," warned the Commission in 1970, "we can hardly wonder at the
great vogue for the separatist movement among young people."[2]

French and English versions of Canadian history have differed on almost
every important subject. In one part of the country Louis Riel was a hero,
in the other he was a villain. In one part of the country the rebels of 1837
were *patriotes* fighting for their rights, in the other they were misguided
traitors. In English Canada Lord Durham was a far-sighted statesman; in
Quebec he was an apologist for assimilation. Most English Canadians
accepted, however reluctantly, the invocation of the War Measures Act in
October 1970 as a necessary step to deal with political terrorism. In Quebec,
Prime Minister Trudeau's use of the armed forces against his own people
was an unforgiveable betrayal.

No event, however, has contributed as much, in its interpretations, to
the creation of the "two solitudes" as the Conquest. When British troops
scaled the cliffs above the St. Lawrence River early on the morning of
September 13, 1759 and surprised the French into engaging in a brief,
disastrous skirmish on the Plains of Abraham, the long war for control of
New France was virtually over. The battle itself took only a few minutes.
But the significance of those minutes has echoed down through Canadian
history ever since, creating a broad and enduring gulf between French and
English understandings of the country. "The Conquest," Ramsay Cook has
written, "is the burden of Canadian history."[3]

I

The facts of the Conquest are easily stated. During the eighteenth century,
France and England were at war almost constantly, each hoping to destroy
the other as a commercial rival. In North America, where the thirteen
English colonies were expanding and threatening to overrun the French
settlements, this long-running contest began its final phase in 1758 when
the British navy threw up a sea blockade which cut off Canada from all

assistance from France. The British then beseiged and captured the fortress
at Louisbourg and the following year, 1759, sent James Wolfe in command
of a force of almost 200 ships and 8,000 soldiers to take Quebec. During a
summer of hesitant skirmishing, Wolfe unleashed a reign of terror on the
surrounding countryside, burning crops, destroying homes, and murdering
civilians, but he came no closer to capturing the walled city. As freeze-up
approached, he had to do something to break the stalemate. Under cover
of darkness he led his soldiers upriver by boat beneath the looming walls
of the fortress, landing at the foot of a steep pathway at l'Anse au Foulon.
From here, the British clambered up onto the heights, catching the French
completely by surprise. The Marquis de Montcalm, the French com-
mander, played into Wolfe's hands by sending his army out of the city to
engage the enemy. In the brief battle that followed, 1,300 men died,
including Wolfe and Montcalm. The victorious British marched into
Quebec and held it until the following year when the remaining French
forces surrendered at Montreal, ending the war and delivering Canada into
British hands.

If everyone agrees about what happened on the Plains of Abraham, that
is where agreement ends. Was the British victory an unmitigated disaster
for the French colonists, or a blessing in disguise? Did life in the colony
change profoundly, or did it go on much as before? Was the role of French
Canadians in their own society completely stifled, or not affected at all?
These are some of the questions which have preoccupied historians for the
past 150 years, and they are unresolved still. What does seem indisputable
is that most Québecois have viewed the Conquest as a turning point in their
history, the moment when the unique French society which was evolving
on the shores of the St. Lawrence was abruptly overwhelmed by a foreign
power. Ever since, the Québecois have been preoccupied with the survival
of the French language and culture in America. For some, this has meant
nurturing the desire to create their own country and thereby to undo the
events of 1759-60: to reconquer Quebec for the Québecois.

The Conquest has often been called a humiliation for French Canadians.
Words like "shock," "trauma," "wound," and "tragedy" are used to describe
its impact. "Conquest is like rape," writes historian Susan Mann
Trofimenkoff. "The major blow takes only a few minutes, the results no
matter how well camouflaged, can be at best unpredictable and at worst

devastating."[4] Not only were the French colonists conquered by the English, but at the subsequent peace negotiations they were abandoned by France. Instead of taking Canada back, which they could have, the French chose to trade it for Guadeloupe and Martinique, sugar-producing islands in the Caribbean. So the humiliation was a double one: conquered by the English, considered worthless by the French. The Conquest had all the earmarks of a first-rate neurosis-making event. "To this minute," wrote Robert Fulford in 1992, "it remains a sensitive issue, perhaps the only eighteenth-century battle, anywhere, that cannot be discussed without anxiety."[5]

According to the Quebec nationalist reading of Canadian history, the grand humiliation of the Conquest was followed by a series of other humiliations, each designed to thwart the aspirations of French-speaking Canadians. This counter-narrative to the English version of the Conquest draws a direct line between the Plains of Abraham, the defeat of the *patriotes* in 1837, the attempt to assimilate the French with the union of 1841, the execution of Riel, the imposition of conscription during the two world wars, right down to the infamous Night of the Long Knives in 1981 when Ottawa and nine provinces agreed to patriate the constitution without Quebec's consent. The truth of this interpretation is not the issue; what matters is that for many (most?) Québecois it reflects the dominant narrative within their culture.

If most Quebeckers consider the Conquest to be a wound that will not heal, most English-speaking Canadians consider it a scab which the French should stop picking. "Get over it," has long been the collective response in English Canada, where there has been little sympathy for, and little understanding of, French Canada's preoccupation with the humiliation of conquest. For generations, while Quebec historians characterized the Battle of Quebec as a catastrophe, English-Canadian historians described it as a liberation and not a defeat at all. According to the English-Canadian version that I learned in school, the Conquest was a victory for French colonists because it rescued them from the despotic control of the French monarchy. Canada went from being a neglected, economically backward, politically oppressed backwater to a free, prosperous, progressive member of the British Empire. Who could complain about that? After the Conquest, French colonists were allowed to preserve their language and their religion, making them realize, according to the books I was given, just how lucky they had been to lose the war. "It was a happy time for the Canadians," A.L. Burt breezily informed his readers. "They were heartily sick of war, and they enjoyed the blessings of peace. They also made the delightful discovery that the British, whom they had feared as terrible enemies, were really excellent fellows."[6] Some versions actually presented the Battle of Quebec as a symbol of unity, a "bond which now holds French and English united in a Canadian nation"[7]; there are no victors and no vanquished. In this view the Conquest was a favour done by the British for which the Québecois are eternally grateful, as they should be. "They should be thankful for all we've done for them," is a refrain still heard regularly in the debating halls of English Canada.

This benign interpretation of the Conquest received its most fulsome presentation in the works of Francis Parkman, an American writer whose seven long books about colonial North America exerted an enormous influence on historical interpretations in Canada. His series *France and England in North America* (published between 1865 and 1892) was written in a forceful narrative style, full of swashbuckling heroes and dramatic events. Parkman was a Romantic who found the glamour and chivalry of New France's history irresistible, and he embellished it in colourful prose that attracted a wide audience, young and old, scholar and ordinary reader. For Parkman, New France embodied a romantic grandeur, but, as Carl Berger has pointed out, it was "the romantic grandeur of a lost cause."[8] In Parkman's view, New France was irredeemably backward and corrupt. He presented the war between France and England as a titanic struggle between two opposing world views: on the one hand Catholic France, feudal, authoritarian, and priest-ridden; on the other hand Protestant England, rational, progessive, and freedom-loving. Not surprisingly, he viewed the Conquest as a blessing in disguise for the *habitants* of the St. Lawrence, which brought them out of the darkness of French despotism and bestowed upon them the privilege of British liberty. "A happier calamity never befell a people than the conquest of Canada by the British arms," Parkman famously concluded.[9]

Parkman's books won a mixed reception in Quebec. Some French readers admired his storytelling abilities and the romantic glow which he cast over the history of New France; others strongly resented his anti-Catholicism. In 1878, when Laval University intended awarding him an honourary degree, a public controversy erupted, pitting Parkman's supporters against those who believed that he denigrated French-Canadian history. The separatist journalist Jules-Paul Tardivel wrote that "Mr. Parkman has permitted himself to insult our race and our religion; he has applied himself to the task of belittling us in the eyes of the world, of shattering our true national glories; he has falsified our history; he has calumnied our priests. . . ."[10] In the face of the uproar, Laval decided not to proceed with the degree, but the following year McGill, the English-language university, granted Parkman an honourary doctorate.

As the McGill honour indicates, there were no second thoughts about Parkman's work in English Canada, where his books were widely read and his influence on other historians was profound. Drawing on Parkman, English-Canadian writers for decades discovered in the Conquest the basis for an enduring partnership between English and French. By treating the Québecois so well, these writers argued, the English newcomers won their loyalty and their gratitude, creating a model of co-operation which has characterized Canadian society ever since. There was no recognition that the French might be nursing any hard feelings about the outcome of the Battle of Quebec. How could they, since it all ended so much in their favour? "The great battle which decided the future of Canada," wrote Arthur Dorland, "is one on which both English- and French-speaking Canadians can look back with pride."[11] In 1908, Governor-General Earl Grey described the Plains of Abraham as the birthplace of the nation. "It was there that French and British parentage gave birth to the Canadian nation," he said. "Today the inhabitants of the Dominion are neither English nor French. They stand before the world . . . as Canadian."[12]

This was the view of the Conquest taught to English-Canadian schoolchildren for most of this century, the view which I had when I journeyed to Quebec as an exchange student. There was nothing triumphalist about it. As an English Canadian of Irish extraction, I was not taught to take pride in the fact that "we" whipped the French on the Plains of Abraham. The Québecois were never presented as a vanquished enemy. Such an approach would be too divisive in a country that depends on two of its main "founding peoples" getting along. Instead, I learned that France was responsible for the Conquest because it neglected the colony and tolerated its sabotage by corrupt administrators. Unlike Americans, who celebrate unreservedly their victory in the War of Independence, English Canadians have never been allowed to feel that the Conquest was a moment of triumph which set the clock ticking on a great national destiny. We were not allowed to gloat and strut; instead we had to appease and accommodate. And so was born the myth of unity: that French and English were partners, co-operating in building the same Canada.

Unable to lord it over the Québecois, English Canadians have enjoyed patronizing them instead. We did this by constructing a history of the country which consistently condescends to French Canadians. From the late nineteenth century, when history became its own subject in the schools, to at least the 1960s, English-language schoolbooks were almost unanimous in depicting the Québecois as simple, happy-go-lucky bumpkins who loved nothing better than to sing and dance and smoke their pipes all day. These books presented two basic roles for the Québecois. One was the *voyageur*, the workhorse of the fur trade, paddling the great canoes to the far corners of the continent, pausing here and there for a pipeful of tobacco. "Feathers stuck jauntily in their gay caps, the men swung their cedar paddles and sang the songs of New France."[13] Rugged, venturesome, and carefree, these "Caesars of the wilderness" were the romantic heroes of schoolbook history. The other stereotypical Québecois was the *habitant*, the French-Canadian farmer, presented as a stalwart peasant in a blanket coat, pious, cheerful, and contented. The schoolbook *habitant* always lacked ambition, feared change, and was content with the status quo. "He was opposed to change," said a well-used textbook from the 1930s, written by a history professor at Queen's University, "and he asked only to be allowed to live as his parents and grandparents had lived and not to be bothered with the improvements and innovations of the energetic, aggressive English."[14] English-speaking Canadians were educated to imagine the Québecois as a picturesque, fun-loving, and inferior minority who wanted only to be left alone to breed huge families and speak their own particular brand of *patois*. "The *habitants* were happy singing the songs of Old France, and they loved to dance. The fiddler was always popular."[15]

When the French writer Andre Siegfried visited Canada in 1904, he found widespread antipathy toward the French among English Canadians.

"And if you seek to draw the attention of the English to their French fellow citizens," he wrote, "they will discuss them either patronizingly and somewhat disdainfully, or else in tones of harsh severity, seldom sympathetically or without prejudice. They would have you understand that the language of the French Canadians is only a *patois*, and the whole race at least a hundred years behind the times."[16] With time, little changed. In his study of Hollywood movies about Canada, Pierre Berton found that almost all French-Canadians "were presented as untutored children of the forest," dressed in the familiar toque and sash, speaking pidgin English and smoking clay pipes.[17] The journalist Ron Graham, who grew up in Montreal during the 1950s, recalls: "If I thought of French Canadians at all when I was a child, it was in a make-believe way . . . as rural folk who went to church a lot, picked raspberries in summer and chopped wood in winter, loved beer and pea soup, danced to the fiddle, made maple syrup, had dozens of kids and an enviable *joie de vivre* and spoke a peasant tongue that had little to do with 'good' French."[18] These rustic characters were essentially children, not a part of the modern, grown-up world.

II

The infantilization of the Québécois by English Canadians went far beyond the pages of schoolbooks. The patronizing version of Quebec history and society inherited from Francis Parkman and his successors burrowed deep into the unconscious where it coloured all English impressions of Québécois culture for generations. For most English Canadians, Quebec was a quaint folk culture, a province of fiddlers and wood carvers which added a lively, picturesque quality to the staid face of English Canada. (This is the decorative argument for Confederation, still widely heard in the debates about national unity, an argument which holds that we need the quaint, exotic presence of Quebec to keep us different from the United States.)

The rustic image of Quebec was not something created by outsiders, at least not completely. The image was built using raw materials provided by Quebeckers themselves. The superiority of rural living was official ideology in the province at the time of Confederation and for many years afterwards.

During the last half of the nineteenth century, Quebec's economy was in crisis. Good, accessible farmland was just about gone. There was a mass exodus of young people from the countryside to the cities and, when jobs could not be found there, south to the industrial towns of New England. Between 1850 and 1900, half a million Quebeckers left for the United States. It seemed as if the life blood of the French-Canadian nation was draining away. In response to this demographic emergency, the Catholic church, supported by the Quebec government, spearheaded a program to colonize the provincial hinterland with agricultural settlers. Promoters built roads and railways into the isolated backwoods and subsidized families to locate on the land. The objective was to guarantee the survival of French Canada and, secondarily, to strengthen the traditional rural society with its ascendant Catholic clergy. The ideology of the colonization movement, which continued right through the depression of the 1930s, played down the hardships of living on the land, celebrating its simplicity and spirituality instead by claiming that the Québecois could overturn the Conquest by occupying the land and creating a strong French presence throughout the north country.

Although not all that many people took advantage of the colonization program, there was widespread acceptance within Quebec of the argument that the essence of French Canada was to be found in the country parish, not amid the crowded tenements and noisy factories of the modern industrial city. A large body of literature extolled the virtues of rural living. Pre-eminent were the two Jean Rivard novels—*Jean Rivard le défricheur* (Jean Rivard the settler, 1862) and *Jean Rivard, économiste* (1864)—by Antoine Gérin-Lajoie, a leading journalist and public servant. In this pastoral romance, the hero, Jean Rivard, abandons his studies in favour of going back to the land in an isolated parish where he successfully cultivates a farm and enjoys a happy, productive life. The novels, which were enormously successful, explicitly denounce urban life and encourage Québecois to join the colonization crusade. The idealization of rural life also infused Philippe Aubert de Gaspé's nostalgic historical romance, *Les Anciens canadiens* (1863) and, much later, Louis Hémon's classic novel, *Maria Chapdelaine* (1914).

English-speaking Canadians have been more than willing to accept and embellish this version of a rustic, deferential peasant society. Images of the traditional *habitant* proliferate in our culture. Some of the earliest poetry I remember reading in school was by the Montreal doctor-turned-writer William Henry Drummond. As a Grade Ten exchange student I may even have had a volume tucked away in my suitcase.

> Johnnie Courteau of de mountain
> Johnnie Courteau of de hill
> Dat was de boy can shoot de gun
> Dat was de boy can jomp an' run
> An' it's not very offen you ketch heem still
> > Johnnie Courteau!

> Ax dem along de reever
> Ax dem along de shore
> Who was de mos' bes' fightin' man
> From Managance to Shaw-in-i-gan?
> De place w'ere de great beeg rapide roar,
> > Johnnie Courteau!

"Johnnie Courteau," "Little Bateese," "The Wreck of the Julie Plante": though they are not much read nowadays, these are some of the most popular poems ever written by a Canadian. Drummond's books, which appeared between 1897 and his death in 1907, enjoyed phenomenal success. The first, *The Habitant and Other French-Canadian Poems*, which he had to pay for himself, sold 66,000 copies in his lifetime. Another, *The Voyageur and Other Poems*, had to be reprinted four times within a year of publication. As the popularity of his work grew, Drummond abandoned his medical practice for the lecture circuit, reading his poems in halls across the country, in the United States, and in Britain. His unique brand of dialect verse appealed to people who normally would not have paid much attention to poetry. He took as his subject the lumberjacks, boatmen, and backwoods farmers of Quebec and invented for them a fractured English which many readers believed was completely authentic to the speech patterns of Quebeckers. Many of his poems retold traditional stories which he had heard during his years as a country doctor in the Eastern Townships; almost all of them celebrated the simple virtues of rural life.

You bad leetle boy, not moche you care
How busy you're kipin' your poor gran'pere
Tryin' to stop you ev'ry day
Chasin' de hen aroun' de hay—
W'y don't you geev' dem a chance to lay?
                    Leetle Bateese!

Off on de fiel' you foller de plough
Den w'en you're tire you scare de cow
Sickin' de dog till dey jomp de wall
So de milk ain't good for not'ing at all—
An' you're only five an' a half dis fall,
                    Leetle Bateese!

While Drummond himself showed great affection for his subjects—"I would rather cut off my right arm than speak disparagingly of the French Canadian people," he once wrote[19]—it is difficult to read his verse today without flinching at its characterization of Quebeckers as rough-hewn primitives, tending their farms, driving the log booms on the rivers, and leaving the affairs of the modern, urban world to somebody else.

An' here we be stay t'roo de summer day,
        w'en ev'ry t'ing's warm an' bright
On winter too w'en de stormy win' blow lak
        she blow to-night
Let dem stay on de city, on great beeg house,
        dem feller dat's be riche man
For we're happy an' satisfy here, mon chien,
        on our own leetle small cabane.

Drummond's poems found a mirror image in the nostalgic paintings of another Anglo-Quebecker, Cornelius Krieghoff. Krieghoff has been called "the first 'popular' artist in the Canadian art scene,"[20] in the sense both that his paintings appealed to a wide audience and that he took as his subject the daily life of ordinary people. Just as Drummond used dialect to evoke

French-Canadian folk society, so Krieghoff painted anecdotal scenes of *habitants* going about their daily activities. The fact that these canvases are worth hundreds of thousands of dollars to modern collectors suggests that the boisterous, nostalgic image of Quebec society they present retains its appeal. So does the fact that according to the critic Russell Harper, Krieghoff has always been one of the most popular Canadian painters with forgers.[21]

Krieghoff was born in Amsterdam in 1815 and grew up in Germany where his father ran a wallpaper factory. As a young man he studied art but was also talented at music, and when he emigrated to New York in 1837 he was able to scrounge out a living for a while as an itinerant musician. He enlisted in the American army and spent three years in Florida helping to drive out the Seminole Indians. His life in Canada began in 1840 after he met Louise Gautier, a young woman from the south shore of the St. Lawrence River opposite Montreal. The couple (it is not certain they ever married) moved to Montreal and then across the river to Longueuil to be near Louise's family. It was in Longueuil that Krieghoff gained exposure to rural life, and many of his most famous paintings reproduce scenes from the immediate neighbourhood. Still, despite his association with the rural milieu, Krieghoff spent most of his time in Montreal, where he hung around with members of the English-speaking elite of military officers, civil servants, and merchants. In 1853, he moved with his family to Quebec City, where once again he made a congenial social life among the well-to-do English-speaking residents who were the natural market for his paintings. This contented, productive period in Krieghoff's life ended by the mid-1860s when he stopped painting and left Quebec to travel in Europe. After returning briefly to Canada, he moved to Chicago in 1871 to be near his daughter, and he died there the following year.

Krieghoff's first biographer, Marius Barbeau, called him "a painter of ancient Canada"[22], by which Barbeau meant a painter who captured the traditional life of the folk of Quebec. His busy canvases are crammed with detail and spill over with activity: jolly *habitants* carousing in the snow, farm families engaged in chores around their simple dwellings, men playing at cards, women sharing gossip, Indians hunting and fishing. Habitually dressed in wool toques and blanket coats belted with the colourful *ceinture*

18. "Merrymaking" is one of Cornelius Krieghoff's busy canvases. Painted in 1860, it depicts a country inn in Quebec spilling over with drunken revellers. More than any other artist, Krieghoff created an image of the Québecois as happy peasants, religiously devout and innocent of urban cares.

fleche, his *habitants* are archetypes—stereotypes, some might say—of the rustic rural peasant: simple, fun-loving, pious, and hard-working. His meticulous re-creations of country life were extremely popular in his own day. He sold his canvases at public auction, and his less expensive prints decorated the walls of the homes of the English-speaking middle class. It has been suggested that French-speaking Quebeckers resented Krieghoff's one-sided, patronizing depiction of themselves, but outside Quebec his paintings have become iconic images of traditional French-Canadian life.

19. Marius Barbeau is considered the founder of folklore studies in Canada. As shown here, he collected music and stories on a wax-cylinder recording machine, an early form of tape recorder, then transcribed the material in his office.

It is fitting that Marius Barbeau should have chosen to write a biography of Krieghoff. In a way, Barbeau's own attempt to preserve the folk culture of Quebec matched Krieghoff's, whom he called "the father of Canadian painting and our best painter so far."[23] Barbeau (1883-1969) was a native of the Beauce region south of Quebec City. After studying anthropology at Oxford as the first French-Canadian Rhodes scholar, he returned to Canada and got a job as an ethnologist at the Victoria Memorial Museum (now the Canadian Museum of Civilization). Barbeau conducted groundbreaking fieldwork among the Huron of Lorette, and later among the Tsimshian of northern British Columbia, but during World War I he began to indulge his interest in Quebec folklore. He believed that the folk culture of rural Quebec—its songs, its stories, its handicrafts—went back hundreds of years. He wanted to rescue evidence of that culture before it disappeared, believing that it formed the basis for a unique Québecois identity. By rediscovering its ancient folk roots, Barbeau believed, Québecois culture would find a new strength and purpose.[24]

Not content simply to collect the songs and stories of "old Quebec," Barbeau began staging performances of them, using fiddlers, singers, dancers, and storytellers he encountered in his travels around the province. His first soirees, which took place in Montreal in 1919, featured a company of musicians and storytellers, some of them dressed as lumberjacks, performing on stage in the setting of an old Quebec farmhouse. These were the first folk concerts in Canada, perhaps in North America, and were doubly unique for showing off the talents of "real people" as opposed to professional entertainers.[25] Naturally enough, when John Murray Gibbon, the popularizer of the notion of the cultural mosaic, began developing his idea of a festival of folk arts for the CPR in the 1920s, he came to Barbeau. For two years Barbeau collaborated with Gibbon and the CPR, presenting exhibitions of handicrafts and music to entertain the tourists at the Château Frontenac, the railway hotel in Quebec City. The festivals were a great success. Gibbon laid on special trains from Boston, and the Old City hummed with American visitors. But for Barbeau it was too much like hucksterism and not enough about authentic culture. Unlike the CPR, which invented Canadian things in order to attract customers for its railway and hotels, he was not interested in turning the folk culture of Quebec into a tourist attraction, and after two years he returned to his own work. Over the next three decades Barbeau produced a steady stream of magazine articles, lectures, books, and films aimed at introducing his ideas to a broad public.

Barbeau was part of a widespread folklore movement active in different parts of the country during the inter-war period. In Quebec and Atlantic Canada, for example, governments established schools to train teachers to go out into the countryside to teach the skills required to produce traditional handicrafts.[26] From the governments' point of view, this was an economic initiative, undertaken to improve rural economic opportunities and to feed the tourist industry. For Barbeau, it went much deeper. He thought folk practices provided a link to an authentic cultural tradition which imparted authenticity and originality to French-Canadian society. Folklore for him was not some quaint hobby; it was at the very heart of Québecois identity.

Outside Quebec, however, the "folklorizing" of rural society played right into the stereotype of a picturesque, priest-ridden, economically backward people, admirable for their naïve *joie de vivre* and their hooked rugs, but ultimately marginal to the development of modern Canada. The "folklorizing" of Quebec provided a comfortable way for outsiders to imagine it and to incorporate it as a kind of colourful "theme park" into their view of

Canada. Barbeau and Krieghoff did not intend this, of course, but their work contributed to the already widespread tendency of Anglo-Canadians to infantilize Quebec.

III

The history of Canada tells two contradictory stories depending on whether it is viewed from a French-Canadian or an Anglo-Canadian perspective. For the Québecois, history describes a struggle to survive the assimilationist intentions of the English majority. For English-speaking Canadians, history describes the evolution of political freedom in a framework of British justice and parliamentary democracy. The differing interpretations of the Conquest are just one example of the national split personality. Just about every major historical event has elicited divergent views from the two "charter communities." The story of our history reveals the deep division at the heart of the myth of unity.

Not surprisingly, the fact that Canada is a country with two histories has been cited often as a cause of instability. Successive reports and inquiries have worried about the fact that French and English are learning different histories. Disagreement about basic historical events is believed to be a festering source of disunity in the country. The study of history is one of those activities which is supposed to contribute to national unity, it is argued; instead, in Canada, it creates two communities which are unintelligible to each other.

The belief that the study of history can contribute to national unity is one of the most durable myths in Canadian education. It goes all the way back to before the turn of the century. George Ross, Ontario's minister of education from 1882 to 1898 (when he became premier), was a strong proponent of the patriotic aims of history as a subject. "As Canadians, we should teach more of Canada," he declared. "We should have a Canadian history, fearless in exalting the great actions of Canada's greatest men."[27] Ross shared with several other leading educators a dissatisfaction with the way history was being taught in schools. They believed the subject lacked a national perspective, that it was fragmented into histories of the different regions. "I have perused with great care the various histories in use in all the provinces of the Dominion," said Ross, "and I have found them merely to be provincial histories, without reference to our common country . . ."[28] There was an opportunity to unite the country through a common understanding of its past, Ross thought, but only if everyone was learning the same history, and for that they needed the same textbook.

In mid-1893, on Ross's initiative, the Dominion Education Association, a group of teachers and administrators, announced the Dominion History Competition, a call for a new history textbook which would convey to students in every part of the country a single, national view of Canadian history. Top prize was $2,000, and publication. The chair of the organizing committee, William Patterson, explained to the *Montreal Star*: "The promoters of this movement are actuated by a wish to inspire the boys and girls of the Dominion with a true sense of the nobility and grandeur of the heritage of Canadians and so to help to create and maintain a writing of patriotic sentiment."[29]

Of the fifteen manuscripts completed by the contest deadline of July 1, 1895, the committee chose five winners.[30] First prize went to W.H.P. Clement, an Ontario lawyer who later became a judge of the B.C. Supreme Court. Clement's effort, which was published two years later as *The History of the Dominion of Canada*, was by no means a unanimous choice. Its main competitor was a manuscript by Emily Weaver from Toronto, a thirty-year-old author of children's books. Some of the judges preferred her submission to Clement's and wanted to split the prize, but contest rules did not permit a tie so Weaver had to be content with one of the $200 consolation prizes. Other runners-up were J.B. Calkin, director of the Normal School in Truro, Nova Scotia, and Dr. E.J. Eede. A fifth submission came from the eminent poet Charles G.D. Roberts. Roberts had been a school teacher as a young man and at the time of the contest was a professor at King's College in Windsor, Nova Scotia. He thought his text was "the best work that I can do in prose," but the judges found it florid in style and only good enough for an honourable mention. Like all the other winning entries except Eede's, Roberts's was published, appearing in 1898 as *A History of Canada for High Schools and Academies*.

Not surprisingly, the quartet of prize-winning textbooks from the 1890s do not appeal to the modern reader. Writing in *The Literary History of Canada*, historian Kenneth Windsor calls Clement's effort "an incredibly dull and fact-ridden volume."[31] It is a description which is equally valid for the books by Weaver, Calkin, and Roberts. Even a hundred years ago none of the winners made much of an impression. Clement's stolid volume was authorized for use in Ontario schools, but in Quebec the Catholic school system rejected it outright—it apparently did not show enough enthusiasm for the role of the church—and teachers in other parts of the country used it sparingly. When Emily Weaver's entry was published in 1900 as *A Canadian History for Boys and Girls*, it was authorized in Ontario and Nova Scotia. Roberts's book went through several editions, though it never lost the exaggerated prose style and overheated patriotism which put many readers off. Calkin's book was the least successful of the four, but by World War I they had all been surpassed by a new generation of textbooks and had faded from use.

What did not fade was the conviction that if only all Canadians could learn the same history of their country it would usher in a new era of understanding and co-operation. In other words, the country would finally work. It is an extraordinary testimony to our faith in the power of education, and of history. The Dominion History Competition was the first expression of this faith. A more recent example, published in 1968, was A.B. Hodgetts's indictment of the education system, *What Culture? What Heritage?*, a profoundly pessimistic study of the teaching of history and social studies, in which he concludes that "we have not given our students a meaningful sense of the Canadian identity." As a result, Hodgetts said, the country was drifting towards breakup and slow absorption into the United States. Turning to the issue of national unity, he made the by-then familiar point that French-speaking and English-speaking students were learning conflicting versions of history and therefore "cannot possibly understand each other or the country in which they live."[32] Then, in 1970, came the Royal Commission on Bilingualism and Biculturalism. "If Canada is more than ever before threatened with schism," the commissioners concluded, "we believe we must look for the cause very largely in the manner in which today's citizens have learned the history of their country."[33] The country needed a new history, they suggested, dissolving English and French differences in a single, bicultural narrative. We are still waiting for it, though as recently as 1991 Keith Spicer's Citizens' Forum on Canada's Future reminded us that our history remains as much a source of disunity as ever.[34] We share a past but not a history, a situation which seems to put the future very much in doubt.

IV

"The myth I grew up believing," writes Michael Ignatieff, another child of English-speaking Canada, "was that Canada was a partnership between two peoples, two languages, two histories, and two traditions."[35] I grew up with the same myth, we all did, the myth of unity, the belief that there is one Canada sharing not only the same territory but the same sense of itself as well. It was in the service of that myth that I made my pilgrimage to Quebec as a high-school student. Since the Quiet Revolution of the 1960s in Quebec, however, the myth has been harder and harder to sustain. An increasingly assertive Quebec nationalism has staked a claim at least on special status within Canada, perhaps on independence from it. So has the Aboriginal population staked such a claim. It is difficult now to agree with historian W.L. Morton who confidently declared in 1960: "There are not two histories, but one history, as there are not two Canadas, or any greater number, but only one."[36] Clearly there are two histories, perhaps more. There always have been, and despite our best efforts we are unable to reconcile them.

As the myth of unity dissolves, an increasing number of writers, borrowing from the language of cultural theory, have begun referring to Canada as a postmodern, or post-national, nation. In a post-national world it is apparently acceptable, even advisable, not to have a unified sense of identity. "We insist on staying multiple," writes novelist Robert Kroetsch.[37] In the postmodern world—shaped by instant communications and global commercialization—there is no coherent narrative imposing order on experience. Everything is provisional, problematic, open to interpretation. Regions assert themselves against the centre; minorities assert themselves against the mainstream. "In the postmodern world of counter-pointing influences, centres and traditions," declared poet and critic Frank Davey, "the claim that a single tradition can be central or orthodox has become meaningless."[38]

Such a world requires a new kind of nation-state and the postmodernists think Canada fits the bill exactly. "Canadians could be a people who recognize that our country is a state in process," argues Bruce Powe, "rather than a nation with one absolute goal."[39] Our identity comes from not having one. If we say we are this, Powe argues, then we cannot be that. On the other hand, if we keep our options open, we can be everything, anything. "Instead of lamenting our state and status as Canadians in search of an identity," asks critic Linda Hutcheon, "instead of bewailing our fate in the name of some sort of collective cultural inferiority complex, what if we made a virtue of our fence-sitting . . . ?"[40]

The postmodernist doesn't take the debate about Canadian unity that seriously. If we were never united to begin with, how can we be disunited. Robert Kroetsch has even suggested, paradoxically, that "the unity is created by the very debate that seems to threaten the unity."[41] It is our lack of unity, and the constant worrying about it, which unites us, and gives us a sort of identity. Canada is not disintegrating; it has simply transmuted into a new kind of country: decentralized, unstable, pluralistic, truly democratic, personally liberating.

The discourse of literary critics has been directed into more mainstream channels. In his recent book *Nationalism Without Walls*, journalist Richard Gwyn called Canada "the world's first postmodern state," by which he meant "multi-ethnic," politically decentralized, economically integrated into the global marketplace. As a result, Gwyn writes, Canadians have "a far lighter sense of national identity" than most other people.[42] Gwyn seems to regret the fact; true postmodernists revel in it; regardless, the myth of postmodernity seems to be challenging the myth of unity as a way of conceptualizing Canada.

The dream of unity dies hard, of course. Our politicians are still pursuing it with all the blind energy they possess. So were the thousands of earnest flag-wavers who congregated in Montreal a few days before the 1995 referendum in an attempt to convince the Québecois that English-speaking Canadians cared about them. There will be more constitutional conferences, more referenda, more media-enhanced crises. As Canadians, it seems to be our fate—our identity, if you will—to be forever engaged in the same discussion. I think most of us are aware, however, that the unity debate is now mostly about housekeeping, the distribution of power. Like Humpty Dumpty, Canada is broken and will not be put back together again. After all the royal commissions, all the unity rallies, all the student exchanges,

Canada is still not one country. If we ever believed it was, we cannot any longer.

The postmodernists tell us that this may not be a bad thing. They may be right. But most English Canadians, myself included, find it a sad thing. I shared the same myth as Michael Ignatieff, that Canada was "living proof that different races, different languages could live together within the framework of a single state." I was proud that Canada in this regard was "a moral beacon to the whole benighted world." Along with Ignatieff, I now wonder at my naïveté. "It seems extraordinary, in retrospect, that I should have supposed that we—the Québecois and I—actually knew each other well enough to constitute any kind of community at all."[43] Of course, the way English Canada maintained the illusion was to keep Quebec in a state of inferiority, of infantilization. Ever since the Québecois took control of their own destiny they have been telling us that at best our union was a marriage of convenience, not love, and they might end it at any time without tears. This is a bit of a shock and many Canadians outside Quebec, again myself included, are having a hard time forgiving them. This is my country they are breaking up, we say. The United Nations says it is the best in the world. Why don't they want to be part of it? The answer to that question is not available to me. All I know is that the debate has forced me to change the way I imagine the country. Perhaps I am seeing it for the first time as it always was—fragmented, incoherent, permanently in question, never united at all. Or perhaps I am witnessing the end of a noble dream.

CHAPTER FIVE

Divided We Stand
THE MYTH OF HEROISM

Growing up in the 1950s, I enjoyed a fairly typical Canadian boyhood. In other words, all my references were American. My family acquired a television set quite early and my favourite shows included *Leave it to Beaver*, *I Love Lucy*, and *The Honeymooners*. Each Sunday evening we gathered to watch *Father Knows Best*, followed by *The Ed Sullivan Show*. In my mind, my own father and Robert Young, the star of *Father Knows Best*, were basically the same person. I learned to dance by watching *American Bandstand*. My favourite rock star was Buddy Holly. I read about the world in *The Saturday Evening Post* and *Newsweek*. Every autumn my friends and I huddled in groups in the schoolyard listening to the World Series on our portable radios. A Davy Crockett coonskin cap was for a time my most prized possession. We named our cats Ozzie and Harriet.

I was sixteen years old when President Kennedy died. Like everyone else I knew, I idolized him: his apparent liberalism, his sophistication, his hair, his wife, the whole Camelot myth. It was a Friday morning. The principal announced over the public address system that the president had been shot, then some time later that he was dead. We were released from school and I spent the weekend rooted in front of the television set watching the awful story play itself out: the details of the assassination over and over again, the body being flown back to Washington, the endless lineup of mourners snaking past the coffin, Lee Harvey Oswald being shot down right before my eyes, and finally the funeral cortege to the cemetery, the grieving widow, the riderless horse, the volley of rifle fire at the graveside.

That weekend was the most compelling time in my life. Nothing equalled it until the political kidnappings and murder in Quebec in October

1970. I watched those events hour after hour on television as well, and I recall vividly Pierre Trudeau's "just watch me" comments on the steps of the Parliament Buildings, the open trunk of the car which contained Pierre Laporte's strangled corpse, another cavalcade of cars, this time ferrying the "terrorists" to the airplane which would carry them to exile in Cuba. In a real sense I began taking Canada seriously that fall and a large part of the reason was that we had finally made prime time television with our own act of political madness.

In the universe I inhabited as a boy, there were no Canadian stars. There was no room; the skies were filled with the super novas of American history, politics, and pop culture. How could Bobby Curtola and the Plouffe family compete? Canada was a subject you studied in school because you had to, like biology. It was not a place which commanded your attention in real life. When I was looking for "role models" (we didn't use the term then) to admire and emulate, I found them on American television or in the myths of the American West or the comic books about U.S. marines in World War II. It would not occur to me until I was older, and no longer looking for heroes, that my own culture had important stories to tell.

It has often been observed that English Canada has not produced many heroes, by which I mean outstanding public figures from the past who we all agree represent the best of us. The overwhelming influence of American culture on our lives has inhibited the emergence of homegrown greatness. Most people seem to feel that this is a bad thing. It is supposed to indicate that we lack confidence in ourselves and in our worth as a nation. But it is a little more complicated than that. For one thing, Canadian history does not present that many occasions when heroism on a grand scale was necessary. We have evolved historically at a measured pace; by and large, change has occurred gradually, without the turmoil of civil unrest. We have had no civil war, no wild west, no successful revolution, all events which might have provided us, as it did the United States, with a pantheon of heroes. We have also lacked, until quite recently, a myth-making industry, as Robert Fulford pointed out several years ago.[1] Our book-publishing industry was weak and foreign-owned; our film industry was non-existent. The media which create and sustain mythic heroes were not available to us.

Furthermore, in a country like Canada—ethnically diverse, divided by three "founding peoples," fragmented into several regions (not to mention the usual divisions of class and gender)—hero worship is as likely to divide as it is to unite. The history of the country has been a history of conflict and compromise: between French and English primarily, but also between Natives and non-Natives, between the metropolis and the hinterland, between capital and labour, between "charter groups" and newcomers. In such a place, it is difficult to agree on who constitutes a hero. Joseph Howe has been called "the greatest of all Nova Scotians." He was a noted journalist, the father of responsible government in the Maritimes. Yet he fought Confederation tooth and nail and would have led the province out of the union if he had had his choice. Out West and in Quebec, Louis Riel is a folk hero. Statues are raised in his honour; operas and poems sing his praises; there is a persistent movement to have him recognized as a Father of Confederation. Yet there has probably never been a person so widely despised in Ontario; when he was executed for his part in the 1885 Northwest Rebellion, Anglo-Ontarions gloated by burning effigies of him at tumultuous outdoor celebrations. Henri Bourassa, the founder of *Le Devoir* newspaper, is a hero to Quebeckers for his stalwart defence of Canadian independence. Yet in British Columbia, in 1920, a history text-book was banned from the schools because it did not present Bourassa as a traitor to the Empire.[2] A recent public opinion survey discovered that "the greatest Canadian of all time" is considered by many people to be Pierre Trudeau. But surely the sample could not have included any Albertans, who continue to vilify the former prime minister for his National Energy Policy.[3]

Heroes are supposed to be a force for unity; in Canada, a country with a weak national culture, strong regional grievances, and an ethnically diverse population, they are more often than not flashpoints for disunity. Which must partly explain why we are so reluctant to identify them.

Heroism, then, is contested terrain. We like to think that heroes draw attention to themselves simply because their selfless deeds of valour seem to incarnate the values which we all share as members of a community. This is the role of the hero, after all: to represent ourselves at our collective best, to knit the community together in a shared self-regard. But heroism is not so self-evident. In Canada at least, heroic figures have tended to emerge from the regions or from minority struggles against the status quo. By and large they are sticks used by one part of the community to beat on another. As a result, every region of the country has its local heroes, but as a nation we have none.

Louis Riel is an interesting case in point. French-speaking Canadians have always admired him, and used his memory to regret the lack of French-language rights outside Quebec. Anglo-Canadians, on the other hand, early in the century depicted Riel as a madman, a traitor, and a murderer. Gradually his reputation among English-speaking Canadians improved as the point of view of Aboriginal people began to erode the master narrative. Since the 1960s Riel has emerged as an all-purpose hero who manages to be different things to different people, depending on what they want him to be. French speakers see him as a defender of French-Catholic rights against the English-Protestant majority. Natives see him as a defender of Aboriginal rights against the forces of assimilation. Western Canadians see him as a defender of regional rights against eastern expansionism.[4] Riel has achieved heroic status by being completely protean. His significance changes shape depending from what angle you look at him.

Riel is an exception, however. Most figures from the past are unable to perform his complicated trick. In a society which is increasingly fragmented, they have too small a constituency to gain hero status on a national scale. And as the whole nature of heroism changes, there is even less chance that Canadians will discover public figures capable of playing the role.

I

On November 11, 1912, an unusual civil trial opened in Toronto. "The spectators who yesterday frequented the court room were of very different character from the usual habitués of the abodes of justice," one newspaper reported. "There were university professors, litterateurs, exponents of political science, journalists and many members of the legal profession, while a couple of Members of Parliament dropped in for short periods." Among this distinguished crowd sat the sphinx-like figure of William Lyon Mackenzie King, former minister of labour in Wilfrid Laurier's cabinet and a rising star in the Liberal Party. As we shall see, King had more than an academic interest in the proceedings.[5]

The case which attracted the attention of so many intellectuals and political heavyweights pitted William Dawson LeSueur, retired public servant and man of letters, against the descendants of William Lyon Mackenzie, the rebel leader who in 1837 led an armed insurrection against the colonial rulers of Ontario, then known as Upper Canada. The family was trying to stop LeSueur from publishing a biography of Mackenzie which he had written. But the case went much deeper than that. The interested parties were contesting not simply LeSueur's right to publish a biography, but his right to express an interpretation of Canadian history which was at odds with the prevailing wisdom. The court case was an attempt to control the reputation of a Canadian hero.

In 1906, William LeSueur had been engaged by the Toronto publisher George Morang to prepare a biography of Mackenzie as part of Morang's "Makers of Canada" series. In LeSueur's day, Mackenzie enjoyed a positive reputation with many historians. This was a far cry from the version I learned from my 1950s history textbook, which painted Mackenzie as an ineffectual zealot, but history has its fashions and at the turn of the century a common view of the rebel leader was that his insurrection had been completely justified, and that it was largely responsible for the granting of responsible government to the British North America colonies, one of the most important innovations in the constitutional history of the country. Mackenzie, in other words, was a true "Maker of Canada." LeSueur disputed this view. In his opinion, which he expressed forthrightly in the manuscript which he submitted to his publisher in the spring of 1908, Mackenzie had been a bumptious troublemaker who did more to delay reform than to bring it about. "He launched his *opera bouffe* rebellion," LeSueur wrote, "fled incontinently at the first shot, leaving his lieutenants to expiate on the gallows the crime which was chiefly his own, and from the security of the neighbouring Republic completed his efforts on behalf of the Canadian people by organizing bands of ruffians to raid and murder them."

When he embarked on the biography, LeSueur did not count on the determined interference of William Lyon Mackenzie King, future prime minister and proud grandson of the rebel leader, who, as soon as he heard that LeSueur had been engaged to write the biography, launched a campaign to thwart the project. "It was quite clear there was a conspiracy . . . to have Mackenzie written down instead of up," he wrote in his celebrated diary. But it was King himself who was the conspirator. In Toronto he met with Morang and the other editors of the series to try to convince them to give the project to another author. In Ottawa he met with LeSueur to urge him to step aside in favour of someone more sympathetic to the subject. But LeSueur did not agree that biography had to be hagiography, and politely told King so.

Once LeSueur submitted a manuscript to his publisher, it did not take the interfering King long to find out about its contents. "It is a vile production," he declared, and renewed his efforts to suppress it. Having seen the manuscript, Morang got cold feet. He finally recognized that LeSueur's Mackenzie could hardly be called a "Maker of Canada," and that the whole purpose of the series was contradicted by the new manuscript. Accusing the author of exaggerating Mackenzie's defects, he asked for changes. When LeSueur refused, the biography appeared to be dead.

As long as the offending manuscript still existed, however, Mackenzie King and other relatives could not rest easy. There was, they rightly believed, nothing to stop LeSueur from finding another publisher for his manuscript. So they took steps to suppress it. First of all, Morang, now an ally of the family, refused to return the only copy. This left the author no choice but to sue his publisher to regain possession of his own work. The court ruled in his favour, but this turned out to be only the first round. During his research for the biography, LeSueur had consulted a stash of personal papers and old newspapers held by Charles Lindsey, Mackenzie's son-in-law and himself author of an earlier biography of the rebel leader. Initially, Lindsey seemed completely sympathetic to LeSueur's project and even invited him to consult the papers, which were stored in Lindsey's Toronto home. When the manuscript was finished, however, the attitude of the Lindsey family changed completely. By this time Charles had died, but his son George, Mackenzie's grandson, was adamant that the biography should never see print. He accused LeSueur of violating the family's generous hospitality to write a scurrilous and mean-spirited book. Having failed to keep the manuscript away from its author, Lindsey went back to court, asking that LeSueur be stopped from ever publishing his book with any publisher at any time. No wonder this trial, the fourth involving the Mackenzie biography, attracted so much attention from the literary and scholarly communities when it began in Toronto in November 1912.

As the trial unfolded it became clear that the real issue was LeSueur's political beliefs and the fact that King and the Lindsey family did not like them. During four days of evidence, the prosecution depicted him as a hopeless reactionary intent on rewriting Canadian history in a Tory image. Not only had LeSueur had the effrontery to present Mackenzie warts and all, he had come out in qualified support of the Family Compact, depicting them as men of principle, not the reactionary cranks of popular imagination. In other words, LeSueur was taking issue with what was then the interpretation of Canadian constitutional development favoured by liberals such as King. That was his real "crime." As *Saturday Night* magazine wryly noted: "Thus it would appear that literary men of Tory sentiments and lineage are not to be trusted."

In the end the court agreed with the prosecution that LeSueur had fraudulently gained access to the Lindsey family papers and it ruled that he could not publish. After an appeal which supported the original decision, the manuscript passed into the hands of George Lindsey who, instead of destroying it, packed it away with the other family papers which eventually ended up in the Ontario Archives. It was not until the 1970s that historian Brian McKillop stumbled across the handwritten manuscript tied up in brown paper wrapping in the Archives. It was finally published in 1979, seventy years after it was written.

The "Makers of Canada" series was one of the earliest attempts to raise up a pantheon of Canadian heroes. There was pretty widespread agreement early in the century about who our culture's heroes were. Disagreement, as in the case of LeSueur, was dealt with harshly. Heroes were individuals whose efforts had contributed to the development of a self-governing nation. This was the main story-line of Canadian history, the gradual evolution of colony into nation, and the "Makers" was one of the great monuments of the colony-to-nation narrative. The series has been called "the climax of the Victorian practice of biography in Canada"[6] (in other words, stuffy, reverential, moralizing, and prissy). George Morang conceived the series as a history of the country told through the lives of the prominent men whose actions had "made" it. The original series, published between 1908 and 1911, ran to twenty volumes, plus index. Its subjects included a triumvirate from New France: Samuel de Champlain, Bishop Laval, and Governor Frontenac, along with the heroes of the Conquest,

Generals Wolfe and Montcalm, treated together in one volume. There were several British colonial governors—Dorchester, Haldimand, Simcoe, Sydenham, Elgin, and James Douglas as the token "Maker" from British Columbia; three fur traders—Alexander Mackenzie, Lord Selkirk, and George Simpson; three French Canadians—Papineau, Lafontaine, and Cartier; three Maritimers—Leonard Tilley, Lemuel Wilmot, and Joe Howe; a war hero—Isaac Brock; the architect of the Ontario school system—Egerton Ryerson; and a passel of Ontario politicians—John A. Macdonald, George Brown, Mackenzie, Robert Baldwin, and Francis Hincks, the familiar responsible government crowd. In 1926, the series was reprinted with a few alterations: some biographies were discarded, others were replaced, and books on Cornelius Van Horne, Donald Smith (Lord Strathcona), and Wilfrid Laurier were added.

Several things strike one immediately about this list of "great Canadians." First of all, they are all men. Women were virtually absent from the telling of Canadian history until the 1960s. They were present in the background, as pioneer wives making candles and quilts (Homemakers of Canada, if you like), or as King's Daughters brought out from home to marry and breed colonists for New France. But they were not allowed to play a significant role in the story of the development of the country. Two exceptions were Laura Secord and Madeleine de Verchères, both of whom "saved" Canada from foreign invaders and therefore earned the right to be singled out for special mention in most histories of the country.

Secondly, the "Makers" are almost all public men—politicians, generals, and colonial officials. Fur traders aside, there was not one entrepreneur, scientist, engineer, athlete, artist, or scholar among the "Makers" until Cornelius Van Horne, the chief engineer of the CPR, was added as an afterthought. Van Horne was also as close as the series got to a "working man," someone who earned his living from the sweat of his brow. There were no labour leaders or factory foremen or any other representatives of the labouring classes. History, according to the "Makers" approach, was all about politics and constitution-making and the elites which participated in these activities, which I'm sure accounts for why so many people found Canadian history as they learned it in school so boring: it lacked good, exciting stories.

Likewise, to qualify as a "Maker" a man had to belong to one of the two

20. Dr. Frederick Banting (*right*) shared a Nobel Prize with Dr. Charles Best (*left*) and two others for their discovery of insulin, but it was Banting who became a celebrity. He received a knighthood, a lifetime annuity from the federal government, and top billing as the "Greatest Living Canadian" in survey after survey.

"charter groups," French-speaking or English-speaking. Blacks, First Nations people, Asian-Canadians, and other visible minorities were not considered part of the nation-building scenario. The series was, in the words of one historian, "an elaborate enunciation of Anglo-Canadian social and political mythology,"[7] and this mythology did not include visible minorities.

In the contest for cultural hegemony, history is a prize. Whoever wins the contest gets to impose their interpretation of the past. The "Makers" series was an expression of the triumph of a particular view of the past, one which celebrated the achievements of the English, and to a lesser degree the French, elites. Dissenting voices, like LeSueur's, were silenced. The series encapsulated several of the myths which form the backbone of Canadian history: the myth of unity, the myth of the master race, the myth of the CPR, the romance of nation-building.

II

The "Makers of Canada" series was the last successful attempt to construct a pantheon of Canadian heroes. In its wake, heroism became a more hit-and-miss affair, less wedded to a single interpretation of the country's development. Canadians still admired heroic figures, of course, but in

English Canada at least they seemed to be admired more for their character and accomplishments than for contributing to the development of the nation. I am thinking here, for instance, of Frederick Banting, co-discoverer of insulin in 1922. Banting, who shared a Nobel Prize for his discovery, was considered the "Greatest Living Canadian" in at least five public surveys carried out in the 1920s and 1930s. Or Dr. Charles Saunders, the government plant breeder who developed Marquis wheat and also finished high on everyone's most-admired list. Sir William Osler and Norman Bethune are two more examples. The doctor/scientist was a new type of Canadian hero, praised for his contribution to humanity, not to nationhood. Politics apparently no longer produced important stories which provide contexts for heroes.

Following World War I, another new category of hero was added, the war hero. There had been war heroes before: Wolfe, Montcalm, Laura Secord, Isaac Brock charging up the hill at Queenston Heights. But they had been attached to a national myth; they were venerated because they had a hand in preserving the nation from invaders or capturing the nation from occupiers (even, perversely, Montcalm). The new war hero of World War I was a hero solely because of his bravery, his sacrifice. He represented the "best" of Canadian character.

Of course, all soldiers who served in the armed forces during the war were heroes to their fellow Canadians. Monuments went up in small towns from coast to coast commemorating those who lost their lives overseas. But the individual who focussed all this admiration was Billy Bishop, the farm boy from Midland, Ontario, who joined the Royal Air Force as a way of escaping the trenches and went on to become the third deadliest pilot on the Allied side. Bishop's early life follows a traditional pattern for a hero. He was a misfit, an outsider, whose exceptional character only emerged in unusual circumstances. If there had been no war, there is no telling what trouble he might have gotten into. He was a poor student who spent more time hanging around the town pool hall and shooting squirrels than studying. At Royal Military College, where he was described as the worst cadet the college ever had, he was caught cheating on exams and would have been expelled had the war not come along just in time. Once overseas with the army he turned out to be illness- and accident-prone, and was a

21. "The Second Battle of Ypres, 22 April to 25 May, 1915," by Richard Jack, was the first painting commissioned by the Canadian War Memorials Fund during World War I to memorialize Canada's contribution to the war. The painting was completed a year after the battle, by an artist who had not been there and had no photographs of the scene to work with. "In order to glorify the Canadian troops," art historian Maria Tippett has written, "Jack employed every hackneyed nineteenth-century battle art convention: a wounded officer waving his men on into battle; a soldier dying in the arms of his comrade; puffs of smoke indicating distant artillery action (or was this the ominous, yellow-green cloud of chlorine gas?); the villainous faces of the enemy in contrast to the smiling faces of the Canadians; and a silhouetted figure of a Canadian soldier bayoneting a German." (Tippett, *Art at the Service of War*, Toronto: University of Toronto Press, 1984, p.26) Despite the inaccuracies—where are the trenches? why are the men weighed down with backpacks?—the painting was thought to convey the glorious gallantry of the Canadian fighting men. It might also be seen as the final expression of a romantic view of war that the horrors of World War I extinguished forever.

pretty dismal sort of a soldier. When he transferred to the Flying Corps in 1916, he was not even much of a pilot, but he turned out to have incredible eyesight, implacable nerve, and a thirst for combat. Finally he was in his element, and quickly showed himself to be a master at the dogfight. On one occasion he engaged seven planes at once, and shot down two. In one period of twelve days he scored twenty-five kills. Twice he took on the famous Red Baron, and both times escaped with his life, which was something of a victory given the Baron's record. On his last day of active duty at the front Bishop downed five planes in less than fifteen minutes, bringing his total to seventy-two enemy aircraft destroyed.

Bishop's exploits won him several medals and a huge public following. When the war began it was considered ungentlemanly to boast about one's accomplishments in combat. Then the politicians and generals began to realize the propaganda value of the dashing young flyboys and began to publicize their exploits. Bishop was the first hero consciously promoted by the Canadian state for propaganda purposes. In the middle of the war he was brought back to Canada for a series of public appearances designed to boost enthusiasm for the war effort. He was living proof of the country's extraordinary contribution to the war. Not only did he incarnate the gallant young warrior, with more victories to his credit at that time than any other Allied pilot, but he was obviously shy and uncomfortable in the public eye, just the way heroes were supposed to be. "No wonder we cheered," wrote a reporter for the *Globe* newspaper, "and just because he looked so modest we cheered all the more."[8]

Following the war Bishop wrote a book, went on a lecture tour, engaged in a short-lived flying venture with another war ace, Billy Barker, then settled comfortably into a business career, first in England, then back in Canada. In the mid-1930s he became an honourary Air Vice-Marshall in the Royal Canadian Air Force and spoke out for expanded air power. During World War II he was in charge of recruiting for the RCAF; after the war, he resumed his business career. When he died in 1956, his reputation as Canada's leading war hero was uncomplicated and intact.

Times change, and with them the nature of heroism. In 1982, the National Film Board released an eighty-minute film about Bishop called *The Kid Who Couldn't Miss*, written and directed by Paul Cowan. From the beginning the film suggests that there is "some truth, some myth" to the

22. Flying ace Billy Bishop poses beside his plane in 1917, shortly after the controversial escapade that won him a Victoria Cross.

Bishop story. Cowan is interested in the nature of heroism, not in glorifying a hero. The film, which is built around a performance of John Gray's popular anti-war stage play *Billy Bishop Goes to War*, repeatedly describes the slaughter and horror of the war, and blames it on the vanity and ambition of nameless generals and politicians. Bishop comes across as a brave man, but also as a cold-blooded murderer, almost a psychotic. At the same time, he and his fellow pilots are presented as pawns in the game of war, "children sent to the slaughter." At the end of the film the message is made clear that "heroism, like war, is neither as simple nor as glorious as we would like."

The most controversial part of the film turned out to be its questioning of Bishop's famous solo attack on a German aerodrome in June 1917. It was a daring, unprecedented escapade and it won him a Victoria Cross, but there were no witnesses to the incident and Cowan wonders openly whether it ever took place at all. In other words, he raises the possibility that one of Canada's greatest legends was a hyper-ambitious liar who inflated his own achievements for personal glory. Furthermore, the film suggests that senior officials were quite willing to overlook discrepancies in Bishop's account because he was so valuable as an inspiring symbol of Allied pluck.

War veterans reacted to *The Kid Who Couldn't Miss* as if they had been stuck with a sharp pin. The film "is an insulting and disgraceful profile of a national war hero," charged Clifford Chadderton, leader of the counter-attack, which "must be destroyed."[9] The outcry led to two Senate subcommittee hearings at which witness after witness expressed their outrage at Cowan's version of history. At times the anguished sense of betrayal was clearly evident. "Don't you think you should be thoroughly ashamed of yourself?" one of the senators asked François Macerola, then head of the Film Board. "I am saying that in all goodwill to you, because I think you are a bright man within your limits. Aren't you ashamed of yourself?"[10] Historians were brought in and documents presented, all to prove that Bishop was the hero he was supposed to be. Would any other country "allow tampering with their most revered heroes?" asked Clifford Chadderton. "Of course not—and neither should we." For Chadderton there was only one version of history; other versions were destructive and should be suppressed. "If we, as Canadians, allow Paul Cowan to get away with his attempt to destroy Billy Bishop, perhaps we are paving the way for those who would re-arrange our history and ignore the struggle to build this nation, and the on-going challenge to keep it free."[11]

The controversy revealed nothing about Billy Bishop that was not already known. Whether or not he actually carried out the raid on the German air field was not confirmed. All the Senate hearings proved was that we will never know for sure. What the controversy did reveal was a dramatic change in our attitude to heroes since the days of the "Makers of Canada." Unfortunately for Chadderton and the war vets, we live in an age of irony. Not so long ago, heroes were larger than life, performing romantic deeds of bravery and daring. They were beyond reproach, greater than ourselves, which is why we admired them. In the age of irony, however, heroes are flawed, just like the rest of us, and just like the rest of us they are victims. Cowan's film does not deny Bishop's bravery; instead it questions the psychological sources of that bravery, wonders whether it was tainted by extreme ambition and accuses authorities of taking advantage of it for their own purposes. The film, and the controversy it inspired, shows that a gap has opened between those who want to celebrate the heroic, and by extension the master narrative, and those who want to interrogate and subvert it. Young pilots were brave, says the film; they were also murderers and fakes. In the age of irony, motives are mixed; we no longer celebrate heroes, we deconstruct heroism. In the age of irony the master narrative has fragmented and no longer enjoys the unquestioned allegiance it once did.

The controversy over Billy Bishop was reprised in 1992 when CBC Television aired *The Valour and the Horror*, a three-part documentary series about World War II. The first film in the series (*Savage Christmas*, about the battle of Hong Kong in 1941) was reasonably well-received, but the other two, *In Desperate Battle*, about the Normandy invasion in 1944, and especially *Death by Moonlight*, about the aerial bombing of German cities, really got veterans' hackles up. Once again revisionist filmmakers too young to have seen combat, in this case the brothers Brian and Terence McKenna, stood accused of smearing the reputation of Canadian fighting men. Once again the Senate agreed to provide a forum for veterans to orchestrate a public protest against the series. The press jumped in and turned the spotlight on itself by redefining the issue as one of freedom of expression. Historians supporting both camps batted evidence back and forth until it seemed like you needed a Ph.D. in military history to follow the arguments. It was clear that many veterans were deeply and genuinely hurt. They believed that they had been betrayed by a publicly-funded television program that misunderstood and misrepresented their wartime experiences. It was hard not to sympathize with their hurt, even while questioning the wisdom of trying to censor the public airwaves.

For their part, the McKennas were unrepentant. They insisted that they were revealing an untold truth about the war; that time and again ordinary Canadian soldiers had been sacrificed because of the ambition and incompetence of the military leadership. The McKennas seemed genuinely surprised that veterans were upset by the series. They thought they were paying tribute to Canadian courage. The veterans thought they were being portrayed as little better than war criminals by members of a spoiled younger generation who had never been asked to sacrifice anything. ("A petulant flower child," is how one army type described Brian McKenna.[12]) The whole affair had overtones of patricide, at least for the veterans.

III

The controversies surrounding *The Kid Who Couldn't Miss* and *The Valour and the Horror* were about the creation of public memory. How should war and its heroes be remembered? The master narrative presents both world wars as heroic struggles to preserve a way of life from enemies who would overwhelm it. According to the master narrative, the sacrifice of all those young lives was valorous and meaningful. War is horrible, but its horror is redeemed by noble sacrifice. This is the official memory of the war. It is unambiguous and idealistic. It invokes the war to promote unity and patriotism. The belief that Canada "came of age" at Vimy Ridge, for example, sanctions the slaughter, makes it purposeful, repays in part the debt we owe to the men who died there.

For good reasons, most Canadians have accepted the official view. It satisfies a deep need to believe that all the death and sacrifice was worthwhile. To question the war is to dishonour the fallen, and they, after all, died for us. But there has always been a counter narrative, muted but persistent, that found the appalling slaughter pointless, and the people who sanctioned it incompetent, even evil. Examples include the 1930 anti-war novel *Generals Die in Bed* and the activities of the small peace movement. The counter narrative usually claims to speak for the ordinary soldier, as the McKenna brothers did in their film series. It presents a trench-eye view of war, full of ironies and ambiguities. Soldiers are ordinary men just trying to live through the horror, not the saintly warriors depicted in memorial paintings and statues ascending to heaven in the arms of an angel. Opponents of the counter narrative find it intolerable because it blurs the distinction between good guys and bad guys and seems to call into question the notion of a just war. Therefore they respond with all the authority they can muster to reassert the primacy of the official memory. The response to the films also reveals how difficult it is to sustain the myth of heroism in the modern age. The uncomplicated, selfless hero is now a creature of bad fiction. Certainly the military no longer provides an acceptable model, not after the fiasco in Somalia and the sophomoric, sometimes racist, behaviour of soldiers revealed in the videos of hazing "rituals" beamed coast to coast on the evening news.

But if not soldiers, who will be our heroes? Explorers are out of business. Politicians, with the possible exception of Mr. Trudeau, are in bad odour, as are business people. Scientists have always been popular but their achievements do not often interest a large number of people. Athletes, now that they are making such inflated salaries, seem to be motivated more by greed than any of the heroic virtues. In the absence of notable public figures, celebrity has replaced heroism. If you ask people to identify the faces of the prime ministers on our currency, you will discover that many more people recognize Don Cherry than Robert Borden. But celebrities are only famous for being famous, not for accomplishing something worthwhile. Don Cherry, I hope, does not represent anyone's idealized version of what it means to be a Canadian.

"Canadians do not like heroes, and so they do not have them," wrote George Woodcock in 1970.[13] French Canadians have been better at creating national heroes, probably because their society is more homogenous. In English Canada, more often than not, the attempt to celebrate a hero creates an enemy or opens a wound. This is due, in part, to the fragmentation of the master narrative. Heroes arise out of stories, but Canada no longer has a story which everyone agrees sums up our national purpose. I said earlier that Louis Riel is an exception because his story can be interpreted in several different ways to appeal to several different communities. Perhaps it is more accurate to say that Riel is a model of what a uniquely Canadian hero has to be: not a "Maker of Canada" who represents an unambiguous ideal, but rather a shape-shifter, someone whose story is complex enough to appeal to the kind of fragmented society Canada has become.

CHAPTER SIX

The Ideology of the Canoe
THE MYTH OF WILDERNESS

In 1991 the federal government installed a giant bronze sculpture at the entrance to the Canadian Embassy in Washington, D.C. The sculpture, by Haida artist Bill Reid, is called "Spirit of Haida Gwaii" (a copy also rests inside a terminal at the Vancouver airport), and depicts a huge canoe spilling over with an assortment of Haida characters, some human, some animal, most a little bit of both. As the poet Robert Bringhurst observes, this crowded canoe is many things: an ark, a lifeboat, an island, a raft. It also seems to be a cradle, or a womb, out of which a whole world is emerging.[1]

"Spirit of Haida Gwaii" is a magnificent work, but initially I wondered at the government's decision to have it represent Canada at such a prestigious location in the capital city of our closest ally. Why are "we" always borrowing Aboriginal iconography, I muttered to no one in particular, "we" meaning mainstream, white, Euro-Canadian culture? Don't "we" have any stories of our own to tell? Clearly the government was attempting to merge Aboriginal mythology with a general mythology of relevance to all Canadians, Aboriginal and non-Aboriginal alike, but as I thought more about Reid's bronze canoe it became clear to me that the choice was a perfectly appropriate one after all. The canoe, and the story of transformation it embodies, does not belong solely to the Aboriginal people. They are also central emblems of non-Native Canadian culture. Ever since the first European traders and colonists arrived in Canada, the canoe journey into the wilderness has been a consistent theme of our history and our culture. The historian W.L. Morton has written that the "alternate penetration of the wilderness and return to civilization is the basic rhythm of Canadian

23. Bill Reid's mammoth sculpture, "Spirit of Haida Gwaii," stands outside the Canadian Embassy in Washington, D.C.

---

life, and forms the basic elements of Canadian character."[2] This excursion seems to have become for Canadians a metaphorical voyage: the canoe carries us out of our European past deep into the wilderness where we are reborn as citizens of the New World. The canoe emerges as the mother image of our national dreamlife, the symbol of our oneness with a rugged northern landscape, the vessel in which we are recreated as Canadians. As much as the beaver or the Canada goose or the maple leaf, the canoe is presented as our link to the land, to the past, to our Aboriginal forebears, and to our spiritual roots.

I

The canoe is omnipresent in Canadian history and folklore. Almost every First Nations group used it to get around, whether it was the light birchbark canoe of the eastern woodlands or the heavy whaling canoe of the west coast, hewn from a single cedar log. The first European colonists recognized its importance immediately. Fresh off the boat from France, Samuel de Champlain wrote: ". . . in the canoe the savages can go without restraint, and quickly, everywhere, in the small as well as the large rivers. So that by using canoes as the savages do, it would be possible to see all there is, good and bad. . . ." As Harold Innis pointed out, there is a logic to the physical contours of Canada, a logic imposed by the early canoe routes. The border with the United States is not an arbitrary line; the watersheds flow away from it north and east. Following these waterways, the canoe created Canada. "If I were asked the question, 'What did most to pave the way for the development of the Dominion of Canada?'" remarked the writer and CPR publicist John Murray Gibbon, "I should feel inclined to answer, 'The Canoe'."[3] The Ontario heritage activist James Coyne once declared: "That Canada is British today is largely due to the birch bark canoe."[4]

In the days of New France, the *coureurs de bois* used the canoe to carry them far beyond the reach of civilized society deep into Indian Country. "Since all of Canada is a vast and trackless forest, it is impossible for them to travel by land," explained one government official; "they travel by lake and river in canoes . . ." It was recognized even then that this practice was creating a new type of colonist. "They love to breathe a free air," wrote Father Charlevoix in his *Histoire de la Nouvelle France* (1744), "they are early accustomed to a wandering life; it has charms for them, which make them forget past dangers and fatigues, and they place their glory in encountering them often. . . ." Far from home, away from family and loved ones, the *coureurs* sometimes paid spectral visits back to the settled villages of the St. Lawrence aboard a flying canoe, the *chasse gallerie* of Quebec folklore. Legend had it that on New Year's Eve in particular, the spirits of absent, or dead, traders soared above the treetops in ghostly canoes, propelled by Satan himself. William Henry Drummond, the country's leading dialect poet, provided a version of the story in his poem "Phil-o-rum Juneau":

> But it's mak' me lonesome an' scare also, jus'
>   sam' I be goin for die
> W'en I lissen dat song on night lak dis so far

away on de sky,
Don't know w'at to do at all mese'f, so I go
w'ere I have good view,
An' up, up above t'roo de storm an' snow,
she's comin' wan beeg canoe.

The religious counterpart of the *coureurs* were the Jesuit missionaries who ventured into the heart of darkness to bring the word of God to the First Nations. The accounts they sent to their superiors back in France told of punishing canoe trips down rivers and across lakes which no white person had ever seen before. The Jesuits seemed to be in ceaseless motion, paddling days at a stretch, their hands raw with blisters, their backs baking under the hot sun. These French stories, the Jesuits and the others, are allowed to contribute to the English-Canadian "national" story because they conform so nicely to the folkloric, pre-modern images of Quebec contained in the master narrative.

Following in the wake of the missionaries came our familiar textbook heroes, the explorers who struck west across the continent by canoe, seeking out the waterways which led eventually all the way to the Pacific Ocean: Alexander Mackenzie arriving at the coast to scrawl his message on a rock—from Canada by land; Simon Fraser, clinging in terror to the gunwales as he bobs like a leaf through the boiling rapids of the river which bears his name; David Thompson on the banks of the Columbia building his own canoe of rough cedar boards lashed together with pine roots to carry him down to the ocean. The most itinerant trader of them all was Governor George Simpson, the "little emperor" of the Hudson's Bay Company, who was famous for charging across the fur country at breakneck speed in a giant canoe manned by a dozen of the strongest Iroquois paddlers and a Highland piper to announce his sudden arrival at the remote trading posts. It was Simpson's genius that he made the canoe a weapon of bureaucratic tyranny.

The fur trade canoes were modelled on the bark canoes of the eastern woodlands. Recreational canoeists preferred to use a variant on this model, the board canoe made from thin strips of cedar or wide planks of basswood. The process for making these wood canoes was developed along the

Otonabee River northeast of Toronto by several different boatbuilders, all of whom were working on variants of the basic board-and-rib design during the 1850s and 1860s. Eventually the Peterborough Canoe Company emerged as the main manufacturer, winning an international reputation for its beautiful cedar products. Other manufacturers in the eastern United States built wood canoes but covered them with a skin of canvas to improve their durability. This idea migrated north into New Brunswick where the brothers William and Harry Chestnut began making canvas-covered canoes in 1897. The Peterborough Company also utilized this design and in 1923 merged with the Chestnut Canoe Company. [5] Together these manufacturers established Canada as the pre-eminent canoe-making nation of the industrial world.

The wooden canoe, tougher than the bark canoe and lighter than the dugout, was perfectly suited to the cottages and summer camps which were appearing in the northern woods at the end of the nineteenth century. It was at this point that the canoe was appropriated by city dwellers, middle-class urbanites with a taste for the simple life who began escaping the cities during the summer months to take up residence in rustic lakeside habitations. Alternatively, they sent their children away to summer camps to experience the healthful benefits of outdoor living by emulating the life of the early trader-explorers. Camps were usually established by churches, the YM-YWCA, or schoolteachers with a strong belief in the character-building effects of outdoor living—what naturalist Ernest Thompson Seton called "the simple life reduced to actual practice." Youngsters learned life-saving and bushwhacking skills, and a large part of the time they play-acted at being Indians. Camps took vaguely-sounding "Indian" names—Camp Oconto, Camp On-da-da-waks, and Camp Winnebagoe (the first Jewish camp in Ontario)—and counsellors taught archery and other woodcraft skills. One of the most popular camps was Ahmek, established in Algonquin Park in 1921 by Taylor Statten, a former Toronto YMCA official, and his wife Ethel. The Stattens took "Indian" names—Gitchiahmek and To-nakela—dressed in "Indian" clothes and taught campers how to build sweat lodges and perform "Indian" dances. It was as if the Textbook Indian had stepped out of the pages of the young campers' schoolbooks. Canoeing was an important activity at Ahmek, as it was at every camp. During the 1920s the staff included James Edmund Jones, author of *Camping and Canoeing*

(1903), one of the earliest canoe manuals. A later instructor, Ronald Perry, was at Ahmek during the 1930s when young Pierre Trudeau spent two summers there. Perry was a private-school teacher and canoe enthusiast whose *The Canoe and You* became a bible for campers after it appeared in 1948.[6] Ahmek was just one camp; there were many others across the Shield country of Ontario and in the northern parts of other provinces. By the 1920s, summer camp was becoming a typical part of a Canadian urban middle-class childhood.

At the end of the day, as the red ball of the sun sank in the west and the lonely call of the loon echoed across the lake, campers huddled around the crackling fire while the counsellor chanted aloud the words to "The Song My Paddle Sings," by Pauline Johnson—probably the most frequently recited poem ever written by a Canadian:

> Be strong, O paddle! be brave, canoe!
> The reckless waves you must plunge into.
> Reel, reel,
> On your trembling keel,
> But never a fear my craft will feel.
>
> We've raced the rapid, we're far ahead!
> The river slips through its silent bed.
> Sway, sway,
> As the bubbles spray
> And fall in tinkling tunes away.
>
> And up on the hills against the sky,
> A fir tree rocking its lullaby,
> Swings, swings,
> Its emerald wings,
> Swelling the song that my paddle sings.

But camping and canoeing were not just for kids: the "back to nature" movement involved Canadians of all ages. The Ottawa poets Archibald Lampman and Duncan Campbell Scott were avid canoeists, sneaking away to the woods whenever their jobs in the federal bureaucracy allowed.

Lampman evoked the atmosphere of these trips in his poem "Morning on the Lievre":

> Softly as a cloud we go,
> Sky above and sky below,
> Down the river; and the dip
> Of the paddles scarcely breaks,
> With the little silvery drip
> Of the water as it shakes
> From the blades, the crystal deep
> Of the silence of the morn,
> Of the forest yet asleep.

Scott, a senior bureaucrat in the Indian Department, was able to combine business with pleasure on excursions he took into the bush on behalf of the government. On one of these trips, his friend and travelling companion, the literary critic Pelham Edgar, describes Scott seated in the back of a bark canoe reading aloud from the *Oxford Book of Poetry*. "Duncan caught a poem as we were going through Island Lake and is still reeling it in," Edgar joked, though the joke was true enough since Scott derived many of his poems from these official forays into canoe country.[7]

II

The canoe, and the wilderness experience it implies, has been grafted as well to the legend of the Group of Seven. At the very centre of the Group legend is the death of Tom Thomson, who, though never a member of the Group, was its progenitor, and the prototype of the painter as canoeist and backwoodsman. "A modern *coureur de bois*" was how one of his friends described him.[8] Arthur Lismer, another friend, wrote: "He could drop a line in places, and catch a fish where other experienced fishermen had failed. He identified a bird song, and noted changes in the weather. He could find his way over open water to a portage or a camp on a night as black as ink."[9] This was a new, and typically Canadian, way of describing the artist, as an adventurer who went out into the woods and tracked down a painting, much like a hunter going after his prey. Thomson's association with canoeing

24. Artists Tom Thomson (*right*) and Arthur Lismer go fishing on Canoe Lake in Algonquin Park in 1914. It was in the same lake that Thomson drowned three years later.

extended right to his death. In July 1917, an overturned canoe was discovered revolving in the current on Canoe Lake in Algonquin Park. Thomson had taken it fishing a few days earlier, and had not been seen since. A week later, his drowned corpse was found drifting face down in the water.

In 1920, Lismer, A.Y. Jackson, and some others held the first exhibition of the Group of Seven, a group of artists dedicated to portraying the Canadian landscape in ways never before attempted. They drew their inspiration from their friend Thomson and from direct encounters with the land: "the inspiration of the backwoods," was how Fred Housser, the Group's first historian, put it. "While these pictures live," Housser wrote, "we can never forget our cradle-environment."[10] Over the years, paintings by the Group of Seven have become visual clichés—"our national wallpaper" in Robert Fulford's memorable phrase—appearing on posters, coffee mugs, T-shirts, and placemats. At the time they were painted, however, they represented a new way of seeing the land. The Group painted nature in the raw, wild and virile: the country as seen from a canoe.[11] Their scenes of the rocky Shield Country are indistinguishable now from our own image of what Canada looks like. In this sense, the Group invented a characteristic Canadian landscape.

The Group of Seven began to come together in the years leading up to World War I. Appropriately enough the Group's prehistory begins with a painting. In 1911, A.Y. Jackson, a young Montreal painter freshly back from studies in France, exhibited a canvas called "At the Edge of the Maple Wood" at the annual Ontario Society of Artists showing in Toronto. The painting depicted a familiar sugaring-off scene in rural Quebec, but its vigorous colour and texture made a strong impression on several painters who saw the exhibition. Tom Thomson, then working as a photo-engraver in Toronto with the commercial art firm Grip Ltd., later said that Maple Wood opened his eyes to the Canadian landscape. Thomson's colleagues at Grip, J.E.H. Macdonald and Arthur Lismer, both praised its fresh approach to a familiar subject. "Jackson's contribution was the beginning of a kinship and a movement in Canada," Lismer said.[12] Lawren Harris later wrote that "It stood out from all the other paintings as an authentic, new expression."[13]

Harris, wealthy son of an Ontario farm machinery manufacturer, did not forget Jackson's painting, and two years later he bought it, thereby inaugurating a friendship which would transform Canadian art. The painting was a turning point, not just for the Group of Seven but for the country. "'The Edge of the Maple Wood' was to Canadian art what 'Le Dejeuner sur l'Herbe' or 'Les Demoiselles d'Avignon' was to French art," the artist Harold Town has written. "Its plangent colour and effortless virtuosity, its sense of absolute Canadian place, galvanized a grumble of dissatisfaction into a tumble of revolt."[14]

The sale of the painting occurred at a crucial moment for A.Y. Jackson, who had been contemplating a life in exile south of the border. Instead, he was persuaded by Harris to visit Toronto first, which he did in May 1913. Immediately he was swept up in the energy of the new movement of artists centred on the Arts and Letters Club. He spent that summer and fall sketching on Georgian Bay where he met James MacCallum, a Toronto ophthalmologist and art enthusiast who was becoming the patron of the new movement. MacCallum invited Jackson to use his cottage on Go Home Bay, then offered to pay all of his expenses if Jackson, instead of going to the States, remained in Toronto.

In Toronto, Jackson, who was then thirty-one years old, found a group of artists who were ardently committed to the idea of painting Canada. "We lived in a continuous blaze of enthusiasm," Lawren Harris wrote. "We were at times very serious and concerned, at other times, hilarious and carefree. Above all, we loved this country, and loved exploring and painting it."[15] When the Studio Building opened on Severn Street near Bloor and Yonge early in 1914, it became the clubhouse for the new movement. Several of the commercial artists from Grip worked at the building. Fred Varley wrote his sister: "We are all working to one big end. We are endeavouring to knock out of us all of the preconceived ideas, emptying ourselves of everything except that nature is here in all its greatness, and we are here to gather it and understand it if only we will be clean enough, healthy enough, and humble enough to go to it willing to be taught."[16]

"Every day was an adventure," Jackson recalled of this period.[17] He shared a space with Thomson and the two artists became friends. They painted together, went to the movies together, conspired to become famous together, and began making sketching trips together to the bush country of Algonquin Park north of the city. Thomson had discovered this wilderness setting in the spring of 1912 and had spent the summer of 1913 camping out in the park at Canoe Lake. The following year two of Thomson's colleagues from Grip joined them: Fred Varley and Arthur Lismer. "The country is a revelation to me and completely bowled me over at first," Varley confided in a letter.[18] Lismer was equally affected. "The first night spent in the north and the thrilling days after were turning points in my life," he wrote.[19] A definite Algonquin School of painting was taking shape.

At this early stage Thomson provided the spark of inspiration. His style, with its audacious use of vivid colour and blunt brush strokes, was seen to embody the raw energy of the northern landscape. All the better that he was self-taught and completely ignorant of modern painting. The others considered him the prototype of what the new Canadian artist should be: an untutored genius whose art sprang from an intuitive understanding of the land. The others all came from cities, but Thomson was a country boy, raised on a farm near Georgian Bay where he learned to handle a paddle, a hunting rifle and a fishing rod with equal facility. His familiarity with the outdoors impressed his clumsier, less robust painting companions.

Things were different when winter forced Thomson out of the woods back to Toronto, where he lived in a shack behind the Studio Building, with a minimum of creature comforts, staying in all day, venturing out at night to tramp the snow-filled ravines of the Don Valley on snowshoes. It was here that he completed some of the most famous paintings in Canadian history, paintings such as "The West Wind" and "The Jack Pine," paintings which have become iconic images through which Canadians recognize themselves.

All the elements were present as early as 1914 for the formation of the Group of Seven, though at this point it probably would have been called The Algonquin School. It did not happen, only because World War I happened first. The war scattered the Algonquin painters in several directions. Some enlisted, others remained at home. They were all stunned in the summer of 1917 by the unexpected death of Tom Thomson. In those horrible war years death itself was no surprise; it was the way Thomson died which was so shocking. He was renowned as a woodsman, an expert canoeist; it didn't make sense that he should fall into the water and drown.

While his death left Thomson's friends profoundly saddened, it seemed to stiffen their resolve to continue along the path they had chosen. World War I derailed the new movement temporarily, but it did not alter its direction. Unlike their European counterparts, thrust by the spiritual crisis of the war into nihilistic experimentation, most evident in Dada and Surrealism, the Canadians regrouped in Toronto more determined than ever to paint the native landscape.

There is no account by any of the participants of the decisive meeting at Lawren Harris's house which led to the formation of the Group of Seven in mid-March 1920. The name was probably borrowed from similar groups which existed in New York (The Eight, or Ashcan School) and Berlin. The first use of the name was in a letter dated March 21 from Arthur Lismer to Eric Brown, director of the National Gallery in Ottawa. "Harris, Jackson, MacD[onald], Johnston, Carmichael, Varley and myself," Lismer ticked off the names of the founding members. "'Group of Seven' is the idea. There is to be no feeling of secession or antagonism in any way, but we hope to

25. Members of the Group of Seven conspiring together at the Arts and Letters Club in Toronto. They are, clockwise from left front: A.Y. Jackson, Fred Varley, Lawren Harris, Barker Fairley (not a member), Frank Johnston, Arthur Lismer, and J.E.H. Macdonald. Only Franklin Carmichael is absent.

get a show together that will demonstrate the 'spirit' of painting in Canada."[20] There was nothing like a formal vote or a decision to incorporate. The Group of Seven was a movement, not an organization. What bound the artists together was not membership in an exclusive club but a shared commitment to certain ideas about painting.

The first exhibition of the Group opened at the Art Gallery of Toronto, May 7, 1920. Subsequently the Group and its supporters concocted a legend that the new movement was beseiged by adverse reviews and viciously negative criticism. According to Lawren Harris, they were "attacked from all sides."[21] The initial exhibition created "an uproar," Jackson claimed many years later. "There was plenty of adverse criticism, little of it intelligent."[22] In fact, the response was favourable, if less enthusiastic than the painters had hoped. Only about 100 people a day came to see the show, but the critics were polite. The National Gallery purchased three of the canvases and helped to organize a smaller touring exhibition in the United States. Clearly the 1920 show did not receive the critical mugging which its participants later claimed it did.

This should come as no surprise. Members of the Group of Seven, while they liked to see themselves as young rebels, were actually all established painters who by 1920 had been part of the Toronto art scene for a decade or more. Macdonald, the eldest, was forty-seven years old; he had been showing his paintings since before the War. So had Harris, Jackson, and Lismer, all of whom were approaching middle age. Both the Ontario government and the National Gallery had purchased their work. Several of the Group made their living as commercial artists and their illustrations appeared in such mainstream magazines as *Maclean's* and *The Canadian Magazine*. Wealthy patrons were expressing interest. Still, despite all this evidence of support, members of the Group insisted throughout its life, and for many years after, that critical opinion had been overwhelmingly against them.

In retrospect it is clear that the Group exaggerated the antagonism of one or two critics into a wholesale conspiracy against modern art. This way of describing their own history worked very much to the Group's advantage. It provided the public with a way of "understanding" the Group, even when it did not understand the artistic issues involved. According to their own version of reality, members of the Group were young rebels fighting to establish a modern, "Canadian" outlook in the face of overwhelming opposition from an ignorant press and a backward-looking Old Guard. In 1926, with the appearance of Fred Housser's book, *A Canadian Art Movement: The Story of the Group of Seven*, this interpretation of events was enshrined in history. Housser, a financial journalist, was an ardent supporter of the Group. His book described their break with European traditions, their struggle to develop a new style through "direct contact with Nature herself," their disputes with critics and "the entire press of the country," and their ultimate emergence as the first important art movement to arise in Canada. The Group triumphed, wrote Housser, because it was unafraid to express the native landscape in entirely new ways. "Just as European artists have long gone to Europe's past for inspiration, so this Canadian group drew its inspiration from the past of this country, the wilderness."[23] For Housser, the new movement represented a great leap forward in the history of the country. No artists before the Group were mature enough to take Canada as its own subject, he claimed, on its own terms. By changing all that, wrote Housser, the Group represented the coming of age of Canada as a culture.

Housser's book was a work of propaganda, not scholarship. Much of what he said about the Group was simply not true. As he himself admitted, the critical reception of their work had actually been pretty favourable. They were not the pariahs of the art world they made themselves out to be. Nor were they the first to attempt to paint in a distinctively "Canadian" style. Artists before them had chosen similar subject matter, although presented in the manner of the civilized landscapes of Europe. Nor were members of the Group as innocent of European training and ideas as Housser claimed. Jackson, Harris, Lismer, Varley, and Carmichael all studied abroad. Tom Thomson was the only one who was truly self-taught, and he was not strictly speaking a member of the Group. Regardless, Housser's book went a long way to reconciling the public to the new movement. Its publication roughly marks the transformation of the Group from delinquent sons to patriarchs of the family. "No longer can the Group enjoy the vilification that is the reward of the precocious few," observed playwright Merrill Denison in 1928, "because the many have now joined them and the calliope has become merely an overcrowded bandwagon."[24]

The Group's success was due to other factors besides good public relations. Most importantly, of course, they were tremendously talented artists who produced some of the most beautiful and evocative paintings in the history of Canadian art. But success usually requires more than talent. The public embraced the Group because it so successfully attached itself to a nationalistic agenda. The Group claimed to be creating not just art but a new national consciousness. This was Macdonald's "big idea": the creation of a national purpose through an appreciation of the rugged Canadian landscape. "We believe wholeheartedly in the land," they declared.[25] In this respect the Group perfectly matched the spirit of their times. During the 1920s Canadians were seeking new ways of imagining themselves as a mature, independent nation. They were receptive, therefore, to a movement of artists which claimed to find in the local landscape a distinctive national identity, and claimed to have found a uniquely Canadian style for expressing it.

The Group's down-to-earth approach to painting also endeared them to a broad public. They were seen to be "modern *coureurs de bois*," not effete intellectuals starving in their garrets. They spoke of art as an energetic, manly activity; they identified painting with adventuring and exploring. (The reality was somewhat different. Jackson, for example, described J.E.H. Macdonald as "a quiet, unadventurous person, who could not swim, or paddle, or swing an axe, or find his way in the bush."[26]) They presented their work in simple, accessible language. One of their pre-war exhibitions made no apology for offering "pictures which are suitable for home use, such as one could live with and enjoy."[27] These were all attitudes which appealed to Canadians who wanted to feel proud of their youth and vitality, not shamefaced at their lack of sophistication. Charles Hill points out that the Group's tame subject matter was another factor contributing to its wide acceptance.[28] No one had to avert their eyes. There were no nudes descending staircases, no Mona Lisas with moustaches. Admirers could be modern, without being "modern," *au courant* without being immoral and nihilistic like those scandalous Europeans. This was modern art that was clean and bracing and stood for something. And what it stood for was the myth of wilderness: the conviction that the essence of Canadianness was present in the land, in the canoeable Canadian landscape.

III

During the 1930s, Tom Thomson's mantle as the pre-eminent Canadian canoeist fell to Grey Owl, the Englishman who claimed to be an Iroquois/Ojibway trapper from northern Ontario. Grey Owl published a series of books about his life as a guide, "riverman" and conservationist which won him a wide audience not just in Canada but internationally. His message was simple: wilderness was being destroyed by the inexorable advance of a civilization that placed more value on economic development than it did on the preservation of the natural world. He spread this message not just in books but in lectures, films, and as a caretaker in the national parks, always posing as an Indian. His deception did not take in most Native people, who saw through it but were content to allow Grey Owl to keep up his masquerade because he so effectively drew attention to issues they thought were important as well. When it was revealed after his death in

26. Grey Owl, the Wilderness Man, sat for this portrait in Montreal in 1931. Grey Owl's experience as an Englishman who went Native is a metaphor for the experience of all non-Natives who face the challenge of becoming North American. He is a symbol for our problematic relationship with the Canadian wilderness.

1938 that Grey Owl had been living a hoax, and that his real name was Archie Belaney, his admiring white public didn't much care either. What he stood for was more important than who he was. "He made pure Canada, the Canada outside the concrete urban enclosures, come alive," explained his publisher, Lovat Dickson.[29]

Grey Owl believed in approaching the wilds in a spirit of reverence. "Man should enter the woods, not with any conquistador obsession or mighty hunter complex," he wrote, "neither in a spirit of braggadocio, but rather with the awe, and not a little of the veneration, of one who steps within the portals of some vast and ancient edifice of wondrous architecture."[30] It was understandable, therefore, that for him the canoe was an almost holy vessel. He once said that it was not prayer that stoops the Canadian but long hours kneeling at the paddle. Grey Owl connected to an imagined long line of restless misfits, stretching back to before the *coureurs de bois*. Probably no one else has written as eloquently about the simple pleasures of taking to the woods by canoe.

Pierre Trudeau's lifelong fascination with the canoe was very much in the mold of Grey Owl. I am reminded of the images of the former prime minister in the television documentary based on his *Memoirs* (1993), kneeling in a canoe on some northern lake wearing a fringed buckskin jacket and pausing in mid-paddle stroke. Is that the call of a loon he hears? (Or is it the siren song of the Canadian electorate, luring him back to public service?) After learning canoecraft at Camp Ahmek as a teenager, Trudeau made many trips into the Canadian North. Following his defeat in the 1979 federal election, for instance, he immediately went canoeing to recover from the disappointment. "Canoeing forces you to make a distinction between your needs and your wants," he wrote in the *Memoirs*.

> When you are canoeing, you have to deal with your needs: survival, food, sleep, protection from the weather. These are all things that you tend to take for granted when you are living in so-called civilization, with its constant pressures on you to do this or that for social reasons created by others, or to satisfy artificial wants created by advertising. Canoeing gets you back close to nature, using a method of travel that does not even call for roads or paths. You are following nature's roads; you are choosing the road less travelled by, as Robert Frost once wrote in another context, and that makes all the difference. You discover a sort of simplifying of your values, a distinction between values artificially created and those that are necessary to your spiritual and human development. That's why, from my youthful expeditions right up to the present day, canoeing has always been such an important activity in my life.[31]

Forty-nine years earlier (in an essay called "Exhaustion and Fulfilment: The Ascetic in the Canoe," 1944), Trudeau had written: "Travel a thousand miles by train and you are a brute; pedal five hundred on a bicycle and you remain basically a bourgeois; paddle a hundred in a canoe and you are already a child of nature."[32]

While he was prime minister, Trudeau was a friend and neighbour of the filmmaker Bill Mason, another guru of the canoeing fraternity.[33] During the 1970s, Mason made a series of instructional films about canoeing for the National Film Board. It was a period when many Canadians were being swept up in the environmental movement and many others were becoming almost fanatically addicted to physical fitness. Canoeing, which combined respect for nature with a suitable level of physical exertion, enjoyed renewed popularity, and Mason's films brought him international celebrity and a British Academy Award. He later adapted the canoeing series as a book, and was much in demand on the lecture circuit. Fans in Salt Lake City even

27. Just as Grey Owl is a symbol for our problematic relationship with the Canadian wilderness he is obviously also a role model for wilderness lovers like former prime minister Pierre Trudeau.

named a film festival after him. With his floppy hat, plaid shirt, and deep commitment to Christianity, Mason was the latest incarnation of a familiar cultural icon: the wilderness man who finds escape and spiritual comfort in the simplicity of the canoe.

My own experiences with canoes have been uniformly less pleasant than Pierre Trudeau's or any of these other enthusiasts. When my wife and I were university students, we decided to plunge into the outdoors by joining the canoe club, newly organized by a science professor from Australia. First time down the Chilliwack River all our canoes upset. As I drifted downstream on an upturned hull, I began to panic at the thought of drowning in a turbulent rapid or pitching headlong over a foaming waterfall. My life was saved, however, when my fellow canoeists, who had reached shore safely, yelled at me to try standing up: it turned out that the river was only knee deep.

Once we had dried out and convinced ourselves that we had had the time of our lives, we decided to raise funds for our club by building fibreglass canoes for sale. The instructions were easy to follow and at the end of the day we had a brand spanking new canoe to sell. Only later did my wife and I realize that we had failed to put hardener in the batch of fibreglass we were using. I have often imagined the looks of puzzled amazement which must have crossed the faces of some unsuspecting paddlers as their canoe began slowly to disintegrate beneath them as they crossed a remote lake or negotiated a difficult stretch of white water.

Several years later we joined a group of schoolteachers on a spring wilderness excursion to LaVerendrye Park in northwestern Quebec. During the final leg of the trip we were crossing a wide lake when a strong breeze blew up, whipping the surface into whitecaps. There was no putting into shore, so we plunged ahead, barely making headway against the wind and waves. At last, shaking with fatigue, we attained the beach and threw ourselves gratefully onto dry land. For the second time I had been spared a watery death. I got the message: it was time to take Stephen Leacock seriously. In one of his popular satires, Leacock pokes fun at "the Bush Mania," embodied in the character of Billy, an enthusiast of the "Open Woods." "He offers to take me to the head-water of the Batiscan," writes Leacock. "I am content at the foot. He wants us to go to the sources of the Attahwapiscat. I don't. He says I ought to see the grand chutes of the Kewakasis. Why should I?"[34]

Many, probably most, Canadians share Stephen Leacock's (and my own) suspicion of canoe adventuring. In fact, a large body of literature suggests that Leacock's response to the outdoors is much more typically Canadian than Grey Owl's or Pierre Trudeau's. In her 1972 survey of the national literature, *Survival*, Margaret Atwood concluded that Canadians perceive nature to be fearful, hostile, threatening, and best avoided whenever possible. Northrop Frye agreed, finding in the national literature "a tone of deep terror in regard to nature," and a "garrison mentality," in which every individual is a small frontier outpost surrounded by a malevolent wilderness.[35] More recently, cultural historian Gaile McGregor has argued that Canadians are self-delusional when it comes to the natural world. We tell ourselves that we find the wilderness peaceful and rejuvenating, but our history and our culture reveal just the opposite, that nature in the raw scares the wits out of us. And because we think we aren't supposed to feel this way, we are afflicted with massive guilt.[36]

All these critics see something almost pathological about Canadians' response to the wilderness. They say we are obsessed with our own limitations and, ultimately, our own death. And there is no denying the evidence they are able to marshal in defence of this reading. There is, however, another narrative in Canadian culture, every bit as convincing, which reveals a much more positive attitude toward the wilderness. Since the days of the earliest colonists, Canadians have expressed an attraction to the wilds by taking to the woods in search of adventure, rejuvenation, or simple peace and quiet. The modern wilderness canoe trip, complete with

28. Mr. Dress-up, Ernest Thompson Seton, in "Indian" garb, 1917. Seton originated the League of the Woodcraft Indians, a youth movement which emphasized teaching youngsters how to survive in the wilderness like Indians.

Goretex outerwear and freeze-dried vegetables, is a variant on a very old impulse. The wilderness has always been a place of refuge for Canadians, whether it was to shed the restrictions of polite society or, more commonly in this century, to shed the anxieties and debilities of urban living. The industrial revolution which swept Canada at the end of the nineteenth century left an ambivalent aftertaste. No sooner had the railways abolished distance and the factories transformed the world of work than people began to grow nostalgic for the simple life. This discontent with the fruits of progress, and especially with the modern city, manifested itself in the growing popularity of outdoor activity. Mountain climbing, canoeing, bicycling, and summer cottaging all became fashionable in the pre-World-War-I era and after, as urban dwellers sought solace in nature from the hustle and bustle of modern life. Then came the automobile, which increased our ability to get away from it all and combined with the general prosperity of the post-World-War-II period to create a mania for camping and outdoor recreation. To take just one indicator: during World War II there were eight provincial parks in Ontario; by 1961 there were seventy-seven parks being used by an estimated 6.2 million visitors each year, triple the number from just five years earlier.[37] Judging by the continued popularity of all kinds of outdoor recreational activities, there is no indication this love affair Canadians have with the wilderness is losing any of its ardour.

One of the variants on this theme has been the desire to "go native." Canadians have always identified Aboriginal people with the wilderness, believing that Aboriginals enjoyed a special, some believe mystical, relationship with the land. It was natural, therefore, to think that Aboriginals

29. One of Edward Curtis's photographs of a Northwest Coast native. Curtis (1868-1952), a Seattle photographer, spent thirty years making a comprehensive record of North American native peoples from Alaska to the American Southwest. The resulting photographs were published in a series of twenty books, titled collectively *The North American Indian*. Curtis's objective was to capture images of "traditional" Indians before they disappeared forever. He photographed his subjects in romantic poses, performing traditional activities, in an attempt to re-imagine what it was like in America before the whites came. These images became extremely popular as expressions of innocent spirituality and a harmonious relationship with nature.

might provide a model for living in North America, a model which non-Natives could emulate by becoming Indian, by "going native." Grey Owl is the best example of a European who came to the New World and took on an Indian identity. The fact that he did so helped to give his conservationist message a credibility it would not have had if he was simply an Englishman whining about the high price of progress. Another example is the writer Ernest Thompson Seton, who created a very popular youth movement, the League of the Woodcraft Indians, a precursor to the Boy Scouts. The League presented the Indian as an ideal for North Americans, quite the opposite of the bestial Textbook Indian presented in the classroom. At meetings and summer camps, youngsters learned a version of the "Indian life," becoming "little savages" who could put up teepees, rub sticks to make a fire, read smoke signals, and perform a variety of other "bushwise" chores. Seton and Grey Owl were moral reformers who advocated the spiritual transformation of modern society by the application of what they took to be "Indian" values, by which they meant wilderness values. Indians, Seton once wrote, were "the most heroic race the world has ever seen, the most physically perfect race the world has ever seen, the most spiritual Civilization the world has ever seen."[38]

The weekend, or weeks long, canoe trip remains a common way for Canadians to "go native" and to get back to nature. The rhetoric of canoeing reveals that the myth of wilderness continues to exert a strong attraction. In a recent CBC Radio documentary about the canoe, called "Perfect Machines," Kirk Whipper, who is known as the "godfather of Canadian wilderness canoeing," explained why he likes to go paddling. "You're removed entirely from the mundane aspects of ordinary life; you're witnessing, first-hand, beauty and peace and freedom—especially free- dom—and I always say that the flirtation with the wilderness is a contact with truth." Another enthusiast interviewed for the broadcast compared canoeing to a spiritual pilgrimage and described instances of people under- going "miraculous cures" for different illnesses by going on extended canoe trips.[39] No matter how overwrought these claims might appear, they are part of a consistent theme in Canadian culture: the myth of wilderness, the belief that our link to the land is a defining national characteristic.

IV

"Only those who have had the experience can know what a sense of physical and spiritual excitement comes to one who turns his face away from men towards the unknown. In his small way he is doing what the great explorers have done before him, and his elation recaptures theirs."[40] The historian Arthur Lower wrote these words about his own experience venturing north by canoe to James Bay. They sum up the several attractions which the canoe expedition has always had for Canadians.

First of all, it is a healthy adventure, an opportunity to escape the mundane realities of urban living and lose oneself in physical exercise. Canoeing is good medicine for whatever ails you. The backwoods of canoe country, a writer once declared, are "a great open-air sanatorium" where nerves are soothed, muscles toned, priorities reorganized.[41] According to

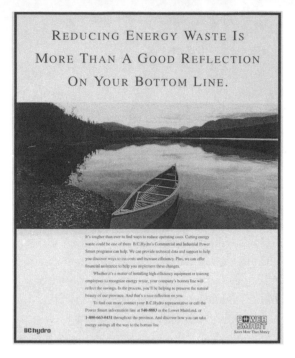

30. As this recent advertisement for BC Hydro suggests, the canoe remains a potent symbol of the unspoiled Canadian wilderness.

the ideology of canoeing, one returns to the workaday world a better, saner person.

Next, as Lower suggests, the canoe trip is an encounter with history. Canoeists believe they are experiencing the country in almost exactly the same way that the early explorers did. Indeed, many expeditions are planned explicitly to follow the routes first taken by these pioneer travellers. They are trips into the wilderness, but they are also trips back in time. The canoe trip is partly an attempt to recapture a past world. It is tinged with nostalgic regret at the loss of a simpler way of life. We believe our ancestors had a more authentic relationship with the natural world; the canoe trip is one means we have of trying to recapture it.

Third, the canoeing excursion is a discovery of national identity. Canadian artists and writers consistently locate the essence of our nationality in the northern landscape. Our cities belong to the global, post-industrial world of traffic, computers, and highrise towers; they are indistinguishable from cities anywhere. Our wilderness, on the other hand, is our own. It is a unique landscape which imparts to us a unique set of characteristics which we recognize as Canadian. When we enter the canoeable Canadian land-scape, we believe we are rediscovering and reinforcing our national virtues. "I know a man whose school could never teach him patriotism," wrote Pierre Trudeau, "but who acquired that virtue when he felt in his bones the vastness of his land, and the greatness of those who founded it."[42] (One might also say that the whitewater canoe trip is the perfect metaphor for the country's perennial state of constitutional angst. "We are in the rapids, and must go on," declared D'Arcy McGee 130 years ago, perfectly capturing the feeling familiar to all Canadians that we are in the grip of powerful, capricious forces over which we have no control.)

And last, the canoe trip is a spiritual quest. It is an opportunity to get away from the banality of everyday life in order to commune with nature and with our spiritual selves. As William James puts it in his essay "The Quest Pattern and the Canoe Trip," the trip follows the circular pattern of the religious quest: the excursionist departs for an unknown country where various ordeals (leaky tents, long portages, blackflies, etc.) must be endured before the successful return to civilization with an enhanced self-knowledge and spiritual awareness. "Thus the perilous journey may lead to a purification of the self, or the dissolution of past images of the self."[43] Every canoeist is a mythic hero in this perpetual playing out of a centuries-old narrative.

Which brings us back full circle to Bill Reid's massive sculpture, "Spirit of Haida Gwaii," with a new understanding of how deeply many Canadians feel that the canoe is a fundamental icon of our nationality, representing as it does our links to our history, to our land, and to our better selves. We think of ourselves as down-to-earth, middle-of-the-road, non-ideological people. We don't have passions like other countries. Not so. Hidden beneath our placid reserve is a secret ideology, a set of ideas which are so basic to our understanding of ourselves that we take them for granted: the ideology of the canoe. Not everyone shares this ideology, of course. It belongs principally to the urban middle class which, no longer having to struggle with the wilderness on a daily basis, has elevated it to the level of romantic myth. Nonetheless, the purchase by the government of the Reid sculpture and its placement in Washington suggest to me that the canoe, with all it implies, has been adopted as the official symbol of the country.

CHAPTER SEVEN

Great White Hope
THE MYTH OF NORTH

To a Canadian, North is more than a point on the compass. It is a region, a territory, a vast intimidating part of the country somewhere beyond easy comfort. Officially, the North extends from the 60th parallel of latitude all the way to the Pole: the Yukon, the Northwest Territories, Nunavut, the Arctic archipelago. Unofficially, it occupies our imagination, filling it with dreams of high adventure and fabulous wealth. To a Canadian, North is an idea, not a location; a myth, a promise, a destiny.

Since at least Confederation there have been people—writers, politicians, intellectuals—who believed that it was its northernness which made Canada distinct. From the beginning, "Canada had a distinct, a unique, a northern destiny," wrote historian W.L. Morton.[1] For these people Canadian history has a particular purpose. "Canadian history is not a parody of American, as Canada is not a second-rate United States, still less a United States that failed. Canadian history is rather an important chapter in a distinct and even a unique human endeavour, the civilization of the northern and arctic lands."[2]

When Europeans first arrived in Canada they convinced themselves that it was a northern site of fabulous wealth such as the Spanish had found in the South. Jacques Cartier believed in the fanciful Kingdom of Saguenay, rich in gold and diamonds, some of whose inhabitants knew how to fly. Martin Frobisher was convinced that Baffin Island was rich in gold; Samuel Hearne's epic trek across the Barren Lands was a search for an imaginary copper mine. In the twentieth century, modern explorers came looking for oil and gas deposits, while most recently the Barrens are rumoured to contain the largest crop of diamonds in the world. Canada was born of these quests for mythical treasures.

Secondarily, the North was rumoured to provide a passage to the riches of Asia, if only someone could find it. For more than 400 years, scores of sea-going expeditions probed the ice-choked rivers and coastal passages of the Arctic seeking a maritime route to Cathay. Their explorations have provided us with many of our examples of heroism and tragedy so necessary to the creation of a national mythology. Mackenzie, Franklin, Amundsen, Stefansson: the names roll out through the history books.

From the creation of the country the North has been central to our sense of ourselves. Our national anthem declares Canada to be "The True North strong and free." Our most popular sport is played on ice. Thinking of ourselves as northern gives us a unique place in North America. Novelist Rudy Wiebe has written that "North is both the true nature of our world and also our graspable destiny,"[3] the one sure thing that makes us different from the United States. It doesn't matter that most of us never travel there, that those of us who know nothing about the North far outnumber those who do. There is "a north of the mind"[4] which exists independently of the geographic North and has always provided an identifiable marker for Canadianness. It imparts an element of freedom to Canadian life, even for those who never go there, a "psychic freedom" in Robert Fulford's phrase, "that forms the real basis of Canadian life."[5]

I

The "cult of the North" gained coherent expression for the first time shortly after Confederation with a short-lived but influential group of young nationalists who called themselves Canada First.[6] The members of Canada First—there were only five originally—were writers and intellectuals who met in Ottawa in 1868 and discovered that they shared a desire to articulate the "new nationality" they hoped would take shape in Canada. Wanting the country to be more than just an expedient political arrangement, they conspired to provide for it a high-minded destiny. According to the Canada First credo, one of the most important characteristics of the new Dominion was its northern climate, which imparted to the people living here a strength of character shared by other circumpolar "races."

"We are the Northmen of the New World," declared one of the Firsters, Robert Grant Haliburton, the inheritors of a long Anglo-Saxon tradition of liberty and racial superiority.

Canada First did not last long as an organized movement, but what today we recognize as the Aryan Nation theme it articulated gained great popularity in subsequent decades. It was believed that the struggle to survive in a northern climate created a set of national characteristics, including self-reliance, physical strength, stamina, and virility, which set us apart as a separate people. The northern air was supposed to stimulate intelligence and encourage initiative, qualities necessary for the creation of political freedom and democracy. Canadians should never complain about their weather, thought the Canada Firsters; it was the climate which weeded out the weak and the lazy and discouraged members of the "southern races" from settling here. The North imposed a form of natural selection which was constantly reinforcing the quality of the nation, "the True North, strong and free."[7]

Though the racist implications of the "cult of the North" are clear, the idea was attractive to more than a fringe group of nationalist intellectuals. During the years leading up to World War I, for example, the federal government actively promoted Canada's northern, wilderness image to attract immigration. Its chief propagandist in this project was James Oliver Curwood, a writer of popular fiction and, curiously enough, an American. Curwood was born in Owosso, Michigan, in 1879 and grew up on a backwoods farm in Ohio. He was another of those people who dreamed of "going native." As a boy he loved to play hookey from school so that he could spend all his time in the woods. "Under my white skin I was almost an Indian," he wrote.[8] At the same time he developed an ambition to become a writer, and the words poured out of him. By the time he was fifteen years old, he had written over one hundred adventure stories, none of which was published. Finally, in 1898, he sold his first story to a magazine for five dollars, and the career of one of North America's most successful pulp writers was launched. He went on to produce twenty-six novels and dozens of film scripts based on his stories until his death in 1928.

Curwood wrote in his autobiography that from his earliest days he was "possessed of an overwhelming desire to express myself in stories of brave men and beautiful women who dared much, loved greatly, and died

31. In 1924, a Hollywood movie crew at Moraine Lake in Banff National Park shoots a scene for *The Alaskan*, a feature film based on a James Oliver Curwood novel.

bravely."[9] This turned out to be just the kind of wholesome melodrama which appealed to the Canadian government, and sometime after 1900 the federal immigration department retained Curwood's services for $1,800 a year (about three times the income of an average working family), plus expenses, to write about the prairies and the North as a way of attracting settlers to these territories. For a decade Curwood spent a few months each year travelling around, as he put it, "as a prairie and wilderness freelance for the Canadian government."[10] Curwood came up with the term "God's Country" to describe the Canadian wilderness; he was never very specific about its exact location. God's Country was a place of the imagination, "the land where the lean wolves run," he once called it. For his readers, and for the many viewers who saw his films, it became synonymous with Canada itself.

In 1918, Curwood teamed up with Ernest Shipman, the country's leading filmmaker, and his wife Nell, an actress who had already starred in a film version of one of Curwood's stories, *God's Country and the Woman* (which was filmed in California but set in the Canadian North). According to the terms of the new arrangement, Nell Shipman acquired rights to Curwood's stories in return for agreeing to appear exclusively in films based on them.[11] The first, and as it turned out only, result of this partnership was *Back to God's Country* (1919), filmed at Calgary and Lesser Slave Lake. The movie was a hit with audiences, but the Shipmans separated soon after and the deal with Curwood lapsed. He, meanwhile, formed his own production company and made two of his own films, *Nomads of the North* (1920), with Lon Chaney, and *The Golden Snare* with Lewis Stone and Wallace Beery (1921). Other Curwood-inspired movies included *The Girl from God's Country* (1921), *God's Country and the Law* (1921), *Jan of the Big Snows* (1922), *The Broken Silence* (1922), and many more. Surprisingly, Curwood continues to inspire filmmakers. As recently as 1989, French director Jean-Jacques Annaud released *The Bear*, a wildlife adventure story based on one of Curwood's action-packed stories.

Curwood was not the only person writing about the Canadian North. At the turn of the century there was a vogue for the memoirs of adventurers describing their personal encounters with the Frozen North. Typically, these "purposeful wanderers" were wealthy Englishmen or Americans who travelled to the Barren Lands to do a bit of exploring and to hunt caribou and muskox.[12] They usually got themselves into trouble, either through incompetence or bad luck, but this only made the books they wrote more exciting. Examples of this genre include *The Barren Ground of Northern Canada* (1892) by Warburton Pike, *Exploration in the Far North* (1898) by Frank Russell, Casper Whitney's *On Snow-shoes to the Barren Grounds* (1896), and *Sport and Travel in the Northland of Canada* (1904) by David Hanbury. The Tyrrell brothers, Joseph and James, were atypical of the others, both because they were government scientists and because they were Canadians. But the memoir of their excursion down the Dubawnt River, *Across the Sub-Arctics of Canada*, published in 1898, was very much in the mainstream of the genre, describing the starvation, the fear of local "cannibals" (who always turn out to be friendly Natives), the back-breaking portages through mosquito-infested swamps, the several near-death experiences as food and strength run low, and finally the emergence from the wilderness back to a world which had given them up for dead. All these books were gobbled up by a public hungry to experience, at a safe second-hand, the perilous North.

With the discovery of gold in the Klondike in 1896, Canada's reputation as a northern nation was secured. As the rush to the gold fields turned into a headlong stampede, Canada became the centre of international attention, much as it had been a half-century earlier during the search for John Franklin and his crew in the Arctic Islands. Once again that attention was rivetted on the northern part of the country. The whole world was watching and absorbing the message that Canada was a vast wilderness of snow and ice.

More important than the gold rush itself, which lasted only a couple of years, was the fact that so many writers and, later, filmmakers were attracted to the story. It was, after all, an incredible tale of greed and adventure, set against one of the most spectacular landscapes in the world. The novelist Jack London joined the rush, and used his experiences as background for several of his popular novels. Charlie Chaplin also was attracted to the story, though he shot his 1925 film *The Gold Rush* in the Sierra Nevadas and on a Hollywood backlot. But no one more successfully mined the Klondike for literary gold than Robert Service, the poet laureate of the Rush. Service, a ranch hand turned bank clerk, did not reach the Yukon until 1904 and was not transferred to Dawson City, the centre of the Rush, for another four years. By that time the stampede was long over, and almost everyone had gone home, leaving the poet free to create his own reality, in poems which achieved greater sales than any other poet in Canadian history.

Service's first poem about the Klondike was the famous "Shooting of Dan McGrew," which he wrote all of a piece in one night.[13]

A bunch of the boys were whooping it up in the Malamute saloon;
The kid that handles the music-box was hitting a jag-time tune;
Back of the bar, in a solo game, sat Dangerous Dan McGrew,
And watching his luck was his light-o'-love, the lady that's
    known as Lou.

He followed it up with "The Cremation of Sam McGee," and by the end of 1906 he had enough poems to put together in a small book. The Methodist Book and Publishing House in Toronto, knowing that poetry did not sell, accepted the manuscript with the proviso that Service would have to pay for the printing himself. That was before one of the salesmen took a copy of the book along on a sales trip out West. He began reading the verses to other passengers on the train, and then to bookstore owners, and pretty soon so many orders were flowing in that the publisher decided to add the book to its regular list. *Songs of a Sourdough* went through fifteen printings in its first year of publication. It was subsequently published in New York and London, and one estimate put total sales at three million by 1940. A critic in *Saturday Night* dubbed Service "the Canadian Kipling" and the name stuck. By 1908 he was making $4,000 a year in royalties, roughly four times his salary at the bank. People in Dawson, who knew Service only as a mild-mannered clerk who liked to be left alone, were astonished to encounter tourists brandishing copies of the book and wanting to know where to find the author to autograph them.

Service repeated his initial success with a string of others. His total output includes thirteen books of verse, six novels, two volumes of autobiography, even a book about keeping fit, and every one of them was a bestseller. He left the Yukon in 1912 and spent almost all of the rest of his life in Europe, mainly in Paris and on the Riviera, though his gold-rush experience continued to provide fuel for his imagination. Hollywood made several of his poems and books into movies and in his day he enjoyed enormous celebrity, as well as enormous wealth. He inhabited a two-storey, five-bedroom apartment in Paris where he lounged around town in expensive tailored suits and a monocle. At a party in Nice he ran into the anarchist Emma Goldman who greeted him by saying: "You're the man who makes poetry pay." To which Service admitted, "I make rhyming remunerative."

Robert Service died in 1958. His poetry still enjoys enormous popularity. Volumes of verse are republished with regularity, and no less a critic than Ronald Reagan proclaimed Service his favourite poet. Whatever its literary merit, his homespun Klondike verses have been read for almost a century, during which time they played an important part in creating and reinforcing an image of Canada as a place where it's always forty below and people get around under the northern lights by dogsled. There is a strong echo of

Canada First in Service, especially his contention that the hard, northern climate welcomes only the strongest, bravest inhabitants. Such is the "Law of the Yukon":

> Send me the best of your breeding, lend me your chosen ones;
> Them will I take to my bosom, them will I call my sons;
> Them will I gild with my treasure, them will I glut with my meat;
> But the others—the misfits, the failures—I trample under my feet.

Service wrote about many other things, but his most popular works were the Klondike poems, whose message went far beyond the adventures of a few miners and dance hall girls. They painted a land of opportunity and adventure where men, and sometimes women, learned to recognize their true potential only if they were worthy enough. Service's verse expressed the fascination which the North exerted over the imagination. In one of his most well-known poems, "The Spell of the Yukon," the gold rush becomes a metaphor for the process of settlement. He could be writing the entire history of the country.

> You come to get rich (damned good reason);
>   You feel like an exile at first;
> You hate it like hell for a season,
>   And then you are worse than the worst.
> It grips you like some kind of sinning;
>   It twists you from foe to a friend;
> It seems it's been since the beginning;
>   It seems it will be to the end.

Another enthusiast for the North who enjoyed a popularity with the public almost equal to that of James Curwood and Robert Service was the explorer/anthropologist Viljhalmur Stefansson. Whereas writers like Curwood and Service dramatized the North as a place of danger and romantic adventure, Stefansson, the scientist, took the opposite approach. It was his contention that people misunderstood the North when they saw it as a frozen wasteland inimical to settlement and civilization. "There are two kinds of Arctic problems," Stefansson once wrote, "the imaginary and the

32. Viljhalmur Stefansson in northern garb, 1914.

real. Of the two, the imaginary are the more real."[14] He wanted to convince government and the public that the North, and particularly the Arctic, was benign and economically productive.

Stefansson was born in Arnes, Manitoba, in 1879; he moved with his parents to the United States when he was very young and grew up in a log cabin in the Dakota Territory. After studying anthropology at Harvard, he made his first trip into the North in 1904 when he visited Iceland to study the relationship between diet and tooth decay. Subsequently he made three excursions into the Canadian Arctic between 1906 and 1918 in search of undiscovered lands and people. During this time he often lived with the Inuit, developing a great admiration for their temperament and survival skills. He also developed his northern thesis, encapsulated in the title of one of his books, *The Friendly Arctic* (1921). Despite the fact that eleven men died during one of his expeditions, the worst death toll of any Arctic expedition since Franklin, Stefansson maintained all his life that the Arctic was not nearly as inhospitable and fearsome as southerners believed. The Arctic Ocean, he predicted, would one day become a new Mediterranean, surrounded by prosperous settlers living off the fat of the land. So upbeat was he about the North that a New York newspaper reporter once accused him of passing off the Arctic as "an ideal summer resort."[15]

Stefansson was the last of what Robert Peary called "the old school of arctic explorers, the workers with the dog and the sledge." He travelled light, relied on local food resources as much as he could, and put his faith in the knowledge of the local people. In other words, he went native. As a result, posterity has granted him less of a reputation than other explorers whose ignorance and ethnocentrism led them into many tragic "adventures" which Stefansson's competence helped him to avoid. In his own day, however, he was a bona fide celebrity. At his lectures he was billed as one of the "World's Greatest Heroes."[16] The books which he wrote about his expeditions were bestsellers, and his controversial theories about "Blond" Eskimos and the virtues of an all-meat diet kept him in the public eye. Other scientists generally disapproved of what they considered to be his self-promotion, and they disagreed with many of his ideas about the benign North. ("Of all the fantastic rot I have ever heard of," Roald Amundsen once told a newspaper reporter, "this comes close to the top."[17]) In 1923, four young men died while taking possession of remote Wrangel Island for a company organized by Stefansson. This disaster was blamed on him and he lost whatever good will he had left with Canadian government officials. From then on he was more or less *persona non grata* in Canada, but there was no denying his abilities as a northern traveller or his popularity with the public as a prophet of the North.

Stefansson's vision of a friendly Arctic connects with the essence of the myth of the North: that Canadians are unique because we are northern, that northward lies our true destiny. In his book *The Northward Course of Empire* (1922), Stefansson made a case for the huge economic potential of the Arctic. "There is no northern boundary beyond which productive enterprise cannot go," he declared, forecasting that Canada would become a world power based on the exploitation of its northern location and resources.[18] This optimism about the future of the North was later picked up by John Diefenbaker, whose "northern vision" galvanized voters during the federal election campaign in 1958. Diefenbaker promised to build "roads to resources" to make the North the new frontier of economic development. "I see a new Canada—a Canada of the North," he proclaimed. "This is my vision."[19] With the instincts of a master politician, Diefenbaker was appealing to the enduring fascination Canadians have with their northland. Just a few years earlier, *Maclean's* magazine had given over an entire issue to the subject of the North. According to Pierre Berton, who

33. "Icebergs Davis Strait," 1930, is one of Lawren Harris's Arctic images, portraying the North as a source of spiritual transcendence.

---

was editor of the magazine at the time, it sold more copies than any issue in twenty years.[20] In 1956, Berton's book on the same subject, *The Mysterious North*, won him his first Governor-General's Award.

At the same time that James Curwood, Viljhalmur Stefansson, and Robert Service were making Canada synonymous with North in the popular imagination, the Group of Seven was accomplishing the same feat at the level of "high culture." "Our art is founded on a long and growing love and understanding of the North," wrote Lawren Harris, the Group's acknowledged leader, in 1929.[21] Harris was a theosophist and mystic who believed that the North was a source of spiritual energy and insight, especially for the artist. "The Canadian artist . . . is aware of the spiritual flow from the replenishing North and believes that this should ever shed clarity into the growing race of America," he wrote: "The North to him is a single, simple vision of high things."[22] Harris's luminous portraits of icebergs and Arctic peaks made the Far North a symbol of spiritual transcendence.

To his fellow members of the Group of Seven, of course, and to many people who admired their canvases, the North meant something a little less ambitious. When they used the term it usually meant anywhere north of Toronto. The wild landscape on which the Group made its reputation is now cottage country; the storm-tossed surface of Georgian Bay dotted with water skiers and sailboats. Nonetheless, as we saw in the previous chapter, the Group successfully implanted the notion that the authentic Canadian landscape is a rough northern wilderness of tree, rock, and sky, not a pastoral view of field and parkland.

II

If Canadians were supposedly "the Northmen of the New World," what about the actual inhabitants of the North, the Inuit who had been living there since long before recorded history began? What did southerners think about these real northerners?

For a long time outsiders only paid attention to the Canadian North when an explorer got lost there. Otherwise the territory and its Native inhabitants were left in peace. Very little was known or thought about them. In fact, so isolated were the Inuit from the rest of the world that in 1910, Viljhalmur Stefansson could still encounter a group of them who had never seen a white person before.

Stefansson's encounter aside, by the end of the nineteenth century the Inuit were being absorbed into the wider world. American whalers had moved into the Arctic, followed by fur traders, missionaries, and finally government agents of various kinds. Concerned about its hold over the area, the Canadian government opened police posts and initiated regular ship patrols of the coast. As interest in, and knowledge of, the North expanded, an image of the Inuit came into sharper focus. This image crystallized in the character of Nanook, the noble Inuit hunter and star character in Robert Flaherty's 1922 quasi-documentary film, *Nanook of the*

North, which has been called "the most famous Eskimo movie ever made."[23]
Nanook was shot on location on the east coast of Hudson Bay, and claimed
to portray realistically the traditional life of the people, who were represented in the film by local Inuit. Like so many other non-Native artists,
Flaherty (1884-1951) wanted to show Aboriginals as he imagined them to
have been before the intrusion of outsiders. "I am not going to make films
about what the white man has made of primitive peoples," he wrote. "What
I want to show is the former majesty and character of these people, while
it is still possible—before the white man has destroyed not only their
character, but the people as well."[24] As Viljhalmur Stefansson delighted in
pointing out, the film was riddled with ethnographic errors, but it was a
success with the public and with critics internationally. It presented an
idealized image of a cheerful, industrious people struggling for survival in
a hostile environment. This image was reinforced subsequently by a string
of Hollywood movies and even in documentaries such as Doug Wilkinson's
National Film Board film *Land of the Long Day*. Wilkinson's movie, which
was also the basis for a book of the same name, featured a "typical" Inuk
hunter, Joseph Idlouk, whose parka-clad image became familiar to every
Canadian when it was reproduced on the two-dollar bill. Nanook's smiling
image was also widely reproduced, on the wrapper of the Eskimo Pie
ice-cream bar.

Flaherty, Wilkinson, and many others portrayed the Inuit as an igloo-
dwelling, seal-eating, nose-rubbing primitive: natural man in mukluks.
This Imaginary Inuk was cheerful, strong, brave and resourceful. According
to the stereotype, Inuit inhabited one of the most hostile environments on
earth, yet were capable of amazing feats of endurance and survival. Of
course, outsiders found them uncivilized and uneducated. But this was their
attraction. In his book *The People's Land*, Hugh Brody argues that most
whites still believe in this romantic image of an authentic "Eskimo" existing
apart from modern life. Brody, a writer and filmmaker who spent several
years in the North, reports: "Newcomers to the north are continuously
reminded of the distance between themselves and the Eskimos by stories
woven out of these romantic and romanticized views. The people and the
land are mythical—the 'real Eskimo,' a strange and wonderful being, utterly
remote from the familiar places of the storytellers, far off in the heart of
the land, where he takes nature's rhythms and makes them his own, a figure

invested with wild dignity and powers, a force of nature himself, leading a life that could scarcely be more different from the settlement and its warm, protective homes."[25] According to Brody, this respect for a mythic Eskimo coexists in most whites with a complete disrespect for Inuit people, chiefly because they do not conform to the romantic stereotype. The paradox is that while whites worked to bring "civilization" to the North, they were disappointed when their work succeeded in producing "modern" Inuit. The explorer Roald Amundsen, who completed the first voyage through the Northwest Passage in his vessel the *Gjoa* in 1906, expressed this view: "During the voyage of the *Gjoa* we came into contact with ten different Eskimo tribes in all, and we had good opportunities of observing the influence of civilization on them, as we were able to compare those Eskimos who had come into contact with civilization with those who had not. And I must state it as my firm conviction that the latter, the Eskimo living absolutely isolated from civilization of any kind, are undoubtedly the happiest, healthiest, most honourable and most contented among them."[26]

The by-and-large positive image of the Inuit was tempered by a breath-taking arrogance on the part of southerners who treated the North as if it was their private domain. No incident illustrates this attitude better than the absurd assembly convened by Mounted policeman Major J.D. Moodie on the shores of Hudson Bay in 1904.[27] Moodie explained to his audience of twenty-five Inuit about the "big chief" across the water (i.e., King Edward VII) who was in charge of things and had their welfare at heart as long as they did "what was right and good." Then Moodie proceeded to hand out a set of woollen underwear to each adult present, with mittens and a toque for every child. According to a witness, the Inuit received these gifts "open-mouthed with various expressions." It is not hard to imagine why. Take as another example the painter A.Y. Jackson, who tagged along on a visit to the Arctic in 1927 aboard the supply vessel *Beothic*. Explaining the role of the RCMP in the North, Jackson wrote: "It was also part of their task to restrain the Eskimos from throwing away girl babies and leaving their old people to die of starvation, and to advise the hunters of the folly of killing more game than they could use."[28] Assuming the worst about the Inuit, southerners invariably thought that they knew better how to live in the North than the people who had been there for generations.

Following World War II, government interest in the North increased dramatically, chiefly because of the Cold War and the perceived threat of missile attack over the Pole. At the same time there was a recognition that the Inuit had suffered from contact with outsiders. Tuberculosis and other diseases were widespread among the people; game animals were depleted and starvation common; jobs were not available; alcohol abuse wreaked havoc with family life. These medical and social problems began to conjure up another image of the Inuit in the minds of many southerners. The Imaginary Eskimo went from being a happy-go-lucky, independent hunter to a welfare-dependent bum. Henry Larsen, captain of the famous RCMP vessel St. Roch, expressed this new image in a letter to his superiors in 1951. "The Eskimo as we knew them a few years ago are quickly disappearing, and in their stead we have a sadly dejected race, undernourished, ill-clad, living in filth and squalor, with no immediate hope of any improvement in conditions."[29] Nanook had become a social problem.

All kinds of schemes were put forward in the post-war period to "help" the Inuit, ranging from the tragic—relocation of entire settlements from one part of the Arctic to another—to the ludicrous—a plan to turn Inuit into pig farmers at DEW Line sites. One of the most successful projects turned out to be the encouragement of Native arts and crafts. The story has often been told how James Houston came into the North on behalf of the Canadian Handicraft Guild to purchase Inuit crafts, how he encouraged the carvers and printmakers to produce marketable items, then helped to set up craft centres where Native artists produced work which became sought after by galleries and collectors the world over. The outside world imagined the Inuit to be natural artists, authentic, intuitive, in touch with the forces of nature. It was an image which corresponded almost exactly with the earlier view of the Inuit as noble primitives.

These two images—the Inuit as self-reliant hunter (or master craftsman) and the Inuit as tragic victim of progress—seem to be diametrically opposed, but one does not necessarily contradict the other. It is possible to hold both in the mind at the same time. The reality of modern developments in the North may have altered Inuit society forever, but it is still possible to believe in the Imaginary Eskimo which Brody describes, the Platonic ideal of an Eskimo which still exists at the heart of all our imaginings about the North. Even people like Captain Larsen who despaired at the plight of the Inuit did not blame the people themselves. They faulted the government, or the Hudson's Bay Company, or "civilization" itself. No matter how tarnished the image of the modern Inuit, the image of the noble primitive persists, probably because it represents an idealized image that Canadians have of themselves as a northern people.

III

A corollary of the northern myth is the myth of hockey. Like nothing else, hockey allows us to celebrate our northernness. To virtually everyone who has ever written about the game, hockey expresses something basic about Canada. It is "Our Game," the "Home Game," "the game of our lives," our "national religion," our "national theatre," the "Canadian metaphor." Lovers of the sport impose on it a terrific weight of significance. The hockey rink, write Ken Dryden and Roy MacGregor, "is a place where the monumental themes of Canadian life are played out—English and French, East and West, Canada and the U.S., Canada and the world, the timeless tensions of commerce and culture, our struggle to survive and civilize winter."[30] Hockey is clearly more than just a game; it has become "one of this country's most significant collective representations—a story that Canadians tell themselves about what it means to be Canadian."[31]

There are several elements to the myth of hockey. First of all, it is Canada's game; we invented it. Not only that, it is pretty much the only sport we're any good at on an international level. For years our teams dominated the world and even now, when the outcome of international competitions are problematic, we are always in the running. Hockey allows Canadians to be proud of ourselves, to puff up our chests and feel we are the best at something.

Hockey is our game not just because we hold the patent on it but because it embodies the northern landscape. Whether it is played on frozen ponds or indoor arenas, it speaks to us of winter, Canada's season. The blank expanse of ice represents the vast, frigid, dispassionate wilderness, or so the metaphorically-inclined tell us, and every game dramatizes the struggle for survival in such a difficult land. "In a land so inescapably and inhospitably cold, hockey is the dance of life, an affirmation that despite the deathly chill we are alive."[32] Hockey, writes the New Brunswick novelist David Adams Richards, "is the non-intellectual impulse for life."[33]

Hockey also provides a parallel, improved version of Canadian history. More Canadians know about the glory days of the Maple Leafs or the Rocket Richard riot than can recall a single reason for Confederation or any of the clauses of the Meech Lake Accord. Our "where were you when?" question is, of course, where were you when Paul Henderson scored The Goal that beat the Soviets in 1972? (I was huddled around a television set in a student lounge at Carleton University where, appropriately enough, I was majoring in Canadian Studies.) Close behind the FLQ kidnappings in the running for the most traumatic moment in Canadian history must surely be The Trade, when Peter Pocklington dealt Wayne Gretzky to Los Angeles. In the hockey version of history, Canada has always been a superpower, and its citizens all enjoyed an idyllic childhood playing on frozen ponds and dreaming of a career in the NHL. Hockey is a sport bathed in nostalgia for a simpler time when players didn't wear helmets and Foster Hewitt was still doing the play-by-play and places like Anaheim and Phoenix had never heard of hockey; a time when we owned our own heroes and controlled our own culture. At least we think we did.

Hockey would not be Canadian if it also was not expected to make a contribution to national unity. A passion for the game is considered to be one of the rare things that brings Canadians together. He Shoots, He Scores becomes the national motto, rather than From Sea to Sea. In this reading, *Hockey Night in Canada*, the most popular radio, then television, show in Canadian history, is much more than entertainment; it is a weekly reconciliation of our differences, be they regional, linguistic, ethnic or class. Hockey's special contribution is that it brings together French and English in a mutual recognition of something that unites rather than separates. "There was no other cultural form," write hockey scholars Richard Gruneau and David Whitson, "no other popular practice, that brought the 'two solitudes' into regular engagement with each other in quite the same way."[34]

Notice the past tense. There is certainly a feeling nowadays among observers of the game that like almost every other Canadian myth, the myth of hockey is crumbling. The intrusion of commercial values is usually blamed, by which most people mean that the Americans have hijacked "our" game, brutalizing and commercializing it in order to attract an audience which is ignorant of its grace, subtlety, and history. As well, we no longer dominate hockey as we once did. Perhaps inevitably, other countries are producing players every bit as good as our own. NHL teams are filled with players from northern and eastern Europe. We used to console ourselves that even if the majority of the teams were based south of the border, at least almost all the players came from Up Here. Now even the Americans are getting proficient at our game and we fear that someday hockey will be like basketball: invented by a Canadian but assimilated by the Americans.

Along with its internationalization, hockey is losing its connection to winter, to North. The game has become a product, marketed wherever there are enough consumers, which means in large American cities and not small Canadian ones. The game continues to be as popular as ever with Canadian youngsters and old-timers, but how can it stand for all the things we used to think it stood for when it is so popular in places like Phoenix and Florida, places where the only ice is in your drink, places without winter? The natural connection between hockey and North is being severed. It remains only for the Stanley Cup to become the property of Disneyland for the final demise of the myth of hockey.

IV

In an article in *Saturday Night* magazine in 1936, historian and political commentator Frank Underhill warned Canadians against growing "false hair on the chest," by which he meant taking too seriously the "cult of the North," an idea he dismissed as "pure romanticism at its worst." Underhill pointed out that "the normal Canadian dreams of living in a big city where he can make his pile quickly and enjoy such urban luxuries as are familiar to him in the advertising columns of our national magazines."[35] Romanticizing the "supposed virtues of the North," grumbled Underhill, was a form of escapism, a way of avoiding the realities of contemporary urban life. Were he alive today I am sure that Underhill (who died in 1971) would be as dismayed as ever that the "cult" he so mistrusted, the "cult of the North," still exerts such a strong attraction for so many Canadians, even if only in their imaginations.

Justice Tom Berger pointed out in his 1977 report on the Mackenzie Valley pipeline proposal that southern Canadians have always imagined the

North to be their frontier, a place of almost limitless potential wealth.[36] The "conquest" of the North, by which is meant the extraction of all this wealth, is believed to be our national destiny. More than that, southerners have also imagined the North to be a source of spiritual strength. Whether we ever visited it or not, having the North there made us better as a people, or at least gave us a future in which we might become better. The North is "a window which opens out onto the infinite—on to the potential future," wrote Andre Siegfried.[37] It is also a refuge, a sanctuary, a place to seek renewal in contact with elemental nature, a place where modern industrial society has not reached. The North, says Pierre Berton, who has written about it extensively, "to most of us in the south continues to appear as haunting and as mysterious as the jungles of Borneo or the shifting sands of the Kalahari."[38]

This is the imaginary North, the "Mysterious North" of Robert Service and James Curwood, full of fabulous wealth and high adventure. The paradox is that while Canadians have held strongly to the myth, they have more or less ignored the reality. As Farley Mowat has angrily observed, behind the myth "lies a real world, obscured by drifts of literary drivel and buried under an icy weight of obsessive misconceptions; yet the magnificent reality behind the myth has been consistently rejected by most Canadians since the day of our national birth."[39] (Many people think that Mowat has contributed his own fair share of misconceptions about the region, but that is another story.) In 1953, Prime Minister Louis St. Laurent famously commented that government had administered the North "in an almost continuing state of absence of mind." Canadians may think that we are a northern people, but blessed little attention has ever been paid to the area or its inhabitants; unless, that is, the Americans show an interest in it, or there appears to be a possibility of some gigantic mineral discovery.

But surely that is just the point. The power of a myth does not rely on its correspondence to the real world. The belief that the North shapes the Canadian character reoccurs too often in the master narrative to believe that it is not something constant and basic. The fact that most of us know so little about the region is precisely why it exerts such a fascination. It remains "the great, big, broad land 'way up yonder'," as Robert Service called it, full of potential, free of the petty conflicts which bedevil the rest of the country, a frontier that never closes. There are many forces which divide Canadians—language, region, class, skin colour. The myth of North is appealing because it promises to unite us, to dissolve all our differences in a great white hope for the future. Much more likely, however, is that the myth will lose some of its tenacity as contact increases between northern and southern parts of the country. We see this happening already with the emergence of Inuit accounts of their own history which undermine the master narrative of North and reveal a different understanding of what it means to be a "northern people." As the North gains its own voice, and ceases to be exclusively a place about which people in the south fantasize, the master narrative will have to change to accommodate it.

CONCLUSION

History in an Age of Anxiety

This book began as an attempt to locate and explore some of the core myths of Canadian history. What I discovered is that the story of Canada, as it was taught to me, was a fraud, or at least only part of the story. Time and again when I traced one of the important narratives back to its source I discovered that it was invented by some large corporate body for its own purposes. The myth of the RCMP, for instance, has been used for years to obscure the coercive power of the state. The CPR turns out to have inflated a railway into a national dream as a highly successful public relations ploy, and incidently to have created the myth of the mosaic to increase its tourist potential. The myth of North and the myth of the master race were used to secure the pre-eminence of Canada's British heritage while minimizing the role of other cultural groups. I am not suggesting that these myths were imposed by groups of shadowy conspirators. I recognize that they were willingly embraced by generations of Canadians as our national dreams, the truths of our history. They provided an explanation of our past and satisfied a deep need to feel that we were engaged in an important national enterprise. Those of us at the centre of these myths were comforted and inspired by them. And why not? They were about us.

The master narrative excluded many people, however, who did not see themselves reflected in the stories; or worse, felt belittled by them. These people—Aboriginals, minorities, working people, women—have had to force their way into the story of Canada by inventing narratives of their own. For someone like myself, raised on the conventional narratives, it is tremendously invigorating to witness this process. I am thinkng here of

Howard Adams's classic history of Canada from a Métis perspective, *Prison of Grass* (1975). Or Maria Campbell's memoir *Halfbreed* (1973). Or Eva Hoffman's tart recollections of her Polish family's transplantation to 1960s Vancouver in *Lost in Translation* (1989). Or Mina Shum's film about a Chinese-Canadian family, *Double Happiness* (1995). Or any number of other books, plays, movies, and magazines emerging from previously-ignored corners of the culture which are thickening Canadian history with stories from "beyond the pale."

At the same time, the old master narrative does not give up without a fight. People with a vested interest, emotional or otherwise, in the old myths resist their subversion by new voices. As a result there is a high level of anxiety evident in the culture these days, a feeling on the part of many people that the familiar Canada they have always known is under seige. They are right, of course. Canada is being reimagined. But this should be a cause for celebration, not concern.

I

Psychologists use the term "perseveration" to describe the repetitive use of the same word or idea in response to a stimulus, even when the stimulus changes. It is considered a sign of psychiatric illness. An associated phenomenon known as "perseveration of memory" occurs when we insist on "remembering" the details of an event even after we have been informed that the event did not happen or did not happen in the way that we remember. The "memory" is so basic, so ingrained, or so comforting, that it overrides any attempt to correct it.

Many Canadians are afflicted by perseveration of memory. They repeat the familiar myths of our history even as they must know that they no longer explain much about us. In 1991, a judge of the British Columbia Supreme Court actually ruled that First Nations people before contact lacked all the "badges of civilization" and that their life was "at best, 'nasty, brutish, and short.'" His judgement, in other words, was an eloquent expression of the myth of the master race. In 1996, Diane Francis, editor of *The Financial Post*, published a book, *Fighting for Canada*, in which she characterized the movement for Quebec independence as a criminal conspiracy by a few people who have duped a majority of Quebeckers into following their mad scheme. I don't know how many times I have heard people say that if only ordinary Québecois knew "the truth," they would never want their own country. This delusion may comfort English-speaking Canadians, but it represents a continuing infantilization of the Québecois which contributes nothing to the reduction of political tensions in the country. Likewise, many people deplore the end of railway passenger service, even though virtually no one rides the trains any longer. Or they solemnly debate whether the RCMP should allow officers to wear turbans, as if the Mounties were still an imperial police force charged with keeping down the "natives." The myths we have used to explain our history no longer make much sense. We "remember" them as a kind of habitual tic, like the repetitive speech of a disturbed psyche, but they represent a nostalgic hankering for the past rather than an accurate understanding of it.

It is not that the master narratives, or "core myths," are no longer true; literal truth was never a measure of their power or their usefulness. It is that they no longer explain anything. It is pointless to wish it were different, to complain that no one is honouring the old traditions, to make a to-do when the trains get shut down or the Queen gets dissed or Quebec wants to rearrange Confederation. We can't go back. Many people seem to believe that the problem is that our kids are not being taught the old myths. I say, thank God they are not. The story of Canada I learned from my schoolbooks is totally inadequate for understanding Canadian society as it is today.

When I returned to live in Vancouver in the mid-1980s after a long absence, a friend told me a story to explain why he didn't like the city. One day he met two other downtown office workers for lunch. He recommended a nice restaurant, only to discover that it had been replaced by a shoe store. Never mind, another of the trio knew an even better place. This time they arrived in front of a great hole in the ground. The building had been demolished to make way for a new highrise development. On the third try they actually succeeded in finding a restaurant, but it specialized in sushi, not the Italian food it had offered just a month earlier. Exasperated and out of time, the friends bought takeout sandwiches at a deli and returned separately to their offices.

My friend told me this story to emphasize his sense of Vancouver as a city without history, a city which is changing so fast that it is leaving behind no trace of itself. It exists only for an instant, in the present. It seems to me that the same thing is true of many peoples' sense of Canada as a whole. It has become a cliché that change is occurring so fast that we are unable to get a grip on experience. Not just the buildings are being replaced; our values, our institutions, our understanding of the world are all in question. Being told this over and over again naturally makes people anxious, and this anxiety manifests itself in a prevailing sense of unease about the country.

The close of the twentieth century finds Canadians disgruntled, discouraged, pessimistic. Recently I paused in front of a shelf at my local library and was struck by the titles of some of the most recent books about Canada. *Breaking Faith*, *The Betrayal of Canada*, *Faultlines: Struggling for a Canadian Vision*, *Impossible Nation*, *The Trouble with Canada*, *Deconfederation*, *Selling Illusions*, *Derailed: The Betrayal of the National Dream*: the list goes on and on. It is a pretty accurate reflection of the gloom which envelops political discourse in the nineties. Keith Spicer's Citizens' Forum on Canada's Future warns us that: Canada is in crisis. (But when has it not been?) In his recent book, *Nationalism Without Walls*, journalist Richard Gwyn writes: "Our community is at risk now of being disinvented—of being deconstructed."[1] According to Gwyn, the forces arrayed against us include the global economy, neo-conservatism, immigration, multiculturalism, our own indifference. Pick your peril. Canada is tied to the tracks and a big locomotive is bearing down on us.

It is not just the outcome of the latest referendum in Quebec, though that didn't help. Beyond the French-English impasse, a great number of people seem to feel that the country no longer works. I think that some of this unease derives from the fragmentation of the master narrative of Canadian history. Over the past three decades First Nations people have wrestled their way back into the history. Now they are demanding their own legal systems and forms of government. Meanwhile, immigration has changed the face of the country. In the 1950s, seventy-five percent of all Canadians were of either British or French background. It was a familiar, ethnically homogenous society. These numbers have changed dramatically and as a result the original "charter groups" feel threatened. They feel they are losing their hegemony, which they are, and they don't like it. Jacques Parizeau expressed it perfectly after the 1995 referendum in Quebec when he blamed "*les autres*," "the ethnics," for frustrating the aspirations of the

Québecois. He was roundly condemned for this outburst, but English-speaking Canadians who do so are being disingenuous if they do not recognize that Parizeau was speaking for many of them as well.

In an age of anxiety, it is not surprising to find nostalgia flourishing. The people who believe that the "old" way of looking at Canada was the right way fasten on the familiar myths, the ones most of us were raised on, the comforting stories of responsible government, the railway, the Mounties. We are losing touch with these "founding" myths, these people say, and so we are losing touch with our identity. There is consolation in nostalgia, the glance behind to a better time when the world seemed to make sense (largely because "we" were in charge), but there is also danger. If a nation is a group of people who share the same illusions about themselves, then Canadians need some new illusions. It is wrong to think that the old ones have the necessary power to imagine solutions to contemporary problems. English Canada needs to recognize new narratives for understanding itself.

At the moment, for instance, the situation in Quebec seems perilous. The myth of unity said that the French could be content with minority status in a federation of equal partners. This is apparently not true, and attempts in English Canada to cling to this way of imagining the country are doing irreparable damage. Likewise, Aboriginal people are challenging a narrative that sees them as a minority within Canada instead of distinctly separate people with age-old claims to justice which have never been honoured.

History is a representation of the past; it is information transformed into story. Sometimes these stories are told as narratives; sometimes they are embedded in symbols or in art or in specific sites. The stories we tell about the past produce the images that we use to describe ourselves as a community. If we are not telling ourselves the right stories, then we cannot imagine ourselves acting together to resolve our problems.

Nations *are* narrations.

Endnotes

INTRODUCTION: THE STORY OF CANADA

1. Edward Said, *Culture and Imperialism* (New York: Alfred A. Knopf, 1993), p. XIII.
2. Benedict Anderson, *Imagined Communities: Reflections on the Origin and Spread of Nationalism* (London: Verso, rev. ed. 1991; orig. pub. 1983), p. 6.
3. The phrase belongs to cyberpunk novelist William Gibson.
4. James W. Loewen, *Lies My Teacher Told Me: Everything Your American History Textbook Got Wrong* (New York: The New Press, 1995), p. 11.

CHAPTER ONE: MAKING TRACKS

1. Jo Davis, ed., *Not a Sentimental Journey* (Goderich, Ont.: Gunbyfield Publishing, 1990), p. 9.
2. Ibid., p. 17.
3. Pierre Berton, *The Great Railway, 1871-1881* (Toronto: McClelland & Stewart, 1970), p. 12.
4. W. Kaye Lamb, *History of the Canadian Pacific Railway* (New York: Macmillan, 1977), p. 436.
5. R.G. MacBeth, *The Romance of the Canadian Pacific Railway* (Toronto: The Ryerson Press, 1924), p. 172.
6. Robin Winks, *The Relevance of Canadian History* (Toronto: Macmillan, 1979), p. 47.
7. Robert Kroetsch, "Canada is a Poem," in Gary Geddes, ed., *Divided We Stand* (Toronto: Peter Martin Associates, 1977), p. 14.
8. MacBeth, p. 139.
9. David Cruise and Alison Griffiths, *Lords of the Line* (Toronto: Viking Penguin, 1988), p. 1.
10. Lamb, p. 135.

11. Hugh A. Dempsey, "Catching the Sunbeams: An Inventory of Canadian Prairie Photographers to 1900," unpublished paper, Glenbow Museum, 1993.

12. Lamb, p. 1.

13. MacBeth, p. 73.

14. Ibid., p. 9.

15. George Ham, *Reminiscences of a Raconteur* (Toronto: The Musson Book Co., 1921), p. 265.

16. Cited in Doug Owram, *Promise of Eden: The Canadian Expansionist Movement and the Idea of the West, 1856-1900* (Toronto: University of Toronto Press, 1980), p. 123.

17. Michael Bliss, *Right Honourable Men* (Toronto: McClelland & Stewart, 1995), p. 22.

18. Sam Kula, "Steam Movies," in Hugh Dempsey, ed., *The CPR West* (Vancouver: Douglas & McIntyre, 1984), pp. 247-57.

19. Lamb, p. 219.

20. John Murray Gibbon, *Steel of Empire* (New York: Bobbs-Merrill Co., 1935), p. 304.

21. Cited in E.J. Hart, *The Selling of Canada* (Banff: Altitude Publishing, 1983), p. 25.

22. C. James Taylor, *Negotiating the Past: The Making of Canada's National Historic Parks and Sites* (Montreal: McGill-Queen's University Press, 1990), p. 27.

23. Douglas Sladen, *On the Cars and Off* (London: Ward, Lock & Bowden Ltd., 1895), p. 306.

CHAPTER TWO: THE MILD WEST

1. Stephen Osborne, "Pile of Bones," *Geist* (July-Aug. 1994), p. 5.

2. Pierre Berton, *Klondike* (Toronto: McClelland & Stewart, 1958), p. XVIII.

3. Pierre Berton, *Why We Act Like Canadians* (Toronto: McClelland & Stewart, 1982), p. 19.

4. Pierre Berton, *Hollywood's Canada* (Toronto: McClelland & Stewart, 1975), p. 111.

5. Col. S.B. Steele, *Forty Years in Canada* (New York: Dodd, Mead & Co., 1915), p. 57.

6. R.G. MacBeth, *Policing the Plains* (Toronto: 1931), p. 63.

7. W.A. Fraser, "Soldier Police of the Canadian Northwest," *The Canadian Magazine* (Feb. 1900), p. 363.

8. A.L. Burt, *The Romance of Canada* (Toronto: W.J. Gage, 1937), p. 317.

9. MacBeth, p. 30.

10. Ralph Connor, *Corporal Cameron of the North West Mounted Police* (Toronto: The Westminster Co. Ltd., 1912), p. 306.

11. Berton, *Why We Act Like Canadians*, p. 43.

12. Connor, p. 387.

13. MacBeth, p. 40.

14. R.C. Macleod, *The NWMP and Law Enforcement, 1873-1905* (Toronto: University of Toronto Press, 1976), pp. 15-17.

15. Cited in Macleod, p. 165.

16. S.W. Horrall, "The Royal North-West Mounted Police and Labour Unrest in Western Canada, 1919," *Canadian Historical Review* (June 1980), p. 171.

17. National Archives of Canada. Robert Borden Papers. MG26. 56665.

18. Ibid., 56698.

19. National Archives of Canada. Dept. of the Militia. RG24. vol. 2543, Jan. 8, 1919.

20. Ibid., vol. 4527.

21. National Archives of Canada. Sir George Foster Papers. MG27 II D7. vol. 7, May 2, 1919.

22. For the OBU, see David J. Bercuson, *Fools and Wise Men: The Rise and Fall of the One Big Union* (Toronto: McGraw-Hill Ryerson, 1978).

23. *Montreal Daily Star*, March 18, 1919; *Calgary Daily Herald*, March 18, 1919.

24. Zaneth's career is detailed in James Dubro and Robin Rowland, *Undercover* (Toronto: Octopus Publishing, 1991).

25. Borden Papers. 56832.

26. Ibid., 56825.

27. National Archives of Canada. Dept. of the Militia. RG24. vol. 3985, file NSC1055-2-21, vol. 1.

28. Cited in *Robert Craig Brown*, Robert Laird Borden, vol. 2 (Toronto: Macmillan of Canada, 1975), p. 165.

29. Dept. of the Militia. RG24. vol. 2543.

30. *Maclean's*, Jan. 1919.

31. Ibid., August 1919.

32. Theodore Draper, *The Roots of American Communism* (New York: The Viking Press, 1957), p. 254.

33. Canada. Parliament. House of Commons. *Debates.* 13th Parliament, 2nd

Session, vol. I, p. 42, Feb. 26, 1919.

34. Ibid., vol. III, p. 3034, June 2, 1919.

35. For the general strike, see David J. Bercuson, *Confrontation at Winnipeg* (Montreal: McGill-Queen's University Press, 1974) and J.M. Bumstead, *The Winnipeg General Strike of 1919: An Illustrated History* (Winnipeg: Watson and Dwyer, 1994).

36. Foster Papers, June 23, 1919.

37. Gregory S. Kealey, "The Surveillance State: The Origins of Domestic Intelligence and Counter-Subversion in Canada, 1914-21," *Intelligence and National Security* (1992), p. 182.

38. The best source on these events is Lita-Rose Betcherman, *The Little Band* (Ottawa: Deneau, 1982).

39. Pierre Berton, *The Great Depression, 1929-1939* (Toronto: McClelland & Stewart, 1990), p. 142.

40. Ibid., p. 319ff.

41. For this episode, see Reg Whitaker and Gary Marcuse, *Cold War Canada: The Making of a National Insecurity State, 1945-57* (Toronto: University of Toronto Press, 1994).

42. See Jeff Sallot, *Nobody Said No: The Real Story About How the Mounties Always Get Their Man* (Toronto: James Lorimer, 1979) and John Sawatsky, *Men in the Shadows* (Toronto: Doubleday Canada, 1980).

CHAPTER THREE: YOUR MAJESTY'S REALM

1. Emily Weaver, *A Canadian History for Boys and Girls* (Toronto: William Briggs, The Copp Clark Co., 1900), p. 111.

2. Charles G.D. Roberts, *A History of Canada for High Schools and Academies* (Toronto: Morang Educational Co., 1897), p. 355.

3. Ibid., p. 446.

4. Arthur Dorland, *Our Canada* (Toronto: Copp Clark, 1949), p. 413.

5. David Duncan, *The Story of the Canadian People* (Toronto: Morang Educational Co., 1904), p. 219.

6. Roberts, p. 195; W.L. Grant, *History of Canada* (Toronto: T. Eaton Co., 1914), p. 135.

7. Grant, p. 155.

8. William Withrow, *A History of Canada for the Use of Schools and General Readers* (Toronto: Copp, Clark & Co., 1876), p. 169.

9. George Wrong, et al., *The Story of Canada* (Toronto: The Ryerson Press, 1929), p. 166.

10. Dorland, p. 212.

11. J.W. Chafe and A.R.M. Lower, *Canada—A Nation and How It Came to Be* (Toronto: Longmans, Green & Co., 1948), p. 256.

12. Grant, p. 192.

13. Burt, p. 242.

14. Wrong, p. 167.

15. Burt, p. 243.

16. Chafe and Lower, p. 259.

17. Weaver, p. 285.

18. Brown, pp. 383, 388.

19. Dorland, p. 413.

20. W.H.P. Clement, *The History of the Dominion of Canada* (Toronto: William Briggs, 1898), p. 413.

21. Quoted in Carl Berger, *The Sense of Power* (Toronto: University of Toronto Press, 1970), pp. 230-31.

22. Roger Graham, *Arthur Meighen: A Biography*, vol. 1, *The Door of Opportunity* (Toronto: Clarke, Irwin & Co., 1960), p. 198.

23. Cited in Peter C. Newman, *Merchant Princes* (Toronto: Viking Penguin, 1991), p. 138.

24. Cited in Kenneth Coates, *Canada's Colonies: A History of the Yukon and Northwest Territories* (Toronto: James Lorimer, 1985), p. 118.

25. This discussion of Empire Day relies on Robert M. Stamp, "Empire Day in the Schools of Ontario: the Training of Young Imperialists," *Journal of Canadian Studies*, vol. 8, no. 3 (Aug. 1973), pp. 32-42.

26. Quoted in Berger, p. 259.

27. Robert M. Stamp, *The Schools of Ontario, 1876-1976* (Toronto: University of Toronto Press, 1982), p. 93.

28. *Toronto Globe*, 22 May 1909; quoted in Stamp, "Empire Day," p. 38.

29. Robert M. Stamp, "Steel of Empire: Royal Tours and the CPR," in Hugh Dempsey, ed., *The CPR West* (Vancouver: Douglas & McIntyre, 1984), pp. 277-79.

30. Ibid., p. 284.

31. Frederick Griffin, *Variety Show* (Toronto: Macmillan, 1936), p. 58.

32. Stamp, p. 285.

33. See Simon Evans, *Prince Charming Goes West: The Story of the E.P. Ranch* (Calgary: University of Calgary Press, 1993).

34. This tour is described in Tom MacDonnell, *Daylight upon Magic: The Royal Tour of Canada 1939* (Toronto: Macmillan, 1989).

35. F.P. Grove, "Assimilation," *Maclean's*, 1 Sept. 1929, p. 75.

36. From Abee Carter Goodloe, "At the Foot of the Rockies," *Alberta History*, vol. 34, no. 2 (1986); cited in Sid Marty, *Leaning on the Wind* (Toronto: Harper-Collins, 1995), p. 78.

37. Marty, p. 78.

38. W.G. Smith, *A Study in Canadian Immigration* (Toronto: The Ryerson Press, 1920), p. 349.

39. Henry H. Miles, *The Child's History of Canada* (Montreal: William Dawson, 1910), p. 22.

40. J. George Hodgins, *A History of Canada and of the Other British Provinces in North America* (Montreal: John Lovell, 1857), p. 123.

41. Miles, p. 22.

42. George Wrong, et al., *The Story of Canada* (Toronto: The Ryerson Press, 1929), p. 14.

43. John Calkin, *A History of the Dominion of Canada* (Halifax: A & W MacKinlay, 1898), p. 3.

44. Duncan McArthur, *History of Canada for High Schools* (Toronto: The Educational Book Co., 1927), p. 2.

45. W.L. Grant, *History of Canada* (Toronto: T. Eaton Co., 1914), p. 51.

46. E.L. Marsh, *Where the Buffalo Roamed* (Toronto: Macmillan, 1923), p. 2.

47. William Withrow, *A History of Canada for the Use of Schools and General Readers* (Toronto: Copp, Clark & Co., 1876), p. 19.

48. J.N. McIlwraith, *The Children's Study of Canada* (London: Fisher Unwin, 1899), p. 6.

49. J. Castell Hopkins, *The Story of Our Country* (Toronto: John C. Winston, 1912), p. 52.

50. W.L. Grant, p. 48.

51. Charles G.D. Roberts, *A History of Canada for High Schools and Academies* (Toronto: Morang Educational Co., 1897), p. 129.

52. Miles, p. 20.

53. Agnes Laut, *Canada: The Empire of the North* (Toronto: William Briggs, 1904), p. 171.

54. James W. St.G. Walker, "The Indian in Canadian Historical Writing," *Canadian Historical Assoc. Historical Papers* 1971, p. 37.

55. Hodgins, p. 144.

56. Roberts, p. 28.

57. G.U. Hay, *Public School History of Canada* (Toronto: Copp, Clark Co., 1902), p. 218.

58. Walker, p. 36.

59. Burt, p. 200.

60. Wrong, et al., p. 263.

61. Roberts, p. 256.

62. Ibid., p. 364.

63. Wrong, et al., p. 293.

64. Dorland, *Our Canada*, p. 256.

65. Thomas Berger, *The Report of the Mackenzie Valley Pipeline Inquiry, vol. 1* (Ottawa: Supply and Services Canada, 1977), p. 91.

66. Garnet McDiarmid and David Pratt, *Teaching Prejudice* (Toronto: Ontario Institute for Studies in Education, Curriculum Series 12, 1971), p. 88.

67. Victoria Hayward, *Romantic Canada* (Toronto: The Macmillan Co., 1922), p. 187.

68. Kate Foster, *Our Canadian Mosaic* (Toronto: Dominion Council, YWCA, 1926).

69. Ian McKay, *The Quest of the Folk: Antimodernism and Cultural Selection in Twentieth Century Nova Scotia* (Montreal: McGill-Queen's University Press, 1994), p. 57.

70. Hart, *Selling of Canada*, pp. 108-09; J. Murray Gibbon, *Canadian Mosaic* (Toronto: McClelland & Stewart, 1938); McKay, p. 58.

71. Gibbon, *Canadian Mosaic*, p. VIII.

72. Terrence Craig, *Racial Attitudes in English-Canadian Fiction, 1905-1980* (Waterloo, Ont.: Wilfrid Laurier University Press, 1987), p. 46.

73. W.L. Morton, *The Canadian Identity* (Toronto: University of Toronto Press, 1972), p. 89.

74. Donald Harman Akenson, "The Historiography of English-Speaking Canada and the Concept of Diaspora: A Sceptical Appreciation," *Canadian Historical Review*, vol. 76, no. 3 (Sept. 1995), p. 391.

75. Dorland, p. 425.

CHAPTER FOUR: THE INFANTILIZATION OF QUEBEC

1. Jeffrey Simpson, *Faultlines* (Toronto: McClelland & Stewart, 1993), p. 279.

2. Marcel Trudel and Genevieve Jain, *Canadian History Textbooks: A Comparative Study*, *Studies of the Royal Commission on Bilingualism and Biculturalism #5* (Ottawa: Queen's Printer, 1970), p. 131.

3. Ramsay Cook, *Canada and the French-Canadian Question* (Toronto: Macmillan, 1967), p. 146.

4. Susan Mann Trofimenkoff, *The Dream of Nation* (Toronto: Gage, 1983), p. 20.

5. Robert Fulford, "A Post-Modern Dominion: The Changing Nature of Canadian Citizenship," in William Kaplan, *Belonging: The Meaning and Future of Canadian Citizenship* (Montreal: McGill-Queen's University Press, 1993), p. 111.

6. A.L. Burt, *The Romance of Canada* (Toronto: W.J. Gage, 1937), p. 137.

7. George W. Brown, *Building the Canadian Nation* (Toronto: J.M. Dent & Sons, 1958), p. 165.

8. Carl Berger, *The Writing of Canadian History*, 2nd ed. (Toronto: University of Toronto Press, 1986), p. 4.

9. Francis Parkman, *The Old Regime in Canada* (Boston: 1874), p. 401.

10. Cited in Mason Wade, *Francis Parkman: Heroic Historian* (1942; New York: Viking Press, 1972), p. 420.

11. Arthur G. Dorland, *Our Canada* (Toronto: Copp Clark, 1949), p. 105.

12. J. Castell Hopkins, *Canadian Annual Review of Public Affairs* (Toronto: Annual Review Publishing, 1908), p. 239.

13. George Tait, *Fair Domain: The Story of Canada from Earliest Times to 1800* (Toronto: Ryerson, 1960), p. 392.

14. Duncan McArthur, *History of Canada for High Schools* (Toronto: The Educational Book Co., 1927), p. 243.

15. A. Garland, *Canada, Then and Now* (Toronto: Macmillan, 1956).

16. Andre Siegfried, *The Race Question in Canada* (Toronto: McClelland & Stewart, 1966), p. 96; orig. pub. in English in 1907.

17. Pierre Berton, *Hollywood's Canada* (Toronto: McClelland and Stewart, 1975), p. 82.

18. Ron Graham, *The French Quarter* (Toronto: Macfarlane Walter & Ross, 1992), p. 10.

19. Cited in J.B. Lyons, *William Henry Drummond: Poet in Patois* (Toronto: Fitzhenry & Whiteside, 1994), p. 170.

20. J. Russell Harper, *Krieghoff* (Toronto: University of Toronto Press, 1979), p. XI.

21. Ibid., p. 165.

22. Marius Barbeau, *Cornelius Krieghoff: Pioneer Painter of North America* (Toronto: The Macmillan Co. of Canada, 1934), p. 3.

23. Laurence Nowry, *Marius Barbeau: Man of Mana* (Toronto: NC Press, 1995), p. 307.

24. Ibid., p. 187.

25. Richard Handler, *Nationalism and the Politics of Culture in Quebec* (Madison: University of Wisconsin Press, 1988), pp. 73-74.

26. Ian McKay, *The Quest of the Folk* (Montreal: McGill-Queen's University Press, 1994), p. 158.

27. Cited in Genevieve Jain, "Nationalism and Educational Politics in Ontario and Quebec, 1867-1914," in Alf Chaiton and Neil McDonald, eds., *Canadian Schools and Canadian Identity* (Toronto: Gage Educational Publishing, 1977), p. 42.

28. Cited in George Tomkins, "Canadian Education and the Development of a National Consciousness," in Chaiton and McDonald, p. 15.

29. *Montreal Star*, 26 June 1893.

30. Genevieve Laloux-Jain, *Les Manuels d'Histoire du Canada au Québec et en Ontario, 1867-1914* (Québec: Les Presses de l'Universite Laval, 1973), pp. 84-85.

31. Kenneth Windsor, "Historical Writing in Canada (to 1920)," in Carl Klinck, ed., *Literary History of Canada* (Toronto: University of Toronto Press, 1965), p. 220.

32. A.B. Hodgetts, *What Culture? What Heritage? A Study of Civic Education in Canada* (Toronto: Ontario Institute for Studies in Education, 1968), p. 34.

33. Trudel and Jain, *Canadian History Textbook*, p. 133.

34. Spicer report, p. 123.

35. Michael Ignatieff, *Blood and Belonging: Journey into the New Nationalism* (Toronto: Viking Penguin, 1993), p. 145.

36. W.L. Morton, *The Canadian Identity* (Toronto: University of Toronto Press, 1972) p. 189.

37. Robert Kroetsch, *The Lovely Treachery of Words* (Toronto: Oxford University Press, 1989), p. 28.

38. Frank Davey, *From There to Here* (Erin, Ont.: Press Porcépic, 1974), p. 20.

39. B.W. Powe, *A Tremendous Canada of Light* (Toronto: Coach House Press, 1993), p. 101.

40. Linda Hutcheon, *Splitting Images: Contemporary Canadian Ironies* (Toronto: Oxford University Press, 1991), p. VII.

41. Kroetsch, p. 25.

42. Richard Gwyn, *Nationalism Without Walls: The Unbearable Lightness of Being Canadian* (Toronto: McClelland & Stewart, 1995), p. 243.

43. Ignatieff, p. 145.

CHAPTER FIVE: DIVIDED WE STAND

1. Robert Fulford, "On Myth-making," *Saturday Night* (Sept. 1969), p. 15.

2. See Charles W. Humphries, "The Banning of a Book in British Columbia," *BC Studies*, no. 1 (Winter 1968/69), pp. 1-12.

3. Reginald W. Bibby, *The Bibby Report: Social Trends Canadian Style* (Toronto: Stoddart, 1995), p. 47.

4. Douglas Owram, "The Myth of Louis Riel," *Canadian Historical Review*, vol. LXIII, no. 3 (Sept. 1982), p. 336.

5. The description of this episode is based on A.B. McKillop, ed., *A Critical Spirit: The Thought of William Dawson LeSueur* (Toronto: McClelland & Stewart, 1977) and "Editor's Introduction" in W.D. LeSueur, *William Lyon Mackenzie: A Reinterpretation* (Toronto: The Macmillan Co. of Canada, 1979), pp. VII-XXX.

6. Carl Berger, *The Writing of Canadian History*, 2nd ed. (Toronto: University of Toronto Press, 1986), p. 218.

7. McKillop, "Editor's Introduction," p. XVII.

8. William Arthur Bishop, *The Courage of the Early Morning* (Toronto: McClelland & Stewart, 1965), p. 130.

9. H. Clifford Chadderton, *Hanging a Legend: The NFB's Shameful Attempt to Discredit Billy Bishop, VC* (Ottawa: The War Amps, 1985), pp. x, 51.

10. Ibid., p. 195.

11. Ibid., p. XI.

12. Anne Collins, "The Battle over 'The Valour and the Horror'," *Saturday Night*, vol. 108, no. 4 (May 1993), p. 74.

13. George Woodcock, *Canada and the Canadians* (Toronto: Macmillan of Canada, 1970), p. 319.

CHAPTER SIX: THE IDEOLOGY OF THE CANOE

1. Robert Bringhurst, *The Black Canoe* (Vancouver: Douglas & McIntyre, 1991), pp. 76-77.
2. W.L. Morton, *The Canadian Identity* (Toronto: University of Toronto Press, 2nd ed., 1972), p. 5; orig. pub. 1961.
3. John Murray Gibbon, *The Romance of the Canadian Canoe* (Toronto: The Ryerson Press, 1951), p. 1.
4. C.J. Taylor, *Negotiating the Past: The Making of Canada's National Historic Parks and Sites* (Montreal: McGill-Queen's University Press, 1990), p. 51.
5. John Marsh, "The Heritage of Peterborough Canoes," in Bruce Hodgins and Margaret Hobbs, eds., *Nastawgan* (Toronto: Betelgeuse Books, 1985), pp. 211-22; James Raffan, *Fire in the Bones: Bill Mason and the Canadian Canoeing Tradition* (Toronto: HarperCollins, 1996), p. 63; Kenneth G. Roberts and Philip Shackelton, *The Canoe: A History of the Craft from Panama to the Arctic* (Toronto: Macmillan, 1983), p. 259.
6. The best source on Camp Ahmek is C.A.M. Edwards, *Taylor Statten: A Biography* (Toronto: The Ryerson Press, 1960).
7. Pelham Edgar, *Across My Path* (Toronto: The Ryerson Press, 1952), p. 60.
8. F.B. Housser, *A Canadian Art Movement: The Story of the Group of Seven* (Toronto: Macmillan, 1926), p. 28.
9. Cited in Peter Mellen, *The Group of Seven* (Toronto: McClelland & Stewart, 1970), p. 59.
10. Housser, pp. 63, 156.
11. The history of the Group is thoroughly detailed in Reid, Mellen and most recently Charles C. Hill, *The Group of Seven: Art for a Nation* (Toronto: McClelland & Stewart, 1995).
12. John McLeish, *September Gale: A Study of Arthur Lismer of the Group of Seven* (Toronto: J.M. Dent and Sons, 1955), p. 44.
13. Lawren Harris, "The Story of the Group of Seven," in Joan Murray, *The Best of the Group of Seven* (Edmonton: Hurtig Publishers, 1984), p. 27.
14. Harold Town and David P. Silcox, *Tom Thomson: The Silence and the Storm* (Toronto: McClelland & Stewart, 1977), p. 24.
15. Harris, p. 27.

16. Dennis Reid, *The Group of Seven* (Ottawa: catalogue for an exhibition at the National Gallery of Canada, 14 June-8 Sept. 1970), p. 67.

17. Ibid.

18. Ibid., p. 70.

19. McLeish, p. 48.

20. Reid, p. 132.

21. Peter Mellen, *The Group of Seven* (Toronto: McClelland & Stewart, 1970), p. 99.

22. A. Y. Jackson, *A Painter's Country* (Toronto: Clarke, Irwin & Co., 1958), p. 64.

23. Housser, p. 145.

24. *Toronto Star*, 22 Dec. 1928; cited in Reid, p. 202.

25. Cited in Peter Larisey S.J., *Light for a Cold Land: Lawren Harris's Work and Life* (Toronto: Dundurn Press, 1993), p. 80.

26. Jackson, p. 56.

27. Citied in Reid, p. 33.

28. See Charles Hill, *The Group of Seven: Art for a Nation* (Toronto: McClelland & Stewart, 1995).

29. Lovat Dickson, *Wilderness Man* (Toronto: Macmillan, 1973), p. 239.

30. Grey Owl, *Tales of an Empty Cabin* (Toronto: Macmillan, 1936), p. VI.

31. Pierre Trudeau, *Memoirs* (Toronto: McClelland & Stewart, 1993), pp. 253-54.

32. Pierre Trudeau, "Exhaustion and Fulfilment: The Ascetic in a Canoe," in Borden Spears, ed., *Wilderness Canada* (Toronto: Clarke, Irwin & Co., 1970), p. 4.

33. Mason's life is recounted in Raffan, *Fire in the Bones: Bill Mason and the Canadian Canoeing Tradition* (Toronto: HarperCollins, 1996).

34. Stephen Leacock, *Literary Lapses* (Toronto: McClelland & Stewart, 1971; orig. pub. 1910), p. 121.

35. Northrop Frye, "Conclusion," in Carl Klinck, ed., *Literary History of Canada* (Toronto: University of Toronto Press, 1976), pp. 830-31.

36. Gaile McGregor, *The Wacousta Syndrome: Explorations in the Canadian Landscape* (Toronto: University of Toronto Press, 1985), p. 53.

37. Gerald Killan, *Protected Places: A History of Ontario's Provincial Parks System* (Toronto: Dundurn Press, 1993), p. 105.

38. E.T. Seton and Julia M. Seton, *The Gospel of the Redman* (Sante Fe, NM: Seton Village, 1963), p. 107; orig. pub. 1936 by Doubleday.

39. Transcript of "Perfect Machines: The Canoe." *Ideas* [radio program]. 23 May 1995. Produced by the Canadian Broadcasting Corporation, Toronto.

40. Arthur R. M. Lower, *Unconventional Voyages* (Toronto: The Ryerson Press, 1953), p. 24.

41. Cited in Patricia Jasen, *Wild Things: Nature, Culture and Tourism in Ontario, 1790-1914* (Toronto: University of Toronto Press, 1995), p. 117.

42. Trudeau, "Exhaustion and Fulfilment," p. 5.

43. William James, "The Quest Pattern and the Canoe Trip," in Hodgins and Hobbs, eds., *Nastawgan*, p. 13.

CHAPTER SEVEN: GREAT WHITE HOPE

1. W.L. Morton, *The Canadian Identity* (Toronto: University of Toronto Press, 1972), p. 4.

2. Ibid., p. 93.

3. Rudy Wiebe, *Playing Dead: A Contemplation Concerning the Arctic* (Edmonton: NeWest Publishers, 1989), p. 111.

4. S.D. Grant, "Myths of the North in the Canadian Ethos," *The Northern Review* (Summer/Winter 1989), p. 23.

5. Robert Fulford, "The Lesson of Canadian Geography," in Gerald Lynch and David Rampton, eds., *The Canadian Essay* (Toronto: Copp Clark Pittman, 1991), p. 280.

6. Carl Berger, *The Sense of Power* (Toronto: University of Toronto Press, 1970), pp. 49-77.

7. Carl Berger, "The True North Strong and Free," in Peter Russell, ed., *Nationalism in Canada* (Toronto: McGraw-Hill, 1966), pp. 4-14.

8. James Oliver Curwood, *Son of the Forests* (New York: Doubleday, Doran and Co., 1930), p. 76.

9. Ibid., p. 4.

10. Ibid., p. 219.

11. Peter Morris, *Embattled Shadows: A History of Canadian Cinema, 1895-1939* (Montreal: McGill-Queen's University Press, 1978), p. 104.

12. Margaret Hobbs, "Purposeful Wanderers: Late Nineteenth Century Travellers to the Barren Lands," in Bruce Hodgins and Margaret Hobbs, eds., *Nastawgan* (Toronto: Betelgeuse Books, 1985), pp. 57-82.

13. This discussion of Robert Service is based on James Mackay, *Robert Service, A Biography: Vagabond of Verse* (Edinburgh: Mainstream Publishing, 1995).

14. Cited in Louis-Edmond Hamelin, *About Canada: The Canadian North and its Conceptual Referents* (Ottawa: Canadian Studies Directorate, Dept. of the Secretary of State, 1988), p. 28.

15. Cited in William R. Hunt, *Stef* (Vancouver: University of British Columbia Press, 1986), p. 156.

16. Ibid., p. 153.

17. Ibid., p. 215.

18. Viljhalmur Stefansson, *The Northward Course of Empire* (London: Harrap, 1922), p. 19.

19. *Globe and Mail*, 13 Feb. 1958; cited in Denis Smith, *Rogue Tory: The Life of John G. Diefenbaker* (Toronto: Macfarlane, Walter and Ross, 1995), p. 256.

20. Pierre Berton, *The Mysterious North* (Toronto: McClelland & Stewart, rev. ed. 1989), p. 13; orig. pub. 1956.

21. Cited in Ann Davis, *The Logic of Ecstasy: Canadian Mystical Painting 1920-40* (Toronto: University of Toronto Press, 1992), p. 65.

22. Ibid., p. 66.

23. Ann Fienup-Riordan, *Freeze Frame: Alaska Eskimos in the Movies* (Seattle: University of Washington Press, 1995), p. 47.

24. Cited in Kevin Brownlow, *The War, the West and the Wilderness* (New York: Alfred A. Knopf, 1979), p. 476. For a general discussion of this attitude, see my *The Imaginary Indian: The Image of the Indian in Canadian Culture* (Vancouver: Arsenal Pulp Press, 1992).

25. Hugh Brody, *The People's Land: Eskimos and Whites in the Eastern Arctic* (Markham: Penguin Books Canada, 1975), p. 81.

26. Roald Amundsen, *The North West Passage*, vol. 2 (New York: E.P. Dutton, 1908), p. 48.

27. Described in W. Gillies Ross, "Canadian Sovereignty in the Arctic: The Neptune Expedition of 1903-04," *Arctic*, vol. 29, no. 2 (June 1976), pp. 100-01.

28. A.Y. Jackson, *A Painter's Country* (Toronto: Clarke, Irwin & Co., 1958), p. 116.

29. Cited in Richard Diubaldo, *The Government of Canada and the Inuit, 1900-1967* (Ottawa: Indian and Northern Affairs Canada, 1985), p. 109.

30. Ken Dryden and Roy MacGregor, *Home Game: Hockey and Life in Canada* (Toronto: McClelland & Stewart, 1989), p. 101.

31. Richard Gruneau and David Whitson, *Hockey Night in Canada: Sport, Identity and Cultural Politics* (Toronto: Garamond Press, 1993), p. 13.

32. Bruce Kidd and John Macfarlane, *The Death of Hockey* (Toronto: new press, 1972), p. 4.

33. David Adams Richards, *Hockey Dreams: Memories of a Man Who Couldn't Play* (Toronto: Doubleday Canada, 1996), p. 73.

34. Gruneau and Whitson, p. 101.

35. Frank Underhill, "False Hair on the Chest," *Saturday Night*, vol. 51, no. 48 (3 Oct. 1936).

36. Thomas Berger, *Northern Frontier, Northern Homeland: The Report of the Mackenzie Valley Pipeline Inquiry, vol. 1* (Ottawa: Ministry of Supply and Services Canada, 1977), p. 1.

37. Andre Siegfried, *Canada: An International Power* (London: Jonathan Cape, rev. ed. 1949), p. 25; orig. pub. 1937.

38. Berton, *The Mysterious North*, p. 373.

39. Farley Mowat, *Canada North Now: The Great Betrayal* (Toronto: McClelland & Stewart, 1976), p. 9.

CONCLUSION: HISTORY IN AN AGE OF ANXIETY

1. Gwyn, *Nationalism Without Walls*, p. 254.

Photo Sources

1. Canadian Broadcasting Corporation (Still Photo Collection) RM.5B303.

2. Canadian Pacific Archives Image no. NS.960A.

3. National Archives of Canada C14115.

4. Canadian Pacific Archives Image no. NS.20010.

5. Canadian Pacific Archives Image no. NS.7190.

6. Glenbow Archives, Calgary, Alberta NA-4035-87.

7. Canadian Pacific Archives Image no. A.636.

8. Provincial Archives of Manitoba N2743.

9. *Toronto Star* 016120-9000.

10. Glenbow Archives, Calgary, Alberta NA-2676-6.

11. National Archives of Canada C12248.

12. National Archives of Canada C5456.

13. Confederation Centre of the Arts, Charlottetown.

14. National Archives of Canada C85086.

15. Glenbow Archives, Calgary, Alberta NA-967-26.

16. Whyte Museum of the Canadian Rockies, Banff, Alberta V689/NA66-1846.

17. Canadian Pacific Archives Image no. A.6187.

18. The Beaverbrook Canadian Foundation, Beaverbrook Art Gallery.

19. Canadian Museum of Civilization, image number J-4840.

20. National Archives of Canada c1350.

21. Canadian War Museum.

22. National Archives of Canada pa1651.

23. Tom Abrahamson.

24. McMichael Canadian Art Collection Archives.

25. Art Gallery of Ontario, Toronto n-10980#2.

26. Archives of Ontario s14459.

27. Jean Demers, 1993.

28. Royal British Columbia Museum pn2790.

29. National Archives of Canada pa185770.

30. BC Hydro.

31. Whyte Museum of the Canadian Rockies, Banff, Alberta v90 na66-2121.

32. National Archives of Canada c86406.

33. McMichael Canadian Art Collection 1971.17.

Sources Consulted

MANUSCRIPTS

National Archives of Canada, Ottawa:
  Robert Borden Papers, MG26
  George Foster Papers, MG27 II D7
  Newton Rowell Papers, MG27 II D13
  Thomas White Papers, MG27 II D18

GOVERNMENT RECORDS

National Archives of Canada, Ottawa:
  Dept. of the Chief Press Censor, RG6 E
  Dept. of Immigration, RG76
  Dept. of Justice, RG13
  Dept. of Labour, RG27
  Dept. of the Militia, RG24 RCMP, RG18

BOOKS AND ARTICLES

Akenson, Donald Harman. "The Historiography of English-Speaking Canada and the Concept of Diaspora: A Sceptical Appreciation." *Canadian Historical Review*, vol. LXXVI, no. 3 (Sept. 1995): 377-409.

Altmeyer, George. "Three Ideas of Nature in Canada, 1893-1914." *Journal of Canadian Studies*, vol. 11, no. 3 (Aug 1976): 21-36.

Amundsen, Roald. *The North West Passage*. 2 vols. New York: E.P. Dutton, 1908.

Anderson, Benedict. *Imagined Communities: Reflections on the Origin and Spread of Nationalism*. London: Verson, rev. ed. 1991; orig. pub. 1983.

Atwood, Margaret. *Survival: A Thematic Guide to Canadian Literature*. Toronto: Anansi, 1972.

_____. *Strange Things: The Malevolent North in Canadian Literature*. Oxford: Clarendon Press, 1995.

Avery, Donald. "The Radical Alien and the Winnipeg General Strike of 1919." In *The West and the Nation*, Carl Berger and Ramsay Cook, eds. Toronto: McClelland & Stewart, 1976: 209-231.

Avery, Donald, Donna Goodman, Ronald Kirbyson and J. Richard Young. *Canada in a North American Perspective*. Toronto: Prentice-Hall, 1989.

Barbeau, Marius. *Cornelius Krieghoff: Pioneer Painter of North America*. Toronto: The Macmillan Co. of Canada, 1934.

Bell, David V.J. *The Roots of Disunity: A Study of Canadian Political Culture*. Toronto: Oxford University Press, 1992; orig. pub. 1979.

Bercuson, David J. *Confrontation at Winnipeg*. Montreal: McGill-Queen's University Press, 1974.

_____. *Fools and Wise Men: The Rise and Fall of the One Big Union*. Toronto: McGraw-Hill Ryerson, 1978.

Bercuson, David J. and S.F. Wise, eds. *The Valour and the Horror Revisited*. Montreal: McGill-Queen's University Press, 1994.

Berger, Carl. "The True North Strong and Free." In *Nationalism in Canada*, Peter Russell, ed. Toronto: McGraw-Hill, 1966: 4-14.

_____. *The Sense of Power:Studies in the Ideas of Canadian Imperialism, 1867-1914*. Toronto: University of Toronto Press, 1970.

_____. *The Writing of Canadian History*. Toronto: University of Toronto Press, 2nd ed. 1986; orig. pub. 1976.

Berger, Thomas. *Northern Frontier, Northern Homeland*, 2 vols. Ottawa: Supply and Services Canada, 1977.

Berton, Pierre. *The Mysterious North*. Toronto: McClelland & Stewart, 1989; orig. pub. 1956.

_____. *Klondike*. Toronto: McClelland & Stewart, 1958.

_____. *The Great Railway, 1871-1881*. Toronto: McClelland & Stewart, 1970.

_____. *Hollywood's Canada*. Toronto: McClelland & Stewart, 1975.

_____. *Why We Act Like Canadians*. Toronto: McClelland & Stewart, 1982.

_____. *The Great Depression, 1929-1939*. Toronto: McClelland & Stewart, 1990.

Betcherman, Lita-Rose. *The Little Band*. Ottawa: Deneau, 1982.

Bibby, Reginald. *The Bibby Report: Social Trends Canadian Style*. Toronto: Stoddart, 1995.

Bishop, William Arthur. *The Courage of the Early Morning*. Toronto: McClelland & Stewart, 1965.

Bliss, Michael. *Banting: A Biography*. Toronto: McClelland & Stewart, 1984.

_____. "Privatizing the Mind: The Sundering of Canadian History, the Sundering of Canada." *Journal of Canadian Studies*, vol. 26, no. 4 (Winter 1991/92): 5-17.

Bringhurst, Robert. *The Black Canoe*. Vancouver: Douglas & McIntyre, 1991.

Brody, Hugh. *The People's Land*. Markham, Ont.: Penguin Books Canada, 1975.

Brown, George W. *Building the Canadian Nation*. Toronto: J.M. Dent & Sons, 1942.

_____, Eleanor Harman and Marsh Jeanneret. *Canada in North America to 1800*. Toronto: Copp Clark Publishing, 1960.

_____. *Canada in North America, 1800-1901*. Toronto: Copp Clark, 1961.

Brownlow, Kevin. *The War, the West and the Wilderness*. New York: Alfred A. Knopf, 1979.

Bryce, George. *A Short History of the Canadian People*. Toronto: The Ryerson Press, rev. ed. 1915; orig. pub. 1887.

Bumstead, J.M. *The Winnipeg General Strike of 1919: An Illustrated History*. Winnipeg: Watson and Dwyer, 1994.

Burt, A.L. *The Romance of Canada: A History*. Toronto: W.J. Gage, 1937.

Calkin, John B. *A History of the Dominion of Canada*. Halifax: A & W MacKinlay, 1898.

Canada and Newfoundland Education Assoc. "Report of the Committee for the Study of Canadian History Textbooks." In *Canadian Education*, vol. 1, no. 1 (Oct 1945): 3-34.

Carpenter, Carole Henderson. *Many Voices: A Study of Folklore Activities in Canada and their Role in Canadian Culture*. Ottawa: National Museum of Man, Canadian Centre for Folk Culture Studies Paper #26, 1979.

Chadderton, H. Clifford. *Hanging a Legend: The NFB's Shameful Attempt to Discredit Billy Bishop, VC*. Ottawa: War Amps of Canada, 1985.

Chafe, J.W. and A.R.M. Lower. *Canada: A Nation and How it Came to Be*. Toronto: Longmans, Green & Co., 1948.

Chaiton, Alf and Neil McDonald, eds. *Canadian Schools and Canadian Identity*. Toronto: Gage Educational Publishing, 1977.

Chambers, Capt. Ernest J. *The Royal North-West Mounted Police: A Corps History*. Montreal: Mortimer Press, 1906.

Christopher, James R. *The North Americans*. Toronto: Oxford University Press, 1988.

Clement, W.H.P. *The History of the Dominion of Canada*. Toronto: William Briggs, 1898.

Coates, Kenneth. *Canada's Colonies: A History of the Yukon and Northwest Territories.* Toronto: James Lorimer & Co.,1985.

Cole, Douglas. "Artists, Patrons and Public: An Enquiry into the Success of the Group of Seven." *Journal of Canadian Studies,* vol. 13, no. 2 (Summer 1978): 69-78.

Collins, Anne. "The Battle Over 'The Valour and the Horror'." *Saturday Night,* vol. 108, no. 4 (May 1993): 44-49, 72-76.

Connor, Ralph. *Corporal Cameron of the North West Mounted Police.* Toronto: The Westminster Co. Ltd., 1912.

_____. *The Patrol of the Sun Dance Trail.* Toronto: The Westminster Co. Ltd., 1914.

Cook, Ramsay. "Landscape Painting and National Sentiment in Canada." *The Maple Leaf Forever.* Toronto: Macmillan of Canada, rev. ed. 1977: 158-179.

_____. *Canada, Quebec and the Uses of Nationalism.* Toronto: McClelland & Stewart, 2nd ed. 1995; orig. pub. 1986.

Craig, Terrence. *Racial Attitudes in English-Canadian Fiction, 1905-1980.* Waterloo, Ont.: Wilfrid Laurier University Press, 1987.

Cruise, David and Alison Griffiths. *Lords of the Line.* Toronto: Viking Penguin, 1988.

Curwood, James Oliver. *Son of the Forests.* New York: Doubleday, Doran & Co., 1930.

Davey, Frank. *From There to Here.* Erin, Ont.: Press Porcépic, 1974.

Davis, Ann. *The Logic of Ecstasy: Canadian Mystical Painting, 1920-40.* Toronto: University of Toronto Press, 1992.

Davis, Bob. *Whatever Happened to High School History?* Toronto: James Lorimer, 1995.

Davis, Jo, ed. *Not a Sentimental Journey.* Goderich, Ont.: Gunbyfield Publishing, 1990.

Deir, Elspeth, Paul Deir and Keith Hubbard. *Canada: Years of Challenge to 1814.* Toronto: Holt, Rinehart & Winston, 1981.

Dempsey, Hugh A. "Catching the Sunbeams: An Inventory of Canadian Prairie Photographers to 1900." Unpublished paper prepared for the Glenbow Archives, Calgary, 1993.

Denny, Sir Cecil. *The Law Marches West.* Toronto: J.M. Dent & Sons Ltd., 1939.

Dewar, Ken. "The Road to Happiness: Canadian History in Public Schools." *This Magazine is About Schools* (Fall 1972): 102-127.

Dickson, Lovat. *Wilderness Man*. Toronto: Macmillan, 1973.

Diubaldo, Richard. *Stefansson and the Canadian Arctic*. Montreal: McGill-Queen's University Press, 1978.

_____. *The Government of Canada and the Inuit, 1900-1967*. Ottawa: Indian and Northern Affairs, 1985.

Donkin, John G. *Trooper and Redskin in the Far North-West*. London: Sampson Low, Marston, Searle and Rivington, 1889.

Dorland, Arthur G. *Our Canada*. Toronto: Copp Clark, 1949.

Draper, Theodore. *The Roots of American Communism*. New York: The Viking Press, 1957.

Dryden, Ken and Roy MacGregor. *Home Game: Hockey and Life in Canada*. Toronto: McClelland & Stewart, 1989.

Dubro, James and Robin Rowland. *Undercover*. Toronto: Octopus Publishing, 1991.

Dufour, Christian. *A Canadian Challenge*. Lantzville, B.C.: Oolichan Books and the Institute for Research on Public Policy, 1990.

Duncan, David. *The Story of the Canadian People*. Toronto: Morang Educational Co., 1904.

Duval, Paul. *The Tangled Garden: The Art of J.E.H. Macdonald*. Toronto: Cerebrus Publishing/Prentice Hall, 1978.

Eaton, Diane and Garfield Newman. *Canada: A Nation Unfolding*. Toronto: McGraw-Hill Ryerson, 1994.

Edgar, Pelham. *Across My Path*. Toronto: The Ryerson Press, 1952.

Edwards, C.A.M. *Taylor Statten: A Biography*. Toronto: The Ryerson Press, 1960.

Entz, W. "The Suppression of the German Language Press in September 1918." *Canadian Ethnic Studies*, vol. 8, no. 2 (1976): 56-70.

Evans, Simon. *Prince Charming Goes West: The Story of the E.P. Ranch*. Calgary: University of Calgary Press, 1993.

Fienup-Riordan, Ann. *Eskimo Essays*. New Brunswick: Rutgers University Press, 1990.

_____. *Freeze Frame: Alaska Eskimos in the Movies*. Seattle: University of Washington Press, 1995.

Fitzgerald, Frances. *America Revised*. Boston: Atlantic/Little, Brown, 1979.

Foster, Kate. *Our Canadian Mosaic*. Toronto: Dominion Council, YWCA, 1926.

Francis, Daniel. *The Imaginary Indian: The Image of the Indian in Canadian Culture*. Vancouver: Arsenal Pulp Press, 1992.

Fraser, W.A. "Soldier Police of the Canadian Northwest." *The Canadian Magazine*, vol. 14, no. 4 (Feb. 1900): 362-374.

Friesen, Gerald. "'Yours in Revolt': The Socialist Party of Canada and the Western Canadian Labour Movement." *Labour/Le Travailleur*, no. 1 (1976): 139-157.

Fulford, Robert. "On Myth-making." *Saturday Night* (Sept. 1969): 15-16.

_____. "The Lesson of Canadian Geography." In *The Canadian Essay*, Gerald Lynch and David Rampton, eds. Toronto: Copp Clark Pitman, 1991.

_____. "A Post-Modern Dominion: The Changing Nature of Canadian Citizenship." In *Belonging: The Meaning and Future of Canadian Citizenship*, William Kaplan, ed. Montreal: McGill-Queen's University Press, 1993: 104-19.

_____. "Regrouping the Group." *Canadian Art* (Fall 1995): 68-77.

Garrod, Stan, Fred McFadden and Rosemary Neering. *Canada, Growth of a Nation*. Toronto: Fitzhenry & Whiteside, 1980.

Gibbon, John Murray. *Steel of Empire: The Romantic History of the Canadian Pacific, the Northwest Passage of Today*. New York: The Bobbs-Merrill Co., 1935.

_____. *Canadian Mosaic: The Making of a Northern Nation*. Toronto: McClelland & Stewart, 1938.

_____. *The Romance of the Canadian Canoe*. Toronto: Ryerson Press, 1951.

Graham, Ronald. *The French Quarter*. Toronto: Macfarlane Walter and Ross, 1992.

Grant, S.D. "Myths of the North in the Canadian Ethos." *The Northern Review* (Summer/Winter 1989): 15-41.

Grant, W.L. *History of Canada*. Toronto: T. Eaton Co., 1914.

Grey Owl. *Tales of an Empty Cabin*. Toronto: Macmillan, 1936.

Griffin, Frederick. *Variety Show*. Toronto: Macmillan, 1936.

Gruneau, Richard and David Whitson. *Hockey Night in Canada: Sport, Identity and Cultural Politics*. Toronto: Garamond Press, 1993.

Gwyn, Richard. *Nationalism Without Walls: The Unbearable Lightness of Being Canadian*. Toronto: McClelland & Stewart, 1995.

Ham, George H. *Reminiscences of a Raconteur*. Toronto: The Musson Book Co., 1921.

Hamelin, Louis-Edmond. *About Canada: The Canadian North and its Conceptual Referents*. Ottawa: Canadian Studies Directorate, Dept. of the Secretary of State, 1988.

Handler, Richard. *Nationalism and the Politics of Culture in Quebec*. Madison, Wisc.: University of Wisconsin Press, 1988.

Harper, J. Russell. *Krieghoff*. Toronto: University of Toronto Press, 1979.

Harrison, Dick. *Unnamed Country: The Struggle for a Canadian Prairie Fiction.* Edmonton: University of Alberta Press, 1977.

Hart, E.J. *The Selling of Canada.* Banff: Altitude Books, 1983.

Hay, G.U. *Public School History of Canada.* Toronto: Copp Clark Co., 1902.

Haydon, A.L. *The Riders of the Plains: A Record of the Royal North-West Mounted Police of Canada, 1873-1910.* Toronto: Copp Clark Co., 1912.

Hayward, Victoria. *Romantic Canada.* Toronto: The Macmillan Co., 1922.

Hill, Charles C. *The Group of Seven: Art for a Nation.* Toronto: McClelland & Stewart, 1995.

Hodgetts, A.B. *What Culture? What Heritage? A Study of Civic Education in Canada.* Toronto: Ontario Institute for Studies in Education, 1968.

Hodgins, Bruce and Margaret Hobbs, eds. *Nastawgan.* Toronto: Betelgeuse Books, 1985.

Hodgins, Bruce and Jamie Benidickson. *The Temagami Experience: Recreation, Resources and Aboriginal Rights in the Northern Ontario Wilderness.* Toronto: University of Toronto Press, 1989.

Hodgins, J. George. *A History of Canada and of the Other British Provinces in North America.* Montreal: John Lovell, 1866.

Hopkins, J. Castell. *Canadian Annual Review of Public Affairs.* Toronto: Annual Review Publishing, 1908.

_____. *The Story of Our Country: A History of Canada for 400 Years.* Toronto: John C. Winston, 1912.

Horrall, S.W. "Sir John A. Macdonald and the Mounted Police Force for the Northwest Territories." *Canadian Historical Review*, vol. 53, no. 2 (June 1972): 179-200.

_____. "The Royal North-West Mounted Police and Labour Unrest in Western Canada, 1919." *Canadian Historical Review*, vol. LXI, no. 2 (June 1980): 169-190.

Housser, F.B. *A Canadian Art Movement: The Story of the Group of Seven.* Toronto: Macmillan, 1926.

Houston, Susan and Alison Prentice. *Schooling and Scholars in Nineteenth-Century Ontario.* Toronto: University of Toronto Press, 1988.

Humphries, Charles W. "The Banning of a Book in British Columbia." *BC Studies*, no. 1 (Winter 1968/69): 1-12.

Hunt, William R. *Stef.* Vancouver: University of British Columbia Press, 1986.

Hutcheon, Linda. *The Canadian Postmodern*. Toronto: Oxford University Press, 1988.

_____. *Splitting Images: Contemporary Canadian Issues*. Toronto: Oxford University Press, 1991.

Ignatieff, Michael. *Blood and Belonging: Journey into the New Nationalism*. Toronto: Viking Penguin, 1993.

Jackson, A.Y. *A Painter's Country*. Toronto: Clarke, Irwin & Co., 1958.

Jasen, Patricia. *Wild Things: Nature, Culture and Tourism In Ontario, 1790-1914*. Toronto: University of Toronto Press, 1995.

Jennings, Francis. "Francis Parkman: A Brahmin among Untouchables." *William and Mary Quarterly*, vol. 42, no. 3 (July 1985): 305-328.

Kammen, Michael. *Mystic Chords of Memory: The Transformation of Tradition in American Culture*. New York: Knopf, 1991.

Kaplan, William, ed. *Belonging: The Meaning and Future of Canadian Citizenship*. Montreal: McGill-Queen's University Press, 1993.

Kealey, Gregory S. "1919: The Canadian Labour Revolt." *Labour/Le Travail*, no. 13 (Spring 1984): 11-44.

_____. "The Surveillance State: The Origins of Domestic Intelligence and Counter-Subversion in Canada, 1914-21." *Intelligence and National Security*, vol. 7, no. 3 (July 1992): 179-210.

Kidd, Bruce and John Macfarlane. *The Death of Hockey*. Toronto: new press, 1972.

Killan, Gerald. *Protected Places: A History of Ontario's Provincial Parks System*. Toronto: Dundurn Press, 1993.

Klinck, Carl F. *Literary History of Canada*. Toronto: University of Toronto Press, 1965.

Kroetsch, Robert. "Canada is a Poem." In *Divided We Stand*, Gary Geddes, ed. Toronto: Peter Martin Associates, 1977.

_____. *The Lovely Treachery of Words*. Toronto: Oxford University Press, 1989.

Lamb, W. Kaye. *History of the Canadian Pacific Railway*. New York: Macmillan Pub., 1977.

Laloux-Jain, Genevieve. *Les Manuels d'Histoire du Canada au Québec et en Ontario, 1867-1914*. Québec: Les Presses de l'Universite Laval, 1973.

Larisey, Peter, S.J. *Light for a Cold Land: Lawren Harris's Work and Life*. Toronto: Dundurn Press, 1993.

Laut, Agnes C. *Canada: The Empire of the North*. Toronto: William Briggs, 1909.

Leacock, Stephen. *Literary Lapses*. Toronto: McClelland & Stewart, 1957; orig. pub. 1910.

_____. *Canada: The Foundation of its Future*. Montreal: The House of Seagram, 1941.

Loewen, James W. *Lies My Teacher Told Me: Everything Your American History Textbook Got Wrong*. New York: The New Press, 1995.

Lower, Arthur R.M. *Unconventional Voyages*. Toronto: The Ryerson Press, 1953.

Lyons, J.B. *William Henry Drummond: Poet in Patois*. Toronto: Fitzhenry & Whiteside, 1994.

McArthur, Duncan. *History of Canada for High Schools*. Toronto: The Educational Book Co., 1927.

MacBeth, R.G. *The Romance of the Canadian Pacific Railway*. Toronto: The Ryerson Press, 1924.

_____. *Policing the Plains*. Toronto: The Ryerson Press, 1931.

McDiarmid, Garnet and David Pratt. *Teaching Prejudice*. Toronto: Ontario Institute for Studies in Education, Curriculum Series 12, 1971.

MacDonnell, Tom. *Daylight Upon Magic: The Royal Tour of Canada 1939*. Toronto: Macmillan of Canada, 1989.

McFadden, Fred, Don Quinlan, Rick Life and Mary Jane Pickup. *Canada: The Twentieth Century*. Toronto: Fitzhenry & Whiteside, rev. ed. 1990.

McGregor, Gaile. *The Wacousta Syndrome: Explorations in the Canadian Langscape*. Toronto: University of Toronto Press, 1985.

McIlwraith, J.N. *The Children's Study of Canada*. London: Fisher Unwin, 1899.

Mackay, James. *Robert Service, A Biography: Vagabond of Verse*. Edinburgh: Mainstream Publishers, 1995.

McKay, Ian. "History and the Tourist Gaze: The Politics of Commemoration in Nova Scotia, 1935-1964." *Acadiensis*, vol. 22, no. 2 (Spring 1993): 102-138.

_____. *The Quest of the Folk: Antimodernism and Cultural Selection in Twentieth Century Nova Scotia*. Montreal: McGill-Queen's University Press, 1994.

McKee, Bill and Georgeen Klassen. *Trail of Iron: The CPR and the Birth of the West, 1880-1930*. Vancouver: Douglas & McIntyre and the Glenbow-Alberta Institute, 1983.

McKillop, A.B., ed. *A Critical Spirit: The Thought of William Dawson LeSueur*. Toronto: McClelland & Stewart, 1977.

_____, ed. *William Lyon Mackenzie: A Reinterpretation*. Toronto: The Macmillan Co. of Canada, 1979.

McLeish, John. *September Gale: A Study of Arthur Lismer of the Group of Seven.* Toronto: J.M. Dent and Sons, 1955.

Macleod, R.C. *The NWMP and Law Enforcement, 1873-1905.* Toronto: University of Toronto Press, 1976.

Marcus, Alan Rudolph. *Relocating Eden: The Image and Politics of Inuit Exile in the Canadian Arctic.* Hanover, N.H.: University Press of New England, 1995.

Marsh, E.L. *Where the Buffalo Roam.* Toronto: The Macmillan Co. of Canada, 1923.

Marty, Sid. *Leaning on the Wind.* Toronto: HarperCollins, 1995.

Mellen, Peter. *The Group of Seven.* Toronto: McClelland & Stewart, 1970.

Miles, Henry H. *The Child's History of Canada.* Montreal: William Dawson, 1910; orig. pub. 1870.

Moir, John S. and D.M.L. Farr. *The Canadian Experience.* Toronto: The Ryerson Press, 1969.

Morris, Peter. *Embattled Shadows: A History of Canadian Cinema, 1895-1939.* Montreal: McGill-Queen's University Press, 1978.

Morton, W.L. *The Canadian Identity.* Toronto: University of Toronto Press, 1972.

Mowat, Farley. *Canada North Now: The Great Betrayal.* Toronto: McClelland & Stewart, 1976.

Murray, Joan. *The Best of the Group of Seven.* Edmonton: Hurtig Publishers, 1984.

Murray, Robert K. *Red Scare: A Study in National Hysteria, 1919-20.* Minneapolis: University of Minnesota Press, 1955.

Newman, Peter C. *Merchant Princes.* Toronto: Viking Penguin, 1991.

Nowry, Laurence. *Marius Barbeau: Man of Mana.* Toronto: NC Press, 1995.

Osborne, Brian S. "Interpreting a nation's identity: artists asa creators of national consciousness." In *Ideology and Landscape in Historical Perspective,* Alan R.H. Baker and Gideon Biger, eds. Cambridge: Cambridge University Press, 1992: 230-254.

Osborne, Kenneth. *"Hard-working, Temperate and Peaceable"—The Portrayal of Workers in Canadian History Textbooks.* Winnipeg: University of Manitoba, Monographs in Education IV, 1980.

_____. "'To the Schools We Must Look for Good Canadians': Developments in the Teaching of History in Schools Since 1960." *Journal of Canadian Studies,* vol. 22, no. 3 (Fall 1987): 104-126.

_____. *Educating Citizens: A Democratic Socialist Agenda for Canadian Education.* Toronto: Our Schools/Our Selves Education Foundation, 1988.

_____. "'I'm Not Going to Think How Cabot Discovered Newfoundland

When I'm Doing My Job': The Status of History in Canadian High Schools."
Unpublished paper presented to the Annual Meeting of the Canadian Historical
Assoc., Calgary (June 1994).

Owram, Doug. *Promise of Eden: The Canadian Expansionist Movement and the Idea of
the West, 1856-1900*. Toronto: University of Toronto Press, 1980.

_____. "The Myth of Louis Riel." *Canadian Historical Review*, vol. LXIII, no.
3 (Sept.1982): 315-336.

Parkman, Francis. *The Jesuits in North America*. Boston: Little, Brown & Co., 1963;
orig. pub. 1867.

_____. *The Old Regime in Canada*. Boston: Little, Brown & Co., 1874.

Parvin, Viola E. *Authorization of Textbooks for the Schools of Ontario, 1846-1950*.
Toronto: University of Toronto Press, 1965.

Pitt, David G. *E.J. Pratt: The Master Years, 1927-1964*. Toronto: University of
Toronto Press, 1987.

Postman, Neil. *The End of Education*. New York: Alfred A. Knopf, 1995.

Powe, B.W. *A Tremendous Canada of Light*. Toronto: Coach House Press, 1993.

Pringle, Allan. "William Cornelius Van Horne: Art Director, Canadian Pacific
Railway." *Journal of Canadian Art History*, vol. 8, no. 1 (1984): 50-79.

Raffan, James. *Fire in the Bones: Bill Mason and the Canadian Canoeing Tradition*.
Toronto: HarperCollins, 1996.

_____ and Bert Horwood, eds. *Canexus: the Canoe in Canadian Culture*.
Toronto: Betelgeuse Books, 1988.

Reeve, G.J. and R.O. MacFarlane. *The Canadian Pageant*. Toronto: Clarke, Irwin
& Co., 1948.

Reid, Dennis. *The Group of Seven*. Ottawa: catalogue for exhibition at the National
Gallery of Canada, 19 June-8 Sept. 1970.

_____. *Our Own Country Canada*. Ottawa: National Gallery of Canada, 1979.

Richards, David Adams. *Hockey Dreams: Memories of a Man Who Couldn't Play*.
Toronto: Doubleday Canada, 1996.

Roberts, Charles G.D. *A History of Canada for High Schools and Academies*. Toronto:
Morang Educational Co. Ltd., 1897.

Roberts, Kenneth G. and Philip Shackleton. *The Canoe: A History of the Craft from
Panama to the Arctic*. Toronto: Macmillan of Canada, 1983.

Ross, W. Gillies. "Canadian Sovereignty in the Arctic: The Neptune Expedition
of 1903-04." *Arctic*, vol. 29, no. 2 (June 1976): 87-104.

Rotha, Paul. *Robert J. Flaherty: A Biography*. Philadelphia: University of Pennsylvania Press, 1983.

Said, Edward W. *Culture and Imperialism*. New York: Alfred A. Knopf, 1993.

Sallot, Jeff. *Nobody Said No: The Real Story About How the Mounties Always Get Their Man*. Toronto: James Lorimer, 1979.

Sawatsky, John. *Men in the Shadows*. Toronto: Doubleday Canada, 1980.

Scully, Angus, John Bebbington, Rosemary Evans and Carol Wilson. *Canada Through Time, Books One and Two*. Toronto: Prentice Hall, 1992-93.

Seton, E.T. and Julia M. Seton. *The Gospel of the Redman*. Sante Fe, N.M.: Seton Village, 1963; orig. pub. 1936.

Siegfried, Andre. *The Race Question in Canada*. London: Eveleigh Nash, 1907.

_____. *Canada: An International Power*. London: Jonathan Cape, rev. ed. 1949; orig. pub. 1937.

Simpson, Jeffrey. *Faultlines*. Toronto: McClelland & Stewart, 1993.

Sladen, Douglas. *On the Cars and Off*. London: Ward, Lock & Bowden Ltd., 1895.

Smith, Donald B. *Le Sauvage: The Native People in Quebec Historical Writing on the Heroic Period (1534-1663)*. Ottawa: National Museum of Man, Mercury Series, 1974.

_____. *From the Land of Shadows: The Making of Grey Owl*. Saskatoon: Western Producer Prairie Books, 1990.

Stamp, Robert M. "Empire Day in the schools of Ontario: the training of young imperialists." *Journal of Canadian Studies*, vol. 8, no. 3 (Aug. 1973): 32-42.

_____. *The Schools of Ontario, 1876-1976*. Toronto: University of Toronto Press, 1982.

_____. "Steel of Empire: Royal Tours and the CPR." In *The CPR West*, Hugh Dempsey, ed. Vancouver: Douglas & McIntyre, 1984: 275-290.

_____. *Kings, Queens and Canadians*. Toronto: Fitzhenry & Whiteside, 1987.

Steele, Col. S.B. *Forty Years in Canada*. New York: Dodd, Mead & Co., 1915.

Stefansson, Viljhalmur. *The Northward Course of Empire*. London: Harrap, 1922.

Stewart, Roderick and Neil McLean. *Forming a Nation, Book One*. Toronto: Gage Publishing, 1977.

Story, Norah. *The Oxford Companion to Canadian History and Literature*. Toronto: Oxford University Press, 1967.

Strong-Boag, Veronica. "Contested Space: The Politics of Canadian Memory." *Journal of the Canadian Historical Association*, vol. 5 (1994): 3-17.

Tait, George E. *Breastplate and Buckskin: A Story of Exploration and Discovery in the Americas.* Toronto: The Ryerson Press, 1953.

_____. *Fair Domain: The Story of Canada from Earliest Times to 1800.* Toronto: Ryerson, 1960.

Taylor, C. James. *Negotiating the Past: The Making of Canada's National Historic Parks and Sites.* Montreal: McGill-Queen's University Press, 1990.

Taylor, M. Brook. *Promoters, Patriots and Partisans: Historiography in Nineteenth-Century English Canada.* Toronto: University of Toronto Press, 1989.

Town, Harold and David P. Silcox. *Tom Thomson: The Silence and the Storm.* Toronto: McClelland & Stewart, 1977.

Toye, William, ed. *The Oxford Companion to Canadian Literature.* Toronto: Oxford University Press, 1983.

Trofimenkoff, Susan Mann. *The Dream of Nation.* Toronto: Gage, 1983.

Trudeau, Pierre Elliott. "Exhaustion and Fulfilment: The Ascetic in a Canoe." In *Wilderness Canada*, Borden Spears, ed. Toronto: Clarke, Irwin & Co., 1970.

_____. *Memoirs.* Toronto: McClelland & Stewart, 1993.

Trudel, Marcel and Genevieve Jain. *Canadian History Textbooks: A Comparative Study.* Ottawa: Studies of the Royal Commission on Bilingualism and Biculturalism #5, Queen's Printer, 1970.

Underhill, Frank H. "False Hair on the Chest." *Saturday Night*, vol. 51, no. 48 (3 Oct. 1936).

Urry, John. *The Tourist Gaze: Leisure and Travel in Contemporary Societies.* London: Sage Publications, 1990.

Vance, Jonathan F. *Death So Noble: Memory, Meaning, and the First World War.* Vancouver: UBC Press, 1997.

Vincent, Sylvie and Bernard Arcand. *L'image de l'Amerindien dans les manuels scolaires du Québec.* Montréal: Editions Hurtubise HMH, 1979.

Vipond, Mary. "A Canadian Hero of the 1920s: Dr. Frederick G. Banting." *Canadian Historical Review*, vol. LXIII, no. 4 (Dec.1982): 461-486.

Wade, Mason. *Francis Parkman: Heroic Historian.* New York: Viking Press, 1972; orig. pub. 1942.

Walden, Keith. *Visions of Order.* Toronto: Butterworths, 1982.

Walker, James W. St. G. "The Indian in Canadian Historical Writing." Canadian Historical Association, *Historical Papers* (1971): 21-47.

Weaver, Emily P. *A Canadian History for Boys and Girls.* Toronto: William Briggs, the Copp Clark Co., 1900.

Whitaker, Reg and Gary Marcuse. *Cold War Canada: The Making of a National Insecurity State, 1945-57*. Toronto: University of Toronto Press, 1994.

Wiebe, Rudy. *Playing Dead: A Contemplation Concerning the Arctic*. Edmonton: NeWest Publishers, 1989.

Wilden, Tony. *The Imaginary Canadian*. Vancouver: Pulp Press, 1980.

Willows, Gerald C. and Stewart Richmond. *Canada: Colony to Centennial*. Toronto: McGraw Hill, 1970.

Winks, Robin. *The Relevance of Canadian History*. Toronto: Macmillan of Canada, 1979.

Withrow, William H. *A History of Canada for the Use of Schools and General Readers*. Toronto: Copp Clark & Co., 1876.

Woodcock, George. *Canada and the Canadians*. Toronto: Macmillan of Canada, 1970.

Wrong, George M., Chester Martin and Walter N. Sage. *The Story of Canada*. Toronto: The Ryerson Press, 1929.

Index

ALSO AVAILABLE FROM ARSENAL PULP PRESS

Bringing It Home *Brenda Lea Brown, ed.*
Deeply personal narratives by women from all walks of life about the impact of feminism on their lives. Includes essays by Kate Braid, Ursula Franklin, Larissa Lai, and Mary Meigs. *$21.95 Cda / $16.95 U.S.*

The Imaginary Indian *Daniel Francis*
A revealing history of the "Indian" image mythologized by popular Canadian culture since 1850, propagating stereotypes of the "noble savage" that exist to this day. *$17.95*

Imagining Ourselves: Classics of Canadian Non-Fiction *Daniel Francis, ed.*
Selections from Canadian non-fiction books that in some way have had a major impact on how Canadians view themselves. *$19.95*

It Pays to Play: B.C. in Postcards, 1950s-1980s *Peter White*
An engaging popular history of British Columbia as depicted in colour postcards, a vehicle for promoting the province as a hotbed of leisure, industry, and tourism. Includes 141 full-colour images. Co-published by Presentation House Gallery. *$24.95*

O-bon in Chimunesu: A Community Remembered *Catherine Lang*
The poignant story of the Japanese-Canadian community of Chemainus on Vancouver Island prior to internment. Winner of the Hubert Evans Non-Fiction Prize. *$18.95*

Out of This World: The Natural History of Milton Acorn *Chris Gudgeon*
The lively biography of one of Canada's greatest poets, exploring and exposing his larger-than-life myths. "A satisfying biography that fills an important gap in Canadian literature." —*Quill & Quire* *$27.95 Cda / $23.95 U.S.*

These and other Arsenal Pulp Press books are available through your local bookstore, or directly from the press (with your Visa or Mastercard) by calling 1-888-600-PULP.

Or send a cheque or money order (add postage: $3.00 for first book, $1.50 per book thereafter; Canadian residents add 7% GST) to:

ARSENAL PULP PRESS
103-1014 Homer Street
Vancouver, B.C.
Canada V6B 2W9

Send for our free catalogue.